WITH JUSTICE FOR ALL

A SOCIAL HISTORY OF DISABILITY IN AMERICA

JACK TRAMMELL

First published in 2023
as part of the Health, Wellness & Society Book Imprint
doi: 10.18848/978-1-957792-67-5/CGP (Full Book)

Common Ground Research Networks
2001 South First St, Suite 201 L
University of Illinois Research Park
Champaign, IL
61820

Copyright © Jack Trammell, 2023

All rights reserved. Apart from fair dealing for the purposes of study, research, criticism or review as permitted under the applicable copyright legislation, no part of this book may be reproduced by any process without written permission from the publisher.

Library of Congress Cataloging-in-Publication Data

Names: Trammell, Jack, author.
Title: With Justice for All: A Social History of Disability in America /
　by JackTrammell, Ph.D., Mount Saint Mary's University (MD).
Description: Champaign, IL : Common Ground Research Networks, [2023] |
　Includes bibliographical references and index. | Summary: ""With Justice
　for All" is a narrative social history of disability in America. This
　book incorporates individual lived experiences, historical figures,
　legal developments, and social movements. The story of disability told
　here is arguably the story of America. Historian Douglas Bayton
　maintained that disability is everywhere-once you begin to look for
　it-and this text attempts to look in many places, some of which have not
　been looked into before by the critical scholarly eye. The story also
　brings the Disability Rights Movement (DRM) into its proper historical
　position, side by side with the Civil and Gender Rights Movements and
　the ongoing imagination of a more equitable America"-- Provided by
　publisher.
Identifiers: LCCN 2023024823 (print) | LCCN 2023024824 (ebook) | ISBN
　9781957792651 (hardback) | ISBN 9781957792668 (paperback) | ISBN
　9781957792675 (pdf)
Subjects: LCSH: People with disabilities--United States--Social conditions.
　| People with disabilities--United States--History. | Sociology of
　disability--United States. | People with disabilities--Civil
　rights--United States. | People with disabilities--Legal status, laws,
　etc.--United States.
Classification: LCC HV1553 .T73 2023 (print) | LCC HV1553 (ebook) | DDC
　362.40973--dc23/eng/20230614
LC record available at https://lccn.loc.gov/2023024823
LC ebook record available at https://lccn.loc.gov/2023024824

FOREWORD

This may be the first book-length historical treatment of disability in America that does not prominently include a large timeline of important events at the forefront. Timelines are not inherently beneficial; nor are they unusually irrelevant. But they do suggest battles that need not necessarily be waged in order to win a war. History is only linear because our understanding of time is limited to our finite human perspective, and to accept the reductionism that goes along with timelines is to ignore the fluid, ongoing, interconnected nature of the fight that still characterizes the ongoing Disability Rights Movement (DRM) and other civil rights movements in America. It ignores the good and the bad that come with every generation and have ripple effects that move forward and backward in time.

There have been breakthrough moments in the DRM, but there have been many other days where victory was not achieved, or there were outright failures, that were just as important. There have been many days where people with disabilities attempted to live their lives without stigma and oppression and were not fully successful.

In spite of this, one can randomly turn through this text and find that the chapters are generally arranged in a linear fashion (and there is an occasional abbreviated timeline), and that will perhaps help begin to frame American's disability experience in ways that seem familiar and comfortable. But a reader may also be curious at the apparently missing chunks of time, where at first glance it might seem that the record player of history skipped across the vinyl (if you're old enough to appreciate that metaphor). Perhaps a reader will notice an important activist, or a pivotal event that somehow escaped recognition.

That is both intentional and unintentional, and completely necessary. Social history is not linear; it is a kitchen table consisting of thousands of veneer strips of wood that overlap but when glued together form what appears to be a smooth and consistent surface. That surface is now a place-setting in an era of neomodernism where the stains and scratches of our disabled past are not truly dissolved or covered over, even though some still are busy vigorously trying to wipe the stains away from the surface. In disability history, the stains and scratches absolutely must remain, even at the cost of diminishing the romantic mood of the dinner.

Social history is only one kind of history, but it is exactly the type of history that disability experience demands be told, especially due to the universality of the disability experience. Doris and Frieda Zames remind us that "handicapism" is the only "ism" we all will experience if we live long enough. Although disability will always arguably be about physical difference (of body, mind, intellect, personality, etc.), its universal nature means that it should logically be the king/queen of identity politics, while in fact, it has long been the pauper. This story helps explain why that was and is, and what America's unique and sometimes unpleasant role in the story is.

Social history eschews dichotomies (us vs. them) and oversimplifications; it generally rejects the perpetration of negative ontologies (disability is bad), even while it demands their full exposure. It instead strives toward reconciliation between what can be known and what can't be known, between every man (and woman) and everyman, and oscillating between the rational and irrational. In one sense, it is a forward moving dialectical expression that looks inward and outward with equal amounts of skepticism and optimism.

If that seems confusing, it is. Disability history is everywhere and nowhere. There are some things we can't ever know, but there are many more that we can and that we need to pursue.

Other types of history (political, legislative, philosophical, biological, biographical, etc.) certainly have their place in the disability story, but only a broader social history can give readers a fuller sense of the deeply emotional and highly individualized journeys that result in disability now more than ever finding itself in the forefront of everything that it means to be human, to live, to love, and to interact with others. The questions disability raises inform the great genetic and bioethical decisions of our times.

This text therefore attempts to not just represent the American experience with disability, but the American experience as it becomes further globalized and still retains uniqueness. The further we move away from 1990 and the passage of the Americans with Disabilities Act (the ADA), the less that demarcating line seems to be distinct and dichotomous, and the more America seems to be an abject case study of identity possibilities in flux, placed squarely at the intersection of the rational and irrational, the qualitative and quantitative, the old and new, the individual and collective, and at the nexus of classic liberalism and neomodernism. In fact, the ADA was reauthorized in 2008, an indication of the constructivist nature of disability policy.

There is also globalization. America's story will increasingly be mankind's story, and it is important to capture the uniqueness of America's experience while we can, and to understand what it contributes to a globalizing disability paradigm.

A quick note about the word disability is in order. I use the word disability consistently throughout the text even though it is a relatively new word in the sense that we use it in speech now. This is to simplify things for the reader so we both know what is being talked about, but I want to make very clear that the word didn't mean those things to Americans and others in prior history. I will address the issue of semantics in several places, but I encourage the reader to always think of it in the context of the person, time and place being discussed.

Telling a story of this magnitude always involves the help of many individuals and organizations, some of whom need to be specifically named here: Lennard Davis, who as a founding figure of disability studies inspires many to pursue important disability narratives; the New York Public Library; The Museum of Disability History in Buffalo, New York; Columbia University Library; Zona Roberts and Paul Hippolitus; the Library and Archives at UC Berkeley; Professor Michael Fischbach, who's excellent historiographical skills informed me constantly; the University of Virginia Library; The New York City Transportation Museum; Douglas Platt and The Disability Museum in Buffalo; and of course, my family and home institution, who supported my efforts fully. This also includes my wonderful current colleagues at Mount Saint Mary's University (MD).

I thank my final readers: Professors Jennifer Bruce (Randolph-Macon College, Emeritus); Michael Fischbach (Randolph-Macon College); and Ernest Solar (Mount Saint Mary's University).

While I would at first say this story is not my own—I feel privileged to be the vessel—I do take responsibility for any of its shortcomings; they belong solely to me, and not to the talented editorial staff, colleagues, and many others who brought this to fruition. And actually, as I think of my own personal and family experience with disability, I realize that it is my story. And yours.

I hope that you as reader will find this story as compelling as I do as author, one that begs for a last chapter that is not yet fully written, and one that suggests an overall theme that still continues to emerge in unpredictable bursts and coalescing visions.

Jack Trammell, Ph.D.
Mount Saint Mary's University
Summer 2022

TABLE OF CONTENTS

Foreword ... iii

Chapter 1: Colonialism, Natives and New World Invasions ... 1

Chapter 2: Birth of American Individualism ... 29

Chapter 3: Deafness, Blindness, and early American definitions of Disablement ... 55

Chapter 4: Civil War Veterans with Disabilities and the Roots of the Modern Disability Rights Movement (DRM) ... 79

Chapter 5: Disease, Dyslexia, and the Globalization of Disability ... 107

Chapter 6: 1965–1975 and the Blossoming of the Disability Rights Movement ... 137

Chapter 7: The 1970s and 1980s and a new Civil Rights Act ... 165

Chapter 8: Conclusion 21st Century Strands of the DRM ... 189

Appendix: Neomodernism for Undergraduate Students ... *215*

Index ... *223*

CHAPTER 1

Colonialism, Natives and Old World Invasions

> "I have cause to be Melancholy, that I am as assuredly damn'd as that there is a God; and no more hopes of me than of the Devils..."
> (Hannah Allen describing her 17th century mental-health disability experience)[1]

Hannah Allen, an Englishwoman with psychological disabilities, penned one of the rare colonial era first-hand accounts of a lived experience with psychological disability. Very little primary source material exists describing disability, comparatively speaking, that illuminates the lived experience in early colonial North America. Existing contemporary accounts relating to disability are mainly drawn from general profiles of medicine at the time, histories of churches and related institutions that sometimes cared for the sick and disabled, and scattered writings of well-known (and literate) figures of the time that sometimes touch on personal disability experiences. Scholars can also draw on Enlightenment sources from Western Europe that generalize to the New World experience, with the caveat again that they are scattered, and not always germane to the unique aspects of the North American experience.

The relative paucity of first-hand sources can make it seem as if disability didn't exist at all in the New World, which was far from reality. Certainly, the term *disability* itself did not exist in the modern semantic sense, although cultural references in popular writings did begin to appear by the late colonial era, where for example in 1749 Henry Fielding wrote in *Tom Jones* that "The coachman was *disabled* from performing his office for that evening. An ancient heathen would perhaps have imputed this disability to the God of Drink" (italics author's). In spite of the sarcasm in this example, most real incidents of what later became termed officially as disability were no doubt more pervasive and impactful, and occurred perhaps

---

[1] Allen, Hannah. *A Narrative of God's Gracious Dealings with that Choice Christian Mrs. Hannah Allen...* Printed by John Wallis in London, 1683, pp. 60–61, as transcribed at http://www.ocdhistory.net/firsthand/allen.html.

at higher rates than in Europe due to the crude frontier conditions and the lack of urban resources. Such disabling events and the subsequent lives experienced over the long-term, though, were very seldom written about, talked about, and the term itself did not yet carry the pejorative cultural implications that it would in the postmodern, identity-driven, 20th and 21st century politics of a new era.[2]

Disability in the colonial era was by and large a family affair, and often a lonely personal experience, with those with the means providing better medical care, comfort, and social stability, and those without means struggling to a much greater degree. The story of disability in colonial America is in part the story of frontier struggle, in part an evolution of the English language to describe such experiences, in part a story of intersections with non-Western native cultures, and in part a segment of the wider human rights or human betterness movement associated with the Enlightenment and the growth of scientific methods to evaluate and treat human wellness.

The evolution of the American-English term "disability" would eventually have a significant impact on the modern disability rights movement itself, becoming an ongoing self-contained semantics battleground, a place where the war over discrimination was fought, and it is therefore worth examining its usage even in its nascent forms in the colonial era. The labels that competed with "disability" for cultural relevance were in hindsight quite easy to identify, mainly including what could best be called quasi-medical terms: handicap, deformity, malady, impairment, cripple, condition, malaise, idiot, lame, moron, lunatic, imbecile, spastic, retardation, etc.[3]

The term "disability" gradually became during the 20th late century the dominant narrative term that encompassed other more specific and outdated terms. But disability was not described one singular way in the colonial era. Another typical use of the term "disability" in early North America can be seen in this segment of a 1643 law passed by the Virginia General Assembly (soon to be known as the House of Burgesses) which rather than describing a medical condition or a cultural burden, employed the term in an older and very traditional English relational meaning:

> Whereas it was enacted at an Asembly [sic] in January 1641, that according to a statute made in the third year of the reigne [sic] of our sovereign Lord King James of blessed memory, and that no popish recusants should at any time hereafter

---

[2] "Disability, noun." *Oxford English Dictionary: The Definitive Record of the English Language*, http://www.oEd.com/view/Entry/53381?redirectedFrom=disability#eid.

[3] Ibid; Gould, Stephen J. *The Mismeasure of Man Revised and expanded edition.* W.W. Norton & Co., 1996, pp. 188–189.

> exercize [sic] the place or places of secret councellors [sic], register or comiss [sic]: surveyors or sheriff [sic], or any other publique [sic] place, but be utterly *disabled* for the same… (italics author's)[4]

The lack of specific language to describe disability and disability experience outside of Enlightenment medical terminology and archaic terms means that rediscovering disability history in early North America is difficult, and requires not only sifting through primary sources, but sifting through the evolution of the American English language itself, as well. The term here, in fact, equates elements of Catholicism with being a person who is religiously disabled. The literary intelligentsia of the New World wrote in rational, Enlightenment-generated medical terminology (such as it was), and therefore that is the obscured record that only with some difficulty can be decoded. Since Americans inherited the Western tradition from Greece, and there is no term for disability in ancient Greek, it is no surprise that semantics has long been an issue in writing about the social history of disability.

Disability was even used as a military term, as Thomas Paine demonstrated in a 1778 letter to Benjamin Franklin:

> … You have doubtless been informed of, which, excepting the Enemy keeping the Ground, may be deemed a drawn battle. Genl. Washington Collected his Army at Chester, and the Enemy's not moving towards him next day must be attributed to the disability they sustained and the burthen of their wounded. On the 16th. of the same Month, the two Armies were drawn up in order of battle near the White horse on the Lancaster Road, when a most violent and incessant Storm of Rain prevented an Action…[5]

Like today, many early disability terms were then synonymous with pejoratives or insults. During constitutional ratification proceedings, James Madison used the term "lame" as an insult to compare the rhetorical efforts of Patrick Henry and George Mason to defeat the Federalists' arguments:

> [Henry and Mason] made a *lame* figure and appeared to take different and awkward ground…[6]

---

[4] *Virtual Jamestown: Laws and Documents Relating to Religion in Early Virginia, 1606–1660*, accessed November 2, 2013: http://www.constitution.org/primarysources/primarysources.html#16.

[5] Paine, Thomas. *Letter from Thomas Paine to Benjamin Franklin*, Sat, May 16, 1778, courtesy of Franklin Papers, accessed online February 23, 2014 at http://www.franklinpapers.org.

[6] Smith, Jean Edward. *John Marshall: Definer of a Nation*. Holt Paperbacks, 1998, p. 127.

Ironically, perhaps, Madison was a great patriot who was unable to serve in the military himself due to a disability, with what appears to have been a seizure disorder that periodically complicated his health. Many others, from Washington to Monroe, made their reputations through their physical and martial accomplishments in war before they became famous patriot political leaders, which he wasn't as readily able to do.[7]

Madison, to his credit, went on later in 1784 as a member of the Virginia House of Delegates (he was term limited from Congress at the time) to support some of the earliest disability legislation in America, "awarding a Virginia state pension 'to all regular or militia officers and soldiers who have been wounded or otherwise disabled in the service of their country.'" He did not consider such veterans "lame" in the same sense he had used the term before politically, it would seem.[8]

Disability, then and now, was mired in a negative ontology that language constantly served to reify and perpetuate, much to the greater oppression of people with disabilities. It was a story dating back to the old world. Language, from in its invention and evolution thousands of years ago when homo sapiens developed pre-frontal cortexes and essentially out-smarted and out-imagined other sapient species and came to dominate, was used in large part to create a system of dominance and labels to control the behavior and status of fellow tribesmen. Our founding figures, as is often true with us today, were only going along with a system that had been in place for a very long time.

Native Americans

Another part of the story of the American disability experience begins before the 1607 founding of Jamestown, with a rich indigenous experience and diversity of culture that quickly and permanently impacted the discursive North American disability experience when Europeans arrived. Native Americans were present on the North American continent long before Europeans arrived, and there is evidence that they developed their own elaborate networks, customs, and resources for coping with disability that significantly influenced the newly arrived Europeans.

In particular, they attended to many immediately disabling conditions like concussions, broken bones, and even more dangerous chronic diseases, with

---

[7] Brockenbrough, Martha. *Alexander Hamilton: Revolutionary*, Square Fish (McMillan), 2017, p. 92.

[8] Madison, James. *The Papers of James Madison*, as quoted in DeRose, Chris. *Founding Rivals: Madison vs. Monroe*. Regnery History, 2015, p. 87.

surprisingly sophisticated care that included both medical, religious, and social prescriptions. In some areas they developed unique communal systems for caring for the injured, mentally ill and disabled that later influenced colonist's attitudes about the disabled (and later how the care of slaves was organized). The eastern Algonquin tribes, and particularly the Chickahominy tribe of Pocahontas fame, set up villages specifically to care for the elderly, the sick, and the disabled. Such camps were often formed at strategically geographic locations considered healthier—on higher ground with a clean freshwater source and moving air. Care was collective, with active hunting parties and younger women supplying food and medicines for the group as necessary.[9]

Warriors by definition suffered a variety of incapacitating injuries in the course of their duties, and in addition to the types of general emergency medicine in practice, they were more likely to have ready access to other supplemental types of ritual healings and recuperative privileges that had a very practical objective—returning them to active duties as soon as possible. Native fighting tactics, later to be famously employed and imitated by American patriots fighting in the Revolutionary War, were designed to protect the most important parts of the body—the legs, and vital organs, for example—from disablement.

Mobility was arguably the most important native fighting weapon/technique, and therefore serious injury or disability of the leg or legs was a traumatic and serious wounding which often carried with it dire consequences. European settlers and explorers also quickly became aware of the dangers of frontier wounds to the limbs, as Nathan Parr discovered in the flats of Grave Creek in what would be West Virginia, when he was struck in the hip by natives firing on him as he hunted, and although he survived the fight, he became a cripple for life, losing the full ability to provide for himself.[10]

It is not perfectly clear that "wounded warriors" were given a free pass on the stigma normally associated with long-term disability in the native system. Operations like the convalescent camps already described must by necessity have been predicated on the majority of the community continuing to function in useful and "normal" ways, hunting, gathering, sowing, harvesting, raising children, fighting, or tending to other important tasks. It's difficult to find any examples of natives "faking" disability, for example, in order to waylay for a

---

[9.] Trammell, Jack. *The Richmond Slave Trade: The Economic Backbone of the Old Dominion*. The History Press, 2012, pp. 22–23, 28–29. Weatherford, Jack. *Indian Givers: How the Indians of the Americas Transformed the World*. Fawcett Columbine, 1988, pp. 177–196.

[10.] Rice, O.K.. *The Allegheny Frontier: West Virginia Beginnings, 1780–1830*. 1969; Brake, Sherri. *The Haunted History of the West Virginia Penitentiary*. Raven Rock, 2011, p. 16.

longer rest period in the care of others, as can be found and often legislated against in the modern era in Western cultures, but it would also be a mistake to assume that the lack of such evidence means that there was not potentially abuse of the disability care system in some cases.

The Native American way, to the extent that it was relatively consistent across tribes, was to make use of every individual in very practical ways that contributed positively to the community's continued survival and security. In some respects, this was what set ancient Egyptian culture apart from their Greek and Roman counterparts. In the pursuit of that practical objective, a variety of social, medical, and organizational efforts were made to accommodate, heal, and convalesce individuals with disabilities. Reintegration or rehabilitation in the modern sense as a separate, tangible social justice concept would have seemed strange, as every individual needed to contribute by default. Ironically, it would take more than two centuries for a postmodern America to adopt any kind of analogous attitude through the efforts of the Disability Rights Movement (DRM).

The Constitution of the Iroquois Nations

Native Americans generally had no written language and relied on strong oral traditions to hand down knowledge and wisdom from generation to generation. In most cases before European settlement, this method worked well for countless centuries; when confronted with the empirical methods of the settlers, however, this system came under tremendous stress due to Colonialism, Empiricism, Enlightenment ideals, and Westernism. Some tribes were better able to reconcile their traditions with this abrupt change than others.

According to historian Gerald Murphy, the democratic principles of the five Iroquois nations had a great influence on the Founding figures as they began to craft an American constitution. The Iroquois had been functioning as a democratic community for hundreds of years prior to American independence.

The native traditions about disability are not easily discerned with absolute certainty, but the codification of their laws during the colonial era gives some insight into their nature. The natives, as Murphy and others have discovered, had a long and complex tradition of social customs that dealt with disability:

> You will find it very difficult to keep in mind that it survives after some 500 or 600 years, and was originated by people that our ancestors mistakenly considered as "savages". Some sources place the origin of the Five Nation Confederacy as early as 1390 AD, but others insist it was prepared about 1450–1500 AD; in any case, it was well before any possible contamination by European invaders. Early explorers and colonists found the Iroquois well established, as they had been for many generations: with a democratic government; with a form of religion that acknowledged a Creator in heaven; with a strong sense of family which was based on, and controlled by, their women; and many other surprises you will soon discover.

In the constitution itself, evidence of disability is quite evident in several places, usually as an expedient for solving leadership problems:

> 21. Certain physical defects in a Confederate Lord make him ineligible to sit in the Confederate Council. Such defects are infancy, idiocy, blindness, deafness, dumbness and impotency. When a Confederate Lord is restricted by any of these condition[s], a deputy shall be appointed by his sponsors to act for him, but in case of extreme necessity the restricted Lord may exercise his rights.

The traditional founder of the nations, a brilliant man named Dekanawida, was considered to have a speech impediment. Hiawatha (not in actuality the famous warrior of Wordsworth fame, but perhaps his inspiration name-wise) joined Dekanawida as official spokesperson, and together they traveled throughout the northeast, spreading wisdom and uniting tribes.

Native American experiences with disability have historically been filtered through the perceptions and recorded history of settlers and colonists. As a result, it is difficult to know on a purely anthropological level exactly how natives typically handled disability on a day to day basis. Evidence like the Iroquois constitution suggests that it was with a mixture of practicality and some compassion.[11]

[11.] Murphy, Gerald Murphy, *About the Iroquois Constitution*, accessed April 28, 2014 at http://www.fordham.edu/halsall/mod/iroquois.asp. Also, see http://www.ratical.org/many_worlds/6Nations/EoL/chp8.html#fn18

There is some evidence that outside of military service or the naturally aged, Native Americans, like many humans across varied cultures and times, beheld other individuals with disabilities with a certain degree of contempt or mistrust. The fact that all individuals were needed for the survival of the tribe did not alter an unspoken human prejudice in favor of the "normally" fit and able-bodied. Postmodern philosophers such as Richard Kearney have debated the degree to which all humans (aka *homo sapiens*) are biologically pre-disposed to such behavior by hard wiring. But the overarching needs of day-to-day survival and a communal lifestyle ensured that disability was not a "social problem" for Native Americans in the classic Western sense.[12]

As the colonial period progressed, European colonists adapted many of the native ways, including the use of local herbs for wellness, a disposition toward communal care, and employing other natural cures. Historians like Martha Robinson make it very clear that even the early European clergy were quite respectful of and often highly aware of native cures and medicines (and there were many more pastors than physicians in most areas, so they were often forced into the role of emergency caregiver). Within native tribes, there were specialized "doctors" or medicine men and women that were recognized as the local healing experts. There are a number of cases where Native American doctors/shamans were called upon to cure a colonist of an ailment such as blindness when a European doctor could not do so successfully, although such medicine men/women were also routinely criticized by more educated Europeans for utilizing superstitious cures and ignoring the burgeoning empirical and medical paradigm or any set of theories to rationally explain illness, treatment and cures. They were dismissive, for example, of natives integrating non-Christian prayer or superstitious rituals into the healing process. Perhaps not surprisingly, lay American colonist healers continuously sought native medical knowledge well into the 18th century, at the same time that formally trained doctors in the European tradition coming to North America became increasingly dismissive of it over time as modernism blossomed and urban centers developed with the attendant post-Enlightenment hospitals and social institutions that would come to dominate them.[13]

An interesting intersectionality across native and European medical cultures was treatment through mineral waters and hot springs. Natives in the mid-Atlantic region, apparently across almost all tribes, saw certain special waters as having healing and enhancing powers and used them frequently to treat ailments and

---

[12] Kearney, Richard. *Strangers, Gods, and Monsters*. Rutledge, 2003; *American State Papers*. Library of Congress, accessed at http://rs6.loc.gov/ammem/amlaw/lawhome.html.

[13] Robinson, Martha. "New Worlds, New Medicines: Indian Remedies and English Medicine in Early America." *Early American Studies* 3, no. 1, 2005, pp. 94–97; Occom, Samson. *Herbal Remedies*. Dartmouth Special Collections, 1754.

disabilities. Having a similar tradition, it is not surprising that European villages often grew up near such sites, as well. According to historian Chris Heidenrich, the city of Frederick, Maryland, for example, was founded near such an area known as:

> Montonqua, meaning "medicine waters," because people believed the springs here were fed by the Great Spirit. Tribes preparing for battle came here to drink the water for strength and courage. Sick people were brought here.[14]

In a similar fashion, Algonquians gathered on the seven hills above the James River which would later become the city of Richmond, Virginia. They used the area as a convalescent camp for the temporary and permanently disabled, and believed the fresh water of local springs and creeks flowing into the James river were refreshing. European settlers would bring old world ideas about water into conjunction with new world ideas about the healing powers of springs and mineral soaks that became powerful cultural markers for avoiding, treating, or reversing disablement. Even today, many people believe in "taking the waters" and that there are sometimes mystical powers to heal through contact with them, in spite of some conventional science now showing limitations on its practicality and impactful benefits. In part, the persistent belief comes out of contact with native medicine.

Colonial Medicine and Mental Health

Americans practiced a unique form of medicine from the very beginning of the New World experience. Although they brought Enlightenment science with them from Western Europe, they also quickly adopted many Native American cures and remedies, and also discovered their own remedies as they experienced and experimented with new animals, plants, and environmental challenges. American medicine essentially became an amalgamation of Native and European traditions in its early phases.

Within a wider medical framework, colonial attitudes about mental health remained more staid and stigmatizing. So-called

---

[14.] Heidenrich, Chris. *Frederick: Local and National Crossroads*. Arcadia, 2003, p. 11.

diseases of the mind were invisible, and only diagnosable as a result of observing external behavior. As a result of the obvious misunderstandings, treatments were crude, sometimes violent, and often followed by social ostracizing (see a later section on Sarah Henry, Patrick Henry's wife).

As a frontier nation, hospitals, infirmaries, or even physicians' offices were practically unknown. In the French colony of New France, citizens had things a little bit better in theory, but still experienced similar frontier hardships:

> Settlers nevertheless enjoyed a good medical infrastructure. Every city had its "hôtel-Dieu," or hospital. Surgeons, doctors, apothecaries and healers worked together with religious congregations to help care for the settlers. The Crown together with the Catholic Church, played a major role in providing health care.[15]

In New Spain, "In a letter dated March 20, 1503, King Ferdinand of Aragon and Queen Isabella of Castile instructed Friar Nicolas de Ovando, the new governor of the island of Hispaniola, 'to erect hospitals for the lodging and caring of poor people, whether Christian or natives, with unmet needs.'"[16]

In Colonial-era Williamsburg, Virginia, the first hospital or home for the mentally ill was established before American Independence through the patronage of Governor Fauquier, with the first patient being admitted in 1773. Although Fauquier argued that such an institution, first called the Public Hospital for the Persons of Insane and Disordered Minds, was for the good of everyone, its twenty-four jail-like cells complete with iron rings for shackles left some wondering if it was actually less effective than treatment by churches and families.

Fauquier addressed the House of Burgesses in 1766:

> It is expedient I should also recommend to your consideration and humanity a poor unhappy set of people who are deprived of their senses and wander about the country, terrifying the rest of their fellow creatures. A legal confinement, and proper

---

[15.] Cesia, Stephanie. "Daily Life: Health and Medicine." *Canadian Museum of History*, 2022. Accessed at https://www.historymuseum.ca/virtual-museum-of-new-france/daily-life/health-and-medicine/

[16.] Risse, Guenter. "Hospitals in Spanish America: Early Historical Perspectives." *Inaugural Conference at the First Ibero-American Congress of the History of Medicine*, 1992, p. 1.

> provision, ought to be appointed for these miserable objects, who cannot help themselves. Every civilized country has an hospital for these people, where they are confined, maintained and attended by able physicians, to endeavor to restore to them their lost senses.[17]
>
> Percival Goodhouse, an early patient, escaped the asylum and fled to the nearby gardens of the Governor's Palace, where he brandished a large knife. He was reportedly hanged for attempting to assassinate the governor, and his body thrown into a nearby field where students frequently disturbed the remains as a school prank.
>
> The Asylum eventually became Eastern State Hospital. The hospital remains in service in the current time with an emphasis on community mental health and wellness.
>
> ---
> [17] Kennedy, John (editor). *Journal of the House of Burgesses of Virginia, 1766–1769.* Richmond, #1096, p. 12.

In the first century of colonization, however, such institutions largely did not exist. Robert Beverly, as quoted by Daniel Boorstin, wrote of native ways as a positive alternative in 1705:

> The planters . . . have several roots natural to the country, which in this case they cry up as infallible. They have the happiness to have very few doctors, and those such as make use only of simple remedies, of which their woods afford great plenty. And indeed, their distempers are not many, and their cures are so generally known, that there is not mystery enough, to make a trade of physick [sic] there, as the learned do in other countries, to the great oppression of mankind.[18]

Although one might argue flippantly that settlers were better off without doctors, amongst the intelligentsia it was quickly recognized as a serious problem. Within a few generations, physicians trained in Europe and transplanted to the New World would be replaced by North American born and regionally trained

---
[18] Boorstin, Daniel. *The Americans: The Colonial Experience.* Vintage Books, 1959, p. 210.

physicians. The Native American imprint, however, would remain, in spite of an unnecessary prejudice against it.

Evolving Attitudes

The English and other New World settlers were much slower than their native counterparts in adopting their own version of communal care for the disabled. This was in part due to increasingly entrenched Western Enlightenment ideas about medicine that were transplanted from Europe—ideas which had at their core a seldom-wavering focus on cures, rather than on relief or accommodation—and also a product of the sparse populations and vast distances between centers of commerce and knowledge. This meant that the early experience of disability in colonial America was inevitably a story of attempts at local and immediate treatments, coupled with more drastic actions like sending the individual away or confining them when treatments failed and a chronic condition developed. In fact, there are many cases of immigrants to colonial America being returned to Europe due to their disabling conditions. There simply were no institutions or alternative accommodations available to start out a New World experience already disabled, and rightly or wrongly, the perception was that they were in danger of becoming part of the problem rather than part of the solution.[19]

Evolving colonial attitudes were also tied to unique aspects of individualism, which steadily crept into the colonial and then later the American psyche. European cultures had long functioned with a certain level of presumed social interaction, a norm, often forced by geographic proximity and shared culture. This tribal-like identity often crossed socio economic class and national boundaries; it was a dynamic, multinational process that had been going on in Europe since the days of the Roman Empire. It fueled wars; it also fused culture.

In the North American colonies, families and individuals by contrast often found themselves in an otherworldly kind of isolation, with significant geographical distance from others, which heightened the calamity of serious disability, and promoted a type of self-reliance and a narrow focus that could in some extreme cases even lead to overtly anti-social or cruel behavior. In this unique social and cultural landscape, disability skewed even more toward being centered in the individual, and away from being a collective social problem.

---

[19] Covey, Herbert. *Social Perceptions of People with Disabilities in History.* Charles C. Thomas, 1998, pp. 261–262. Jaeger, Paul, and Bowman, Cynthia Ann. *Understanding Disability: Inclusion, Access, Diversity, and Civil Rights.* Greenwood Publishing Group, 2005, p. 49.

Ironically, some of the more elaborate forms of communal care in North America originated on larger slave plantations in the colonial South, where slave-owners had economic as well as practical reasons for attempting to secure adequate care for their numerous slaves and preventing disability. In some cases hospitals were established right on the plantation property, although observers often noted that the level of care was significantly better or worse than that afforded to their own families, a situation of which presented a moral and economic quandary. By and large, these hospitals did not deal with permanent disability or chronic disorders, since such conditions could in essence render the slave valueless, and there was no compelling economic reason to keep such slaves or invest any significant capital in them. Therefore, the focus in this type of communal care was on prevention, quick cures and immediate rehabilitation toward work, a theme more fully developed later on a wider scale in the Wilson era for returning veterans of World War I.[20]

Life in colonial America was far from easy, and the average life expectancy generally did not exceed forty years during most periods. As few as one percent of the general population reached the age of seventy-six, which even at that is still significantly below the present-day average American life expectancy (pre-COVID-19). For individuals with disabilities—both visible and invisible—that life was often particularly challenging and considerably shorter in comparison to individuals without disabilities. Sometimes, groups of the disabled in Colonial America were classified as "deserving poor," and integrated into local communities through the shelter of their combined families and sometimes churches or fledgling charitable organizations. These initiatives dated back to the English Poor Laws of 1693. But such individuals were more often not accommodated or fully tolerated in the larger open society. A theme in early America that would carry over into the modern era was one of some occasional and unpredicted tolerances, but more often than not, pervasive social and physical exclusion.[21]

The family assumed an exaggerated importance in the North American colonial experience. In Europe, and particularly in Great Britain and France, the growth of cities and the evolution of a wide network of church-based institutions as well as some minimal urban social safety nets ensured that some families did not have to rely completely on their own resources in extreme cases of disability. In North America, as well as around the globe in other isolated British colonies, many families were almost completely self-reliant, well outside the easy reach

---

[20] Mitchell, Sarah Mitchell. *Bodies of Knowledge: The Influence of Slaves on the Antebellum Medical Community.* Virginia Tech, 1997, pp. 12–13.

[21] Miller, John. *The First Frontier: Life in Colonial America.* Dell, 1966, p. 237; Foreman, Michael, et. al. *Sharing the Dream: Is the ADA Accommodating All?* U.S. Commission on Civil Rights, 1998, Chapter 1, p. 1.

of a few small cities. They relied on home remedies (often borrowed directly from Native Americans in North America), physical isolation of invalids in separate quarters (often in lofts, attics, or separate buildings like kitchens), and intentional social distancing (being left out of trips to court, church, or town). Families coped with disability because they had to, but seldom felt comfortable or supported by the community in doing so.[22]

Some authors like Waltraud Ernst have tracked the rise of Colonialism and positioned it in its later stages as evolving side by side with a wider institutionalization and medicalization of society. The relationships and connections between colonial and medical powers in the modern sense are evident even in this frontier period in important Foucauldian ways within this framework, and Ernst suggests that it is no accident that in some British colonies the inhabitants of hospitals for the mentally and physically disabled were often overrepresented by minorities and natives. Because of how pervasive medical expertise and power has become entrenched in the neomodern era, some have suggested a historical bias against recognition of the family in colonial era disability experience. There can be little doubt, however, that the family consisted of the main hope of intervention in most cases of disability in early America.[23]

The growth of centralized medical expertise also began to speed up the dichotomization of disability and medical labels. In the Revolutionary War, for example, the Continental Congress and shortly thereafter the new American Congress began to heavily legislate what a disability in the armed services literally consisted of. Such dichotomization (you either qualified or you didn't) and formal labeling was not limited to just disability in the military and began to occur semantically in a number of variations in the wider culture, polarizing in ways that were notably different from those in old Europe. In the colonies there were savages and civilized men; whites and blacks; males and females; Christians and non-Christians; free and enslaved; franchised property owners and the disenfranchised. The identity landscape was more complicated and more polarized in several important ways compared to that in Europe.

Disability, injury and chronic illness respected none of these identity boundaries, and instead occupied the nebulous zones of medical crisis and religious

---

[22.] Coleborne, Catharine. *Madness in the family: Insanity and Institutions in the Australasian Colonial World, 1860–1914*. Basingstoke: Palgrave Macmillan, 2010, as reviewed by Gayle Davis in *Australian Historical Studies*, no. 33, 2013, pp. 289–290. Ernst, Waltraud. "Medical/Colonial power: Lunatic asylums in Bengal, C. 1800–1900," *Journal of Asian History*, 40, no. 1, 2006, pp. 46–79; Ernst, Waltraud. "Idioms of madness and colonial boundaries: The case of the European and "Native" mentally ill in early nineteenth-century British India," *Society for Comparative Study of Society and History*, 1997, pp. 153–181.

[23.] Ibid; Foucauldian ways come out of the work of Michel Foucault, and relate to power, bureaucracy, and agency.

superstition, and in the ultimate truism of anthropology, the various native and European cultures in conflict with each other in the New World quickly adopted many of the others' ideas about disability and healing. North American quickly became a unique polyglot of beliefs and practices. In almost all cases, the disabled required resources that were scarcely available even to the healthy in the family.[24]

Religion played a dominant role in both positive and negative fashions shaping colonial attitudes about disability, as Linsenmeier and Moyer suggest in discussing the possibility of infanticide in Colonial America. Religious (a.k.a. Christian) orthodoxy, they argue, would have precluded abandoning disabled children to the state such as it was, ill-equipped to deal with them, or formally reviving the ancient ritual of exposure or other infanticidal practices that continued in some parts of Europe well into the modern era. There was a strong sentiment that disability, especially that which occurred at birth, but of all types, represented the direct will of God, and that parents as well as family members were obligated to confront it on some level as tragedy, but also to stoically accept it. The Salem Witch Trials and similar persecutions also suggest that divine judgment could quickly turn away from pity and charity and transform into outright punishment, scapegoating, and open discrimination in quite unpredictable and socially destructive ways.[25]

In fact, there are more recent scholarly attempts to reframe at least some of the witch hysteria that swept through Massachusetts and other areas in nearby colonies as an awkward, repressive reaction to the unresolved dilemma of invisible mental illness and psychological disability (especially in terms related to gender). Colonial medicine and puritanical norms simply could not reconcile the erratic behavior of the manic depressant, for example, and befuddled authorities often bowed to the social pressure demanding community order, rather than attempt more patient and rational examinations of such behavior (and hence their own medical diagnosis was termed Hysteria). The witch trials remain primary evidence of the colonial disability mindset which was based on an irrational fear of the abject Other, was more often than not gendered, and was most often characterized by its convenient rejection of the empirical positivism the Enlightenment should have and sometimes did advance. To make matters more complex, male religious officials often applied those more structured and reasonable Enlightenment standards to themselves, while reserving superstition

---

[24.] Marriott, Alice, and Rachlin, Carol. *American Epic: The Story of the American Indian.* G. P. Putnam's Sons, 1969, p. 41.

[25.] Linsenmeier, Carol, and Moyer, Jeff. "Reaching Across the Divide: Visual Disability, Childhood, and American History," in *Children with Disabilities in America: A Historical Handbook and Guide.* Greenwood Press, 2006, pp. 29–31.

and religious judgment for all others. None-the-less, recent studies of Salem tend to focus on the phenomenon of witchcraft, or the impact on American Exceptionalism, rather than the underlying anthropology of disability the events signified which is relevant to the modern identity rights movements and the history of the North American disability experience.[26]

"Goody" Glover was hanged as a witch in Boston in 1688. Her story is one that touches on disability as physical or mental difference, as well as cultural Otherness. An indentured Irish laundress, Glover was blamed for her employer's children's illness, and had an emotional confrontation with the family as a result. During her later testimony, she spoke only in Gaelic, which convinced her accusers of her perfidy and contributed to an image of a woman that was out of her mind or possessed by evil forces. In fact, Glover was probably not a witch at all, but persecuted in part for her Catholic faith and cultural Otherness. In reality, her death like those of other accused witches, is a window into a New World mindset that had very little means of reconciling the rational with the irrational.[27]

Contrary to stereotypes, the hysteria over witches and witchcraft extended across regions. In Virginia, for example, Grace Sherwood of Pungo was accused in 1706 of being a witch, and when she failed to drown after being bound and thrown into deep river water, sent to jail. The "Witch of Pungo" was only one of many who exposed the colonial uneasiness with non-traditional identities.[28]

Sarah Shelton Henry, the wife of famed statesman and patriot Patrick Henry, was no witch but suffered from profound and debilitating physical and mental illnesses. Like other women with psychological disabilities of the era, she was subject to the intersectionality of both gender and disability stigma. Although her husband, Patrick, has never been accused of abuse, once Sarah's illness reached the point of complete breakdown, he confined her within a lonely room in the basement of the plantation home, Scotchtown, with a dirt floor, isolated from the rest of the house and accessible only by a secret stair. In fairness, the arrangement was done with safety and isolation in mind. She remained there for years, locked away in the equivalent of a strait jacket much of the time. When

---

[26] Mappen, Marc. *Witches & Historians: Interpretations of Salem.* Malabar, FL: Robert E. Krieger Publishing Co., 1980; Gilman, S.L et.al. *Hysteria beyond Freud.* University of California Press, 1993; Blakemore, Colin, and Jennett, Sheila (editors). *The Oxford Companion to the Body.* Oxford University Press, online 2003; Rowlands, Alison. "Witchcraft and Old Women in Early Modern Germany." *Past & Present*, No. 173, Nov. 2001, pp. 50–89; Adams, Gretchen. *The specter of Salem: Remembering the witch trials in nineteenth-century America.* The University of Chicago Press, 2008).

[27] Rosenthal, Bernard (editor). *Records of the Salem witch-hunt.* Cambridge University Press, 2009, p. 942; "Goodwife 'Goody' Ann Glover," accessed February 21, 2014 at http://www.goodyglovers.com/history.html.

[28] Anonymous. "Virginia Beach: A heritage on the sea." *Ocean 2014–2015*, p. 7.

Sarah died—some said mercifully—Henry was preparing to give his famous "liberty or death" speech in nearby Richmond. It is almost certain, had the roles been reversed, Henry's treatment would have been significantly different than that of his wife. Henry remarried a year later, although the new couple did not make their residence at Scotchtown, which has over the years reputedly been haunted by Sarah's tortured memory.[29]

In the scattered written records, a few case studies taken directly from primary sources across disability types will bear several recurring colonial era themes out more directly. The first instance involves blindness, a fairly common condition of the times. According to a sage observer in 1773, "the infinitely wise author of nature has assigned to the EYES and EARS the most useful and important offices of life..."

> The inestimable blessing and great advantages which attend a perfect enjoyment of the sight and hearing are obvious to all; but deplorable and truly pitiable condition of the blind and deaf is attended with such solitary discomfort, such gloomy ideas, and constant uneasiness of the mind, as no one can be truly sensible of who has not, in some measure, experienced it himself.[30]

The dramatic announcement accompanying this text was the news that Doctor Graham, an occultist [sic] and aurist (eye and ear specialist) would be practicing his learned craft in central Virginia, with expertise "in all disorders of the eye and its appendages, and in every species of deafness, hard of hearing, ulcerations, noise in the ears, etc."

Doctor Graham, in the traditions of the evangelical healing spirit of the Christian gospels, promised to work even with the most vexing congenital cases, especially involving the body:

> Those persons, likewise, who have had the unspeakable misfortune of being born deaf and dumb, and those who labor under any impediment in their speech, by applying personally, will probably be assisted. Those persons whose eyes are utterly perished or sunk in their heads may have the deformity removed by artificial eyes, so curiously fixed and adapted to the orbits, as to have, in appearance, the beauties, motion, etc. of a natural eye in healthy state.[31]

[29.] Crawford, Alan Pell. "The Upstart, the Speaker, the Scandals, and Scotchtown." *Colonial Williamsburg Journal*, Winter 2001–2002, accessed on February 20, 2014 at http://www.history.org.

[30.] *Supplement to the Virginia Gazette*. Williamsburg, VA: Rind, May 6, 1773, 1, c. 1.

[31.] Ibid.

There are several remarkable aspects to this notice, which given the state of medical knowledge at the time, cannot possibly have delivered on its promises. Graham was in Virginia specifically in order to train other doctors, so that there might be at least one *expert per "province"* (italics author's) who could carry on the professional trade after he left. The excitement the announcement generated speaks to the utter lack of formal medical care available to a general population spread across the rural areas of the colonies in this period, and also captures the contradiction of the Enlightenment mindset concerning disability, a paradigm that usually combined pity and loathing with a paternal compassion and persistent scientific curiosity in the rationally explainable.

Also of importance in this notice was the notable emphasis placed on general accessibility, even to the poor:

> The poor who apply, properly recommended, will be assisted *gratis*, with advice, medicines, or manual operations, as their respective cases may require; and for that purpose he will appropriate every morning, Sundays excepted, between the hours of five and seven.[32]

In spite of such notable exceptions, colonists rarely talked about the body or the mind in terms we would readily recognize today. In their writings, bodies and minds were seldom talked about in positive terms, and usually quite the opposite. There was no "Hollywood" effect. In fact, detailed physical descriptions in primary sources are fairly rare from this period.

The story of disability as it related to physical beauty, nuances of gender, or normality was one that either was not present in their own narratives, or that they choose not to record in writing. Although some of the ingredients of the modern social welfare state were already present in nascent forms during this era, as evidenced by the advertisement, contemporary ideas about the mind, disability, gender, and Otherness remain surprisingly difficult to document.[33]

Religion and Charity

Although both the Catholic and Protestant churches in Europe had long been agents of philanthropy in cases of permanent or temporary disability, they had also cloaked their efforts in long-standing traditions of framing disability as

---

[32] Ibid.

[33] Block, Sharon. "Making Meaningful Bodies: Physical Appearance in Colonial Writings." *Early American Studies*, Fall 2014, pp. 524–547.

punishment for sin, and socially constructed disability as a cause for pity. In colonial North America, there were occasional glimmers of a more liberal notion of accessibility-orientation that started to show even before independence from Britain and more related constitutional protections were formalized, due in part to disability's escape from the hegemony of the European Christian orthodoxy. This might be termed a frontier and colonial effect, as distance from one authority and the slow creation of a new one to fill the void inevitably led to practical changes and adaptations.

In North America, the idea of communal charity became increasingly linked to disability during the late colonial period, and while it was a unique North American variation, the movement did connect with larger and similar social forces at work in Great Britain and Europe, where there was also a concurrent diffusion of some church authority. The so-called "Duke's Laws" issued by the Duke of York in 1665 (affecting areas of New York, Pennsylvania, New Jersey, and Delaware) were, according to Claire Liachowitz, a blessing and a curse; an acknowledgement of the community's joint responsibility for the welfare of all, but also trying to reinforce a dangerous and damaging association between charity and disablement that still stains disability perceptions in the post-ADA American landscape. The laws governed different types of disability situations, even including something like an early label for ADHD with people who were termed "distracted persons:"

> That in regard the Condition of Distracted Persons may Prove of Publique Concerne, and for that it is too greate a burthen for one towne alone to bear, It may be taken into Consideration at the Assizes whether the other townes of that riding ought not to Contribute to the Charge.[34]

Overshadowing those glimmers of change was a persistent and vexing tradition of seeing disabilities and chronic medical conditions as disconnected from each other etiologically; there was no universal sense that individuals confronting blindness had anything in common with individuals who were crippled physically, or those who suffered from melancholy (depression). Because these diverse situations had very different medical causes, none of those suffering from them felt connected to anyone outside their narrow experience. There was not yet a nascent Disability Rights Movement (DRM) per se.

---

[34] Liachowitz, Claire. *Disability as a Social Construct: Legislative Roots*. The University of Pennsylvania Press, 1988, pp. 65–67.

This categorical disconnection became one of the most significant barriers to a wider disability rights movement in the 19th and 20th centuries. In early America it meant that each major type of disability was treated as a unique, discrete medical problem, separate from other conditions, and completely separated from a more generalized human experience. It effectively made any wider disability rights movement impossible, even had the idea occurred to anyone.

The case of blindness illustrates disability compartmentalization. American intellectuals in the colonial era considered themselves modern Greeks, or at the very least, the contemporary heirs of a wider Greek Western tradition that valued eyesight well beyond the other four senses as a matter of course. To be blind was to be helpless, not just in the physical world of labor and movement, but also in an esoteric human sense. A case from Newport, Rhode Island illustrates the combination of pity, compassion and morbid interest that colonists experienced in cases of profound blindness:

> Yesterday, in the afternoon we hear there was a very handsome collection in the Church of England, in this town, for the relief of Mr. Thomas Allen, of Prudence, in this colony, a very poor man, whose circumstances are really deplorable, having a wife who by sickness hath been a long time blind, and 11 children, 7 of whom were born blind; which charitable collection is truly laudable, and worthy imitation, and it is hoped will be followed by all other congregations in this town and colony.[35]

Two centuries later the scientific curiosity of the early colonists combined with the pseudo-science of 20th century Eugenics would lead to controversial and discredited programs of sterilization and almost universal institutionalization for those with profound disabilities. Such absolute separation and supra-medicalization eventually led to a postmodern rebellion. The early colonists, however, did not have the science, liberal refinement, or the financial resources to do anything but cope locally, within families, as best as they could.[36]

A second example can be found in the congenitally deaf. In the mid-17th century Europe had witnessed a blossoming of institutes for the deaf and hard of hearing that coincided with renewed scientific attempts to understand the condition's underlying causes. The North American colonies, however, lacked the urban centers and larger philanthropic institutions to make such a movement possible.

---

[35] *Virginia Gazette*. Williamsburg, VA: Purdie and Dixon, March 8, 1770, 2, c. 1.

[36] Watkinson, Patricia. *20th Century Eugenics in Virginia*. Ashland, VA: Randolph-Macon College, February 15, 2012, lecture.

Instead, the deaf and hard of hearing remained isolated in small families or within small communities. Martha's Vineyard in Massachusetts had one of the earliest segregated/congregated deaf communities; Jonathan Lambert, is credited as being the first deaf community member there in 1694.[37]

According to recent ethnographic research, this community was the product of a recessive genetic trait that, when occurring in both parents, led to a significant increase in the number of children born with deafness. In fact, rates of deafness on Martha's Vineyard between 1694 and 1952 were sometimes in excess of one hundred times or more higher than the rates occurring in the general population. Nora Ellen Groce traces the mutated gene to pods of families from the Weald in Kent, England, many of whom immigrated to the Massachusetts colony while keeping those family pods intact, and then settled to Martha's Vineyard. Her research also suggests that unlike in other parts of the North American colonies, at least in this small and isolated community individuals with disabilities like deafness were relatively seamlessly normalized and assimilated into the wider culture. In some situations working onboard dangerous seagoing vessels, the use of hand signals and the ability to ignore auditory distraction was sometimes even seen as an advantage. This was certainly the exception and not the rule during this period of American history.[38]

Citizens on the island, both hearing and deaf, developed a unique sign language referred to as Martha's Vineyard Sign Language, which was spoken as recently as 1952. Both hearing and deaf community members learned it as a matter of course, and the integration was so complete that even the birth records don't always reveal with accuracy who was born deaf, and who was born hearing on the island. Individuals who were deaf were not prohibited from any local vocations, and became some of the many famous whalers and sailors of the maritime community, to cite one example. Alexander Graham Bell, who remained fascinated with deafness as a special case of disability, later studied the island's population.[39]

Accounts of the deaf in the colonial period range the gambit from wealthy to poor, black to white, and the indentured to the free:

> Came to my house some time [sic] in August an Irishman, about 20 years of age, 5 feet 8 inches high, of a swarthy complexion, has on an old brown turnout coat, an old hat, without any brim, and brown linen shirt and trowsers

---

[37] Covey. Pp. 198–199.

[38] Groce, Nora Ellen. *Everyone Here Spoke Sign Language: Hereditary Deafness on Martha's Vineyard*. Harvard University Press, 1985, pp. 4, 42, etc.

[39] Groce. pp. 16, 19, 83.

[sic]; the little toe of his right foot is off. He is quite deaf, and says he is a servant to one John Wayman, in Maryland, and calls his name James Watson. James Gordon.[40]

In contrast to Martha's Vineyard, there is evidence that the deaf were persecuted and shunned in other areas. Mid-19th century reports from institutions for the deaf often position their services as relief from an uncaring wider society, and while somewhat propagandized, by positioning their work in the cause of humanity reinforce this hypothesis.

America Unique

As much as any other factor in North America, a primary determinant of disability experience in the early colonial period was physical distance, as the region was devoid for the most part of large urban centers and transportation networks. In fact, it was often faster to travel by boat on the coast than by any method further inland. Therefore, accommodating disability was almost always a family duty by geographic necessity, and not a shared duty as it could be in the larger cities and social networks in Europe, where hospices, asylums, and other institutions could be formed through the largess of the church and/or on the basis of a large tax base. In the American colony, disability was almost always a private family dilemma, rather than a public societal dilemma, not only because there were very few services, but also because those services that did exist were limited to half a dozen or so eastern seaboard cities. Even churches, which in Europe founded great centers for the treatment of lepers or the blind or the deaf, remained mostly small, local institutions in America that had scarcely more resources than individual families did during this period.

Disability thus remained largely hidden. This was also due in large part to a continuing disability stigma. There were what one can assume at the time to be very practical reasons for avoiding public exposure, according to Frank Bowe:

> Disabled individuals were prohibited from settling in towns and villages of our Thirteen Colonies unless they could demonstrate ability to support themselves independently... Immigration policy effectively forbade entrance into the country of persons with physical, mental, or emotional disabilities. Because popular

---

[40] *Virginia Gazette*. Williamsburg, VA: Pinkney, October 19, 1775, 3, c. 3.

perceptions equated disability with inability [within the colonies and later the states], existence of a disability appeared reason enough to deny a person the right to participate in societal life. Within families, persons with disabilities were hidden, disowned, or even allowed to die through the withholding of life-support services. Within disabled individuals, self-perception inevitably reflected prevailing social attitudes, keeping people from even attempting to become self-reliant.[41]

Although there were evolving medicalized labels that began to legitimize some disabilities, ordinary colonial North Americans did not distinguish between types of disabilities with any degree of sophistication. They relied on outward symptoms that could be physically seen and quickly evaluated: sweating fevers, shortness of breath, or in extreme cases, missing limbs, bleeding wounds, or the obvious loss of eyesight. There were no invisible disabilities per se—only the work of demons and vaporous air filled with foul spirits, as Hannah Allen's case reports—and as a result, disability was a strange combination of a medical-related and superstitious-related experiences. To be disabled was usually to be seriously and obviously sick or injured, and in a world already filled with disease and hardship, it was understood to mean a shorter life span. Doctors remained rare, relatively undertrained, and sometimes did more harm than good.

This wider lack of a sophisticated and systemic understanding of the mind, the body, and individual notions of identity was revealed most horrifically, as previously mentioned, in the Salem Witch Trials, which on the surface might appear to have nothing at all to do with colonial disability, but which in reality were a metaphor for the aesthetic nervousness with which colonials and later early Americans experienced dealing with disability as abject form of Otherness.[42]

One disability treatment common to the colonial era, but now relatively ignored in the 21st century, was the use of hot springs and mineral waters. Although such treatments had been long-known and utilized in England and Europe, they assumed a larger role in colonial life, perhaps due to the Native American influence. "Taking the waters," became a catch-all cure for all types of mental and physical disabilities, ranging from the common cold to summer fevers. A typical newspaper notice informed the public in 1776 of such health opportunities:

---

[41] Bowe, Frank. "An Overview Paper on Civil Rights Issues of Handicapped Americans: Public Policy Implications," *Civil Rights Issues of Handicapped Americans: Public Policy Implications*. A Consultation Sponsored by the United States Commission on Civil Rights, May 13–14, 1980, pp. 8–9; as quoted in Doris Zames Fleischer and Frieda Zames, *The Disability Rights Movement: From Charity to Confrontation*. Temple University Press, 2001, p.11.

[42] Mappen.

> The public are hereby informed, that the new bath, in Louisa County [Virginia], ten miles above the courthouse, is now in good repair, and has every accommodation necessary for Gentlemen and Ladies who are inclined to retire from the lower parts of the country during the unhealthy season. The waters from long experience have been found excellent for removing slow fevers, agues and fevers, and all lingering disorders, and is a speedy remedy for ulcers, inflammations, etc. The utmost diligence will be used to render the place agreeable, by the Public's most obedient humble servant, Nathaniel Anderson.[43]

Many of the founding figures, such as Thomas Jefferson, found comfort and relief in the hot springs and mineral-rich waters of the nearby Appalachian Mountains. The practice was common enough that public notice was frequently made of it:

> Williamsburg, June 27. The Honorable Lewis Burnwell, Esq; President of this colony is returned from the medicinal springs on the frontiers, where he has been some time past for the recovery of his health, and we hear he has received much benefit by the waters—he is now at his seat in Gloucester County.[44]

Jefferson attempted to examine the benefits of medicinal springs with a more scientific eye: "Some ...are indubitably efficacious, while others seem to owe their reputation as much to fancy and change of air...as to their real virtues." (The efficacy of "taking the waters" is still debated today.) Although for the most part disability as medical problem was divorced from disability as lived experience, the persistent fascination with medicinal waters was an area where chronic disease and debilitating conditions were communalized and experienced in consistent ways across demographics and social status. Effective or not, people widely believed in the restorative power of the hot mineral springs, and there are countless reports of people from all walks of life going west or north to "take the waters." It became a ritual for more well-to-do families who could easily afford it, especially if the season correlated with an escape from the hot and humid tidewater summers; the experience even crossed class lines, with slaves being sent to the springs for healing.[45]

In what would become Canadian North America, similar forces were at work, tempered culturally by a French influence, but following parallel tracks

---

[43] *Virginia Gazette*. Williamsburg, VA: Dixon and Hunter, August 10, 1776, 7, c. 1.

[44] *Virginia Gazette*. Williamsburg, VA: Hunter, June 27, 1751, 3, c. 2.

[45] Jefferson, Thomas. *Notes on the State of Virginia*. Bedford/St. Martin's, 2002, pp. 104–106; Mitchell, p. 12, note 10.

to events further south. A frontier mentality, complicated by a cooler climate and even sparser population, meant that disability was a sentence to hardship or worse, and most typically dealt with in the immediate family. As in the thirteen American colonies, there are practically no early primary disability accounts. While culturally distinct and eventually independent as a nation, British colonial Canada, like her neighbors to the south, eventually (but perhaps slightly more quickly) evolved out of primitive conditions and into post-Enlightenment industrialization and institutionalization. Events very mostly mirrored those to the south. Canada, like the U.S., would eventually see disability labels proliferate in the late 19th and early 20th centuries side by side with the growth of public education systems, Progressivism, and the development of a wide eugenics initiative.[46]

Canadian colonial disability history, even more so than American colonial disability history, is largely still waiting to be uncovered. Geoffrey Reaume, disability scholar, characterizes it by pointing out that disabled people who are hidden within families and small rural communities are much harder to find, historically speaking, than those congregated into institutions or cities as happened in the mid to late 20th century. In English and French Canada, as in the American colonies, the rural disability experience was significantly different from the urban experience when cities began to flourish.[47]

Impact of Slavery

A discussion of the colonial era experience of disability can't be complete without considering the evolution of slavery in the new world, and specifically the race-based system that evolved in what would become the United States. There were many reasons slavery did not take hold in French and British Canada, but the elaborate system that grew in the American colonies to the south quickly became something unique in human history—a system characterized by an overwhelming capitalist imperative, a growing dichotomy of color-based

---

[46] McLaren, Angus. "The Creation of a Haven for 'Human Thoroughbreds': The sterilization of the Feeble-minded and the Mentally Ill in British Columbia," *Canadian Historical Review*. 1986, 2, pp. 128–150; *Mad People's History*. course description, Ryerson's School of Disability Studies, accessed December 12, 2013 http://abilities.ca/mad-peoples-history; "Disability historian explores 'mad' people's history," *yFile: York University's News Source*. February 13, 2007, accessed December 12, 2013 http://www.yorku.ca/yfile/archive/index.asp?Article=7892.

[47] Reaume, Geoffrey. "Disability History in Canada: Present work in the field and future prospects," *The Canadian Journal of Disability Studies*. 2012, Vol. 1(1), p. 61; Personal correspondence with Geoffrey Reaume, email, December 12th, 2013.

racism, and an elaborate form of legalized Otherness that would eventually prove indestructible by legislation alone.

American slaves in the colonial era were legally, educationally and socially disabled in a comparable context of modern identity politics as stigmatized Other, but they also were also frequently (and literally) physically and psychologically disabled in the same ways that other non-black Americans were; perhaps even at higher rates, due to the nature of their physical labor, the lack of freedom to access what few wellness resources were available, and due to the actual violence endemic to slavery itself. The literal evidence of this can be found in the military records of the Revolutionary War where blacks who volunteered, or were given permission by their masters to fight, were paid at roughly the same rate that white disabled pensioners were paid (roughly half pay). To be black was to be disabled.

The overwhelming economic imperative of slavery meant that irreconcilable contradictions were built into the system—one slave owner established a well-provisioned hospital complete with a staff physician exclusively for his slaves, while his own family members suffered from a conspicuous lack of adequate healthcare. A disabled slave was a mostly economic commodity that had lost its inherent human value, and therefore resources went into preventative care, but disappeared after permanent disablement. Slave auction lists were required to list any type of disability, large or small: "old and disabled; sickly; a great drunkard; sickly; sickly [with] consumption; etc." one list read. The corresponding monetary value in such cases was considerably less; anecdotal and statistical data suggests that abuse occurred more frequently in the case of disabled slaves, largely due to the perceived loss of utility and economic value. Martin Luther King, Jr. would later see the lingering effects of such disability stigma when black servicemen wounded in foreign wars could not access medical and support services that white soldiers routinely received upon coming home; he considered them twice disabled. To be a black slave in America, and to be or become disabled or chronically ill, meant a double dose of hardship and heightened risk for early death.[48]

Early North Americans, as has been mentioned, simply did not view "disability" (or to use the terms of the times: "illness, injury, malady, sickness," etc.) as a notable dichotomy of identity. Everyone got sick; everyone could die young; accidents were so common as to not be noteworthy. In contrast, the more familiar defining dichotomies of colonial-era identity generally functioned in terms of

---

[48] PBS. *Africans in America*. Accessed February 18, 2014 http://www.psb.org; Trammell, Jack. *The Richmond Slave Trade*. The History Press, 2012.

Christian or non-Christian, wealthy or poor, free or not free, and a very short time after 1607, as black or white. There was no notion of the disabled, or the temporarily abled bodied (TAB).[49]

There is no question, however, that disability occurred to people in early North America at rates at least as high as in the present time, and probably consistent with rates that had been occurring in the West since the days of the Roman Empire. Modern scholars often estimate that as much as twenty percent of the overall population is disabled at any given time. Life on the frontier, and even on small farms in small towns, was far from safe and secure, and the numbers of people suffering regular accidents that debilitated—even caused death—were common enough to escape wide comment, very simply appearing as public notices, if at all, and usually being accepted as routine.[50]

It is also apparent that disability stigma was as prevalent as it had been in previous eras in Western history. Congressional documents reveal that the maximum pay a disabled sailor could obtain, even if his disability was incurred in service to the empire or country, was one half the rate of normal pay. In addition, it was common to dismiss such sailors from service due to their disability, meaning that their potential to earn full pay or a living wage under any circumstances was severely restricted. Such policies are echoed in the 21st century in many disability insurance policies and government benefits that offer only a fraction of the original pre-disability salary to individuals.[51]

There were many *Hannah Allen*'s in the new world, most of whom will never be remembered by history. Even Hannah herself was cynical about what people would do with the information about her mental illness:

> My Aunt sometimes would tell me, that my expressions were so dreadful she knew not how to bear them. I would answer roundly, but what must I do then, that must feel them. I would after say to my Aunt, Oh, you little know what a dismal dark condition I am in; Methinks I am as dark as Hell itself...[52]

As Hannah found out in her own experience, the colonial era in North American disability history can best be characterized as a reflection of larger Western

---

[49] Fleischer, Doris Z., and Zames, Frieda. *The Disability Rights Movement: From Charity to Confrontation.* Temple University Press, 2011, p. 40.

[50] Covey, Herbert. *Social Perceptions of People with Disabilities in History.* Charles C. Thomas Publishers, 1998, p. 4.

[51] *American State Papers, House of Representatives, 13th Congress, 3rd Session, Naval Affairs: Volume 1.* 362, No. 126. "Distribution of prize money." No. 127. "Pension for the greatest disability limited to half pay."

[52] Allen.

European Enlightenment ideals, which emphasized a growing systemization of human anatomy, pursuit of rational cures, and a charity-based, pity-based view of those who became disabled. Unique factors influencing North American disability experience included a New World frontier mentality that heightened the emphasis on physical fitness, on individuality and independence, balanced later with a unique and growing experience with democracy and libertarian ideas that in fits and starts would much later set the stage for much later postmodern identity movements. The uniqueness of the North American experience would become particularly important with the formalization of American independence, after which there was a wider divergence between the British colonial world, New France, New Spain, and an evolving and more singular American Exceptionalism in the United States.

It would only be in the 1970s, in the words of Zames and Zames, that a "new concept emerged: the idea of disability as a social and political force." In the colonial era, however, the experience of disability and social geography of Otherness that would make such a movement possible were only barely beginning to be evidenced. The slivers of light might be seen in disability benefits for those in military service, or the slow creation of Western European style institutions for the sick and disabled, or the eventual creation of the early social sciences interested in bettering mankind. For the most part, however, the colonial era was devoid of great promises that a disability identity would eventually crystalize in the U.S. in the 1960s and contribute significantly to the modern Disability Rights Movement (DRM) in the Western world.[53]

[53.] Fleischer and Zames.

CHAPTER 2

Birth of American Individualism and Disability as Disruption

Our founders still speak to us in many important ways today, from the original American sin of slavery to the Enlightenment innovation in our unique democratic design. Their wisdom as well as their sins have been passed along through the growth of our great republican experiment, and their lives stay with us today through biography, history, and shared memory. But what do the founders tell us about disability? Was disability an interruption or social "disruption" in their lives?

Distinguishing what I call "social history" from the formal practices of historiography is not an absolute task, but it is safe to say that where traditional methods of history are often linear, causal, or focused on grand narratives, social history focuses more on lived experiences, descriptive analysis, and micro narratives. Formal history is often concerned less with anomaly in the sense that Kuhn (1962) described it in *The Structure of Scientific Revolutions*, while social history is by contrast often specifically focused on and fascinated by anomaly or outliers. Kuhn says that "normal science does not aim at novelties of fact" (p. 52). However, social history seeks novelty and individually unique experiences and seeks the discovery of diverse ways of knowing, experiencing and narrating history, all the while remaining connected to larger methodological threads recognizable in both fields.

This does not mean that social history does not involve procedure or rigor. Because one can place social history within a broader sociological framework, it has access to both quantitative and qualitative social methods, as well as access to broader theoretical frameworks which can inform it. Irving Goffman's focus on everyday life, for example, can fit into a social history research framework quite easily, differing from it though in its additional quest to connect with the larger historical threads already mentioned. The important difference is that social history claims to be both history and social analysis, as well as narrative story.

Douglas Baynton famously wrote that when intentionally looking at disability in history it could be found everywhere. His words could not be truer for the case of the founders. Using social history, the founders can be utilized to help tell America's disability story.

America, from its earliest native and colonial beginnings, was defined by individual possibilities and uniquely individual experiences. Between the colonial era and the antebellum period of industrialization and modernization, this was manifested in practical terms by land-grabs, a constant westward expansion, a unique frontier mentality, and a healthy libertarianism that was more than adequately suspicious of the federalized power of the central state. This resulted in a new republic founded on a number of fundamental principles that protected the rights and property of individuals (i.e., white males, at the time) and perhaps *over-valued* (italics author's) individualism.

Americans also built into their democracy entrenched elements of elitism that largely ignored salient issues of race, class, gender, and disability status. It basically ignored any recognition of the status of natives, for example. As a result, modern disability scholars are left to ponder the irony that is the American Constitution, a living document that encapsulates the best and the worst of the early American experience; a document that was not designed in any way, shape, or form at the time to speak specifically to the issue of disability, and yet seems arguably to philosophically sustain a modern disability rights movement.

The founding figures—those who can best be described as the architects of the U.S. Constitution—were not diverse. They were white, male, propertied, by and large wealthy, and sometimes unapologetically elitist. Yet they were also products of the Enlightenment, and accustomed to thinking of themselves as arbiters and protectors of the common good. While their definition of the common good was by 21st century standards narrow and quite flawed, it was in the grander scheme of human history quite benevolent, tolerant, and liberal in the classical sense. The founding figures created through the phrase "we the people"—partially by intent, and arguably partially by serendipity and subsequent lived experience—a document or framework for governance that could and did eventually allow for the birth of all of the modern civil rights movements.

In this chapter from hence forward, the term *founding figures* will intentionally be used to refer to a non-gendered, non-racialized, and to the extent historically possible, a class-free group of Americans. Although the historian must by default grapple with a preponderance of existing primary source material that is almost exclusively skewed toward the white, male, landed perspective, Americans none-the-less experienced revolution and change collectively, and the historian has the difficult but important obligation to seek out the wider American story in spite of the inherent difficulties of showing diverse perspectives.[1]

Even including in this chapter voices of women and people of color does mean that this collection of icons were in any sense fully representative of the typical American at the time. In fact, some of them like General and first U.S. President George Washington actually might be thought of as figures of anti-disability, or anti-liberal, contributing to the myth of what modern scholars like Rosemarie Garland-Thomson call the "normate." Washington, in fact, was quite vain about his physical appearance and mental wellness, to the point at times of becoming a caricature of normality. The "monumental image" came about in part due to Washington's inexplicable and incredible record of immunity to injury in battle, having hardly sustained so much as a scratch during years of dangerous service, often under fire, and also from his own deep well of vanity. He sometimes considered the problems with his teeth the worst physical disability he ever suffered from, and later, real problems with his eyesight did irritate him. But even near his death, "he was always averse to nursing himself for any slight complaint," an aide wrote. Washington's remarkable health and unjustified vanity were not the typical founding story and serve as a reminder about the dangers of over-generalizing from a small sample.[2]

Although far from diverse in many ways, the founding figures generally were at least representative (outside of Washington, perhaps) in the selected range of their personal disability experiences. True to Doris and Frieda Zames' maxim that "'handicapism' (also referred to as 'ableism') is the only 'ism' to which all human beings are susceptible," the founders tended to exceed the period's average life expectancy, and hence exhibited a wide variety of visible and invisible disabilities over time, some of which even required formal accommodations (even, for example, during the events associated with the constitutional convention, to be elaborated on later). In fact, the more historians examine the personal lives of the founding figures, the more apparent it is that their perspective was informed by a wider and very personal disability experience, even if they didn't call it that.[3]

---

[1] Longmore, P.K. and L. Umansky, eds. *The new disability history: American perspectives.* New York University Press, 2003.

[2] Flexner, James Thomas. *Washington: The indispensable man.* Signet, 1984, p. 401.

[3] Fleisher, Doris Zames, and Zames, Frieda. *The Disability Rights Movement: From Charity to Confrontation.* Temple University Press, 2011, p. xix; Smith, J. David. "Diagnosing Mr. Jefferson: Retrospectives on Developmental Disabilities at Monticello," *Intellectual and Developmental Disabilities* 45, 6 (2007), pp. 405–407; Shapiro, Joseph. *No Pity: People with Disabilities Forging a New Civil Rights Movement.* Times Books, 1993, p. 59.

Interpreting the Constitution and Disability

The U.S. Constitution as it was originally published in 1787 says very little if anything about disability, with the exception of the section on presidential succession. It does speak to race through the 13th, 14th, and 15th Amendments, and gender through the 19th Amendment. Many disability advocates have used this apparent disparity as a justification for an argument in favor of passing legislation like the Americans with Disabilities Act, especially in the event an actual amendment could not be passed (and passing an amendment of ANY type has become increasingly difficult…)

Constitutional scholars, however, do connect various parts of the existing constitution with important ideas that are consistent with the overall spirit of the "law of the land." For example, the 14th Amendment was geared toward giving recently freed slaves and all Americans "equal protection under the law." The amendment empowered Congress to pass legislation that carries out that directive, especially in cases where evidence suggests discrimination is likely or recurrent. The 1964 Civil Rights Act, as conceptualized by President John F. Kennedy, and later effectuated by President Lyndon B. Johnson in 1964, is a good example of legislation that descends directly from the spirit of the 14th Amendment.

The 1990 passage of the ADA, and the more recent 2008 Amendments Act, are very consistent with this same clause, as well, and were openly crafted after the model of the 1964 Civil Rights Act. The general language in many sections or amendments also suggests a proactive disability attitude, consistent with the notion that Americans should "promote the general welfare," and treat all Americans with "justice" and share the "blessings of liberty."

Still, many disability advocates in the 21st century worry that the ADA and ADAAA did not go far enough, and that the constitution needs to be more explicit in protecting the rights of people with disabilities. Women's groups, in a similar vein, continue to advocate for an explicit Equal Rights Amendment to the constitution. Since the constitution is considered a living document, amendable by three quarters of the states, there is always the possibility that a disability rights act or similar amendment will be added someday, and a significant number of people would like to see that happen.

Americans were forged as a nationality (a group with a national common interest) during this period, and they looked to these public figures as examples of what was ideal and possible in a uniquely new collective experience. Life, it was true, was often difficult and short, but if a Jefferson could write hundreds of letters and monitor a large estate and business while battling chronic pain and discomfort; if a Franklin could invent his own bifocals to compensate for his fading vision due to presbyopia; if an Abigail Adams could force herself to get up and tend to household needs in spite of her chronic depression; if a Gouvernuer Morris could take his wooden leg and turn it into a social advantage; then average Americans in other challenging situations could also persevere. The theme of "overcoming" would become a uniquely American attribute, with both positive and sometimes quite negative components, and one clearly evidenced in the tensions of the blooming disability rights movement of the 1960s and 1970s. Overcoming itself as a concept would eventually become part of the "super crip" myth that disability radicals would and still do angrily reject. But in early American history, overcoming helped define the overall collective disability experience in a meaningful fashion.

Founding Semantics

The founders inherited and utilized an American English semantic legacy in which the term disability was primarily a political and positional tool in the English Language, and not one associated with a personal identity or consistently with a medically-oriented condition. In fact, if the founding figures are to be read literally, the colonies were in essence "disabled" in their relationship with Great Britain more than individuals were disabled by physical impairment. This usage by Benjamin Franklin is typical of hundreds of examples:

> This wanton destruction of [American] property operated doubly to the *disabling* (italics author's) of our Merchants, who were importers from Britain, in making their Payments, by the immoderate Loss they sustain'd (sic) themselves, and also the loss suffered by their country debtors, who had bought of them the British goods, and who were now render'd (sic) unable to pay. The debts to Britain of course remained undischarg'd (sic), and the clamour continu'd (sic), these knavish Americans will not pay us![4]

[4.] Franklin, Benjamin. *The writings of Benjamin Franklin, collected and edited with a life and introduction by Albert Henry Smyth, Volume X 1789–1790*, London: MacMillan & Company, LTD., 1907, p. 110. "The extract

None-the-less, like a significant number of early Americans, the founding figures generally lived long enough and in dangerous enough environments to experience actual personal disablement. Thomas Jefferson, author of the Declaration of Independence and third president of the new republic, suffered from as many as forty-three separate "disabilities" or medical conditions according to some researchers, ranging from being on the Autism spectrum (ASD) to experiencing chronic migraines. In addition, Jefferson experienced profound personal disability issues vicariously with both his sister and his brother that caused him great mental anguish. Taken as a whole and regardless of the arguments about post-hoc diagnosis and the distance of time, there can be little doubt that disability was a prominent overarching theme in Jefferson's private life.[5]

He frequently wrote about his various ailments and illnesses, as in this 1823 letter:

> The bone of my arm is well knitted and strong; but the carpal bones, having been disturbed, maintain an oedematous (sic) swelling of the hands and fingers, keeping them entirely helpless, and holding up no definite term for the recovery of their usefulness. I am now in the 5th month of this disability.[6]

If one is to accept the correlation between Jefferson's personal complaints and his modern medical analysts, it is a wonder he accomplished anything at all due to pain, discomfort, immobility, and the sickness he constantly wrote about. Still, Jefferson is more typical of the times than Washington, and he also left an open record of his disability experiences, which makes his understanding doubly significant. Other founders, including Franklin, often wrote letters and treatises with an overt eye toward their legacy; Jefferson was usually more honest in his personal writings. Of his various conditions, perhaps Jefferson's headaches—migraines more accurately—feature as often in his complaints as anything:

---

from the Sessions Paper and the first paragraph of this article are written in Franklin's hand, in ink, on the back of a letter to him from T. Barker, dated April 16, 1786. The article seems to be referred to in Franklin to Bishop Shipley, February 24, 1786, and is certainly the paper mentioned in a letter to Le Veillard, April 15, 1787. It is there said to have been written about a year. ED."

[5.] Schneeberg, Norman G. "The Medical History of Thomas Jefferson (1743–1826)," *The Journal of Medical Biography*, 16, 2, 2008, pp. 118–125; Smith, J. David. "Diagnosing Mr. Jefferson: Retrospectives on Developmental Disabilities at Monticello," *Intellectual and Developmental Disabilities*, 45, 6, 2007, pp. 405–407; Doctor Zebra, *The Health and Medical History of President Thomas Jefferson*, http://www.doctorzebra.com/prez/g03.html.

[6.] Gawalt, Gerald W. (Ed.) "Thomas Jefferson and William Short Correspondence," Manuscript Division, *Library of Congress;* Thomas Jefferson to William Short, March 28, 1823, Monticello March 28.23.

> Dear Sir: An indisposition of periodical head ach (sic) has for some time disabled me from business, and prevented my sooner acknoleging (sic) your letter of Mar. 22 and returning that of Feb. 2. 06 which it inclosed (sic).[7]

Jefferson, according to Norman Schneeberg, had a lifelong and intense interest in matters related to medicine and corresponded regularly with doctors and medical experts. His library was filled with medical texts and treatises. He was often critical of the general state of medical expertise, and usually recommended more natural and practical treatments, which included Native American cures. As a result, historians assume that Jefferson frequently treated himself, as well as his slaves and family members, rather than constantly call on the expertise of "trained" physicians. Even his trusted personal physician, Dr. Robley Dunglison, who tended to him late in life admitted to Jefferson's unyielding skepticism of formal medicine, claiming that Jefferson said that where three doctors are gathered there are also buzzards to be found hovering.[8]

Listed amongst his probable conditions and disabilities in addition to those already mentioned are: dysentery, rheumatism, malaria, tuberculosis, diabetes, insomnia, UTO (urinary tract obstruction), anxiety, depression, and Obsessive Compulsive Disorder (OCD). To say that Jefferson was, in 21st century terms, twice exceptional—that is that he had both extreme giftedness and profound disabilities that existed side by side, or 2E in popular vernacular—might be an extreme understatement. He was, in spite of the danger of "super crip" stereotypes, an amazing individual who remains no less amazing in the present time given what posterity knows about him, and all of his human complexities.

In terms of his personal disability identity, one can only speculate, but the letters, notes, and eyewitness accounts that are left to us suggest that Jefferson was a complainer, a bit of hypochondriac, marginally cynical about the human condition in terms of long-term comfort and access to a healthy physical and mental life. It would be an overstatement to say that he was bitter, miserable, or discontent, but there can be little doubt that disability was a constant, less than comfortable companion that Jefferson accepted, but never fully embraced with complete and seamless grace.

Ultimately, Jefferson suffered from the most common human disability of all: old age. As he wrote in the following excerpt from a letter, it kept him from

---

[7] Gewalt, Gerald W. (Ed.) "Thomas Jefferson and James Monroe Correspondence," Manuscript Division, *Library of Congress*, Thomas Jefferson to James Monroe, April 11, 1808, Washington Apr. 11.08.

[8] Schneeberg, Norman G. "The medical history of Thomas Jefferson (1743–1826)," *Journal of Medical Biography*, 16, 2008, pp. 118–125.

volunteering for military service against the British in the War of 1812, though it seems his spirit was quite willing:

> I think we shall have learnt how to call forth our force, and by the next I hope our funds: and even if the state of Europe should not be that time give the enemy employment enough nearer home, we shall leave him nothing to fight for here. These are my views of the war. They embrace a great deal of sufferance, trying privations, and no benefit but that of teaching our enemy that he is never to gain by wanton injuries on us. To me this state of things brings a sacrifice of all tranquility & comfort through the residue of life. For altho' (sic) the debility of age disable me from the services & the sufferings of the field, yet, by the total annihilation in value of the produce which was to give me subsistence and independence (sic), I shall be like Tantalus, up to the shoulders in water, yet dying with thirst. We can make indeed enough to eat drink & clothe ourselves; but nothing for our salt, is on, groceries, & taxes, which must be paid in money.[9]

Jefferson also had complicated views on slavery and race relations that were more than a shadowy prophesy of the intersection of race, gender and disability that would become the focus of a branch of modern sociology (identity studies/intersectionality) and ultimately produce the field of disability studies. For example, he in essence argued that giving healthcare and disability rights to slaves, but then denying it to ordinary working men, was illogical and worked at cross purposes to the wider good (!?). In the following passage written to Clement Caine, he predicts a future that might include the illogical (at that time perhaps) marriage of slavery and union-like disability and health benefits, a future that almost came to pass (in industrial Civil War Richmond) if not for a bloody Civil War:

> Sir,--Your favor of April 2d was not received till the 23d of June last, with the volume accompanying it, for which be pleased to accept my thanks. I have read it with great satisfaction, and received from it information, the more acceptable as coming from a source which could be relied on. The retort on European censors, of their own practices on the liberties of man, the inculcation on the master of the moral duties which he owes to the slave, in return for the benefit of his service, that is to say, of food clothing, care in sickness, and maintenance under age and disability, so as to make him in fact as comfortable and more secure than the

---

[9.] Gawalt, Gerard W. "Thomas Jefferson and William Short Correspondence," Manuscript Division, *Library of Congress*, Thomas Jefferson to William Short, November 28, 1814, Monticello Nov. 28. 14.

laboring man in most parts of the world; and the idea suggested of substituting free whites in all household occupations and manual arts, thus lessening the call for the other kind of labor, while it would increase the public security, give great merit to the work, and will, I have no doubt, produce wholesome impressions.[10]

Clearly, a Jeffersonian sense of social justice differed radically from the early 21st century conceptions of such. But his precognition of intersectionality remains to his credit within the context of his slave-ownership and racialized attitudes.

In spite of or because of those complexities, Jefferson remains an icon of the American spirit, and in the records it is evident that he was an early intellectual critic of medicine and disability, and a personal actor in the American disability experience. While clearly shaped by the times he lived in, and far from perfect in his own humanity, Jefferson was a founding figure who would not have had difficulty understanding some aspects of the modern disability rights movement: the benefits of self-autonomy (perhaps even the "natural" state of humans), the sacred rights and profits of citizenship, the need for a moral foundation to determine what social equity consists of, what human agency is, or especially the need to curtail the governmentality of the body and mind usurped by doctors and professionals' expert status, and allow instead individuals the ultimate power over their bodies and minds.[11]

Even then, he and his family members were not immune to practicing blatant disability discrimination. His daughter Martha described John Marshall's wife, struggling with depression, this way: "Mrs. Marshall, once Miss Ambler, is insane, the loss of two children is thought to occasioned it." According to historian Jean Edward Smith, who quotes the anecdote in his biography of Marshall, Martha's gossip about Polly Marshall did nothing to improve the strained relationship between the two founders. The stigma of mental disability crosses time and cultural boundaries.[12]

The Exceptional Franklin

Benjamin Franklin was if anything more complex than Jefferson. Perhaps more than any other founding figure, he embodied the intricacies of twice exceptionality

---

[10] Ford, Paul Leicester (Ed.), *The Works of Thomas Jefferson in Twelve Volumes, Federal Edition*; Jefferson, Thomas. "Personal Correspondence with Clement Caine," September 16, 1811, Monticello, September 16, 1811.

[11] Tremain, Shelley. *Foucault and the government of disability.* The University of Michigan Press, 2005.

[12] Smith, Jean Edward, *John Marshall: Definer of a Nation*, H. Holt & Co., p. 107.

(2E), being posthumously diagnosed with learning disabilities, ADD/ADHD, and physical disabilities including visual impairment, while at the same time being considered a genius and a luminary. Franklin in his own writings approaches disability and sickness with humor, but also with an unresolved tension quite typical of the late Enlightenment fascination and fear of physical deformity and medical crisis.[13]

Franklin has long been suspected of having Dyslexia, and in some of his letters he mentions that he has not read something yet because he has been "too busy," a clue that he may in fact have been a slow reader, especially when he was younger, or felt embarrassment about his reading deficiencies. His excuse-making could possibly seem to indicate a problem. There can be no doubt he worked very hard once he firmly committed to educating himself and learning to read, and even if he was a slow reader at first he must have improved over time as a result of the sheer amount of reading he eventually did in fact do. He appreciated good access to books as he became a better reader:

> This library afforded me the means of improvement by constant study, for which I set apart an hour or two each day; and thus repair'd (sic) in some degree the loss of the learned education my father once intended for me. Reading was the only amusement I allow'd (sic) myself. I spent no time in taverns, games, or frolicks (sic) of any kind.[14]

Franklin processed disability(s) both as a personal experience and as something that he empirically observed in others. Like many Enlightenment figures, he both feared and was fascinated by it. Here he describes an early encounter with a disabled widow whom he befriended as a young man:

> [She] had lived much among people of distinction, and knew a thousand anecdotes of them as far back as the times of Charles the Second. She was lame in her knees with the gout, and, therefore, seldom stirred out of her room, so sometimes wanted company; and hers was so highly amusing to me, that I was sure to spend an evening with her whenever she desired it.[15]

---

[13]. Franklin, Benjamin. *The autobiography of Benjamin Franklin with introduction and notes edited by Charles W. Eliot LLD P F.* Collier & Son Company, 1909.

[14]. Ibid. Also see popular articles, like this one in the Wall Street Journal, all of which claim Franklin was dyslexic: http://online.wsj.com/news/articles/SB10001424127887324020504578396421382825196.

[15]. Ibid. p. 58 (of 112)

In this case, pity and a charitable concern were Franklin's somewhat predicable reactions. But there was also curiosity, even as he also disingenuously (perhaps) suggested that disability was not something his own family was predisposed to suffer:

> My mother had likewise an excellent constitution: she suckled all her ten children. I never knew either my father or mother to have any sickness but that of which they dy'd (sic), he at 89, and she at 85 years of age. They lie buried together at Boston, where I some years since placed a marble over their grave...[16]

In reality, Franklin was like Jefferson, apparently suffering from numerous disabilities and maladies over the course of his long life. Although he was living in a time period where rugged individualism encouraged people to simply accept their plight, to suffer silently, and families were by default the primary caregivers, he none-the-less was a pioneer in what would eventually become the institutional movement for accommodating the disabled. His support for this dated back to as early as 1751:

> Dr. Thomas Bond, a particular friend of mine, conceived the idea of establishing a hospital in Philadelphia (a very beneficent design, which has been ascrib'd (sic) to me, but was originally his), for the reception and cure of poor sick persons, whether inhabitants of the province or strangers. He was zealous and active in endeavouring (sic) to procure subscriptions for it, but the proposal being a novelty in America, and at first not well understood, he met with but small success...[17]

Franklin went on to explain how a subscription format allowed supporters to give their funding to the project without committing massive public monies, using techniques and logic eerily similar to the political processes utilized in 1990 to pass the Americans with Disabilities Act, which some criticized at the time as creating an unfunded mandate without the resources behind it to make any significant difference:

> This condition carried the bill through; for the members, who had oppos'd (sic) the grant, and now conceiv'd (sic) they might have the credit of being charitable without the expence (sic), agreed to its passage; and then, in soliciting subscriptions among the people, we urg'd (sic) the conditional promise of the law as an

---

[16] Ibid. p. 8 (of 112)

[17] Ibid. p. 74 (of 112)

> additional motive to give, since every man's donation would be doubled; thus the clause work'd (sic) both ways. The subscriptions accordingly soon exceeded the requisite sum, and we claim'd (sic) and receiv'd (sic) the public gift, which enabled us to carry the design into execution.[18]

The establishment of this institution in Philadelphia, and places like the first insane asylum established in Williamsburg, Virginia in 1771, proved to fill a great pubic need even in their rudimentary forms, and served as a model that was soon imitated in other American and Canadian cities. Franklin's charity as a young man, however, would be a favor returned to him in spades as he entered into his golden years and dealt with his own increasing physical discomforts, increasingly reliant on the help of others.

In 1789 during a serious illness, for example, Franklin's secretary penned for him to a correspondent this apology:

> A painful illness has hitherto prevented Dr. Franklin's answering Mr. Merwin's obliging letter. He is extreamly (sic) sensible of the Honour proposed to be done him by the dedication, and requests Mr. Merwin to accept his thanks; but cannot give his consent to the publishing such encomiums on his own conduct, and hopes Mr. Merwin will excuse the refusal.[19]

He also was nagged by failing eyesight. According to one source, "Franklin wrote in August 1784 to his friend George Whatley that he was 'happy in the invention of double spectacles, which serving for distant objects as well as near ones, make my eyes as useful to me as ever they were.'" Franklin invented the glasses for himself more than for anyone else. Although more famous for his inventiveness than his disability(s), Franklin was clearly living a disability experience that impacted much of his life and work, including the self-serving invention of bifocals.[20]

Some have argued that even in the colonial era there was an important dichotomy between impairment and disability, two terms sometimes used synonymously in the present time, but more often than not seen as very different in important semantic, cultural, and medical ways. In the 20th century, the dissimilarity between

---

[18] Ibid. p. 75 (of 112).

[19] Benjamin Franklin, *The writings of Benjamin Franklin, collected and edited with a life and introduction by Albert Henry Smyth, Volume X 1789–1790*, (London: MacMillan & Company, LTD., 1907), 75.

[20] "Electric Ben Franklin: Benjamin Franklin's Inventions, Discoveries, and Improvements." Accessed February 21, 2014, http://www.ushistory.org/franklin/info/inventions.htm.

physical difference (impairment) and the social consequences (disability) became the foundation of the social model of disability, an idea critical to the disability rights movement. Impairment came to be associated with the medical definition of disability, which centered the primary problem within the body of the individual with the disability (known later as the medical model). Men like Franklin and Jefferson were largely unconcerned with such a sophisticated argument, and more concerned with daily living and personal comfort.[21]

In Franklin's time, some cite as an example of the impairment/disability dichotomy an instance when Franklin was carried into the Constitutional Convention of 1787 in a large chair due to his physical immobility. Claire Liachowtiz argues that Franklin was impaired in this situation, but not disabled. The counter argument which is equally defensible is that Franklin was in fact disabled, and he was also accommodated for that disability. To limit him to the simple medical notion of impairment is to take away the lived experience he had with disability that impacted everything he did, including his work at the convention. Many of the figures who in this chapter are being called founding figures had "lived" experiences with disability that superseded labels and medical conventions.[22]

This lived experience with disability most likely heightened Franklin's natural interest in social justice (albeit quasi-benevolent and paternal), which later in life was a more frequently recurring theme in his writings and public initiatives. In explaining the terms with which to treat debtors after the Revolutionary War, he made special dispensation for individuals with disabilities, as just one example, and especially those who had suffered directly from combat injuries visible and invisible. The argument he made was remarkably consistent with modern systems of social welfare:

> With regard to your other debtors, my opinion is, that your best way will be to send over express an active capable man, with a power to collect them where there is ability to pay, and *where there is evident disability to give farther reasonable time*; for it is certain that the severe operations of the war did actually disable many, and I am inform'd (sic) that the person in question had two good houses one in the country the other in town, stript (sic) of their furniture, and burnt to the ground. (italics author's)[23]

[21.] Barnes, Colin; Mercer, Geof; and Shakespeare, Tom. *Exploring Disability: A Sociological Introduction*. Cambridge: Polity Press, 1999.

[22.] Liachowitz, Claire H. *Disability as a Social Construct: Legislative Roots*. University of Pennsylvania Press, 1988, preface.

[23.] Franklin, Benjamin. "Letter to John Sargent" (unpublished). Thursday, May 25, 1786; Franklin Papers. http://franklinpapers.org/franklin//.

Taken in total, Franklin must be seen not only as an intellectual luminary and a remarkable leader, but also as a man who in essence accepted disability as a routine part of the human condition that all would be more or less subject to over time, and a social reality that all should be held accountable for. As in most things, he was imminently practical in his approach.

Founding Diversity

Abigail Adams, a remarkable individual and the spouse of John Adams, experienced disability through a variety of perspectives, and gives insight into the female gendered revolutionary era disability landscape. She not only experienced disability in a deeply personal manner, but also experienced it in the wider community. When she was younger, she and John both witnessed an epidemic of dysentery break out in the Boston region which decimated the U.S. army soldiers stationed there, local citizens, and threatened the entire Adams family:

> Such is the distress of the neighborhood that I can scarcely find a well person to assist me in looking after the sick... ...so mortal a time the oldest man does not remember. As to politics I know nothing about them. I have wrote as much as I am able to, being very weak.[24]

Her biographer wondered at her ability to pen such letters, and care for so many others, even disabled as she was herself by sickness and worry, and her other disabilities. Throughout her long life, her chief worries were often not in politics but the ever-present threat of sickness, accident, or permanent disability. According to David McCullough, she was sick as a child and continued to experience chronic headaches, rheumatism, melancholy and insomnia throughout her long adult life.[25]

"Neither of us appear built for duration," she wrote in a letter to John. "Would to heaven the few remaining days allotted to us be enjoyed together."[26]

It didn't help that Abigail's disabilities, temporary or chronic, were often treated with little or no sophistication psychologically or medically. Once during a winter bout of severe rheumatism, complicated by fever and depression, her

---

[24] Adams, Abigail; as quoted in McCullough, David. *John Adams*. Simon & Schuster, 2001, p. 25.

[25] Ibid., pp. 54, 362.

[26] Ibid., p. 290.

condition was worsened by treatments of severe bleedings, a common therapy of the day, but one which her doctor used to extremes. One can almost imagine her husband's colleague and later friend, Thomas Jefferson, reminding her about the evils of consulting trained physicians.

"How soon may our fairest prospects be leveled with the dust and show us that man in his best estate is but vanity and dust?" she wondered in her letters at the time. It took weeks for her to recover enough to travel, as their lifestyle often demanded of them, a routine that intensified her disabilities. When not traveling, she was often left alone to tend to the rest of the family and the estate, and to recover.[27]

Abigail, like the founding figures in general, enjoyed privileges that many middle class and lower class Americans did not: access to healthcare (such as it was); access to urban resources; a modest wealth; and a lifestyle sometimes protected from the most savage elements of frontier life. In spite of that, her experience would have mirrored that of many ordinary women in the era, who generally suffered many physical and mental disabilities that were mostly untreated, unrecognized, and formulated at best to be a result of the fairer gender also being the presumed weaker sex. In newer terminology, Abigail's gendered disability experiences represented an intersectionality of race (privileged white), gender (she shared power with her husband), religion (she was minority unitarian in more religiously conservative region), and education (she promote a less gendered universal educational system). She didn't represent all women, of course, but she represented a complex and meaningful combination of many female identities that makes her a relevant case study.

Increasingly later in her life, Abigail's troubled health and various disabilities, including severe chronic depression, were a primary cause for great angst in the marriage partnership, even as husband Adams excelled and advanced in his diplomatic and political career. On more than one occasion, she even proclaimed herself possibly on her deathbed. She wrote to him about these chronic illnesses in 1793:

> My days of anxiety have indeed been many and painful in years past, when I had many terrors that encompassed me around. I have happily surmounted them, but I do not find that I am less solicitous to hear constantly from you ... friendship and affection deep-rooted subsists which defies the ravages of time.[28]

---

[27] Ibid., pp. 433–434.

[28] McCullough, p. 440.

Adams himself recognized his spouse's disability-related "ravages" all too well, often finding it difficult to concentrate on his own work as a result. He was occasionally criticized for neglecting his presidential duties as a result of returning home to care for and supervise her health. He wrote in 1796 that:

> Of all the summers of my life, this has been the freest from care, anxiety, and vexation to me. *The sickness of Mrs. A. excepted.* (italics author's)[29]

Abigail eventually succumbed to Typhoid at the age of seventy-four, having survived a long life with a number of recurring ailments, injuries, and sicknesses. Although it can hardly be said that she was drastically more disabled than many of her peers, it is noteworthy that her experience was quite typical for women of the times. Women without the resources Abigail enjoyed would have suffered additional hardships, and perhaps not lived nearly as long as she did, and perhaps been more disabled in the modern sense of the term.

Abigail was also twice exceptional (2E), like so many of the founding figures. Her gifted insights, uncanny intuition, cleverness and love for John made possible the greatness they achieved together. Theirs was truly a remarkable partnership.

Famous Individuals and Post Hoc Disability Diagnosis

At the end of the 20th century, and into the 21st century, a trend to normalize disability has resulted in the post-hoc (after the fact) diagnosis of many famous people with disabilities. The list of historical figures includes such well-known personalities as: Alexander the Great (ADHD), Amadeus Mozart (ASD), Ludwig Van Beethoven (Depression), Dr. Samuel Johnson (Tourette's), Frida Kahlo (Polio and likely Spina Bifida), Hermann of Reichenau (Cerebral Palsy and Spina Bifada), Sir Isaac Newton (Epilepsy), Stephen Hopkins (CP, and signer of the Declaration of Independence with a shaking hand), and many, many others.[30]

Some doctors and psychologists, however, are reluctant to make such hasty determinations without very rich primary source information. In spite of that, the cultural normalization of disabil-

---

[29] Ibid., pp. 462, 508–509, 526.

ity in the early 21st century has resulted in a growing list of historic celebrities who we now think likely were disabled, and all of them are by definition also twice exceptional (2E).

Patriot and founding figure Benjamin Franklin is sometimes advertised as the most famous example of combining many geniuses and many disabilities in one person.

"Perhaps the most innovative thinkers include not only the ones with the greatest intellectual talents, but also the ones who blend that intellect with perceptive dysfunctions that allow them to function beyond the norm," says Kiesa Kay.[31]

[30.] *Famous People with Disabilities*, A list of some famous and well known people with various disabilities and conditions including actors, politicians and writers who contributed to society, accessed August 10, 2015 at http://www.disabled-world.com/artman/publish/article_0060.shtml.

[31.] Quoted in "2E Newsletter," accessed online August 11, 2015 at http://www.2enewsletter.com/topic_2e_thoughts.html.

Phyllis Wheatley was the rarer still African American woman from the period with a profound disability story that can be partially recovered historically. Wheatley, who was brought to America as an eight-year-old slave, eventually was manumitted and became a well-known poet, although she lived a tragically short life, dying from complications of chronic respiratory illness at thirty-one. Ironically, she arrived in the new world in Boston Harbor on a ship filled with many other disabled slaves—more than was typical—who were either not capable of the physical demands of Caribbean or southern plantations, or too young to do the hard physical work (and hence were sent to cooler climes but still as slaves). She was sickly then, too, with the captain of the slave ship reportedly more than happy to get *anything at all* for her and the others when Susanna Wheatley, wife of a tailor, purchased her. Amongst her chronic illnesses, she suffered most from severe Asthma, a potentially fatal disorder for which the dangers were intensified due to the crude understanding of the respiratory system at the time.[32]

Wheatley's poetry was often composed in classic couplets, both iambic pentameter and heroic forms, and was generally well-received by critics. She even traveled to England as a result of her writing talents. She was reportedly the first

---

[32.] Rinaldi, Ann. *Hang a Thousand Trees with Ribbons: The Story of Phillis Wheatley*. Orlando: Harcourt, 2005; The Poetry Foundation, "Phyllis Wheatley biography," accessed February 13, 2014 http://www.poetryfoundation.org/bio/phillis-wheatley.

African American woman to publish a book, and her fame eventually connected her directly to the founding figures—even George Washington complimented her work. But her lived experience as a disabled black woman, enslaved, during the colonial era makes her an important and singular figure.[33]

In one her better-known poems, *Imagination*, she suggests what many individuals with disabilities have known intuitively for countless centuries, that a life of the mind can counter the harsh physical reality of illness, pain and disability:

> Such is thy pow'r, nor are thine orders vain,
> O thou the leader of the mental train:
> In full perfection all thy works are wrought,
> And thine the sceptre o'er the realms of thought.
> Before thy throne the subject-passions bow,
> Of subject-passions sov'reign ruler Thou,
> At thy command joy rushes on the heart,
> And through the glowing veins the spirits dart.

She carried on an international correspondence, and luminaries as distant as Voltaire discussed the importance of her work. Although she has been perhaps unfairly criticized for not taking a stronger stand against slavery after her own manumission, she did in fact articulate an anti-slavery stance that could have easily stood side by side with the radical disability activism of the 1960s that demanded a response from the rest of America regarding the hypocrisies of supposed freedom:

> ...In every human breast, God has implanted a principle, which we call love of freedom; it is impatient of oppression, and pants for deliverance; and by the leave of our modern Egyptians I will assert, that the same principle lives in us. God grant deliverance in his own way and time, and get him honour (sic) upon all those whose avarice impels them to countenance and help forward the calamities of their fellow creatures. This I desire not for their hurt, but to convince them of the strange absurdity of their conduct whose words and actions are so diametrically, opposite. How well the cry for liberty, and the reverse disposition for the exercise of oppressive power over others agree -- I humbly think it does not require the penetration of a philosopher to determine...[34]

---

[33] Notes in Fold3, available through Ancestry.com.

[34] *The Connecticut Gazette*, March 11, 1774, as reprinted in Africans in America, PBS, accessed February 14, 2014 at http://www.pbs.org/wgbh/aia/part2/2h19t.html.

Wheatley was a remarkable individual who died so young as to cut off her own growing fame. Only learning English for the first time when she was eight, she was also learning Latin, for which her master said she had "a great inclination to learn," by the time she was twelve. Although she was freed after her mistress's death in 1774, she was seldom physically healthy enough to enjoy her subsequent marriage, writing career and family life as a free woman. She died in poverty. As in some of her poetry, she seemed to gravitate as in the following letter to escape in the inner life of the mind, where physical and emotional ailments could be daydreamed away for a little while, and the harshness and shortness of life could partially be mitigated:

> The vast variety of scenes that have pass'd (sic) before us these 3 years past will to a reasonable mind serve to convince us of the uncertain duration of all things temporal, and the proper result of such a consideration is an ardent desire of, & preparation for, a state and enjoyments which are more suitable to the immortal mind.[35]

It's not perfectly clear what other specific health problems Wheatley suffered from, although it is abundantly clear from the records that along with severe asthma, these other factors were omnipresent from early childhood until her death. Biographers specifically list asthma among her maladies, and at least one that she died from pneumonia, an obviously-related respiratory illness. Her trip to England was not only to promote her poetry, but also to pursue treatments for her ailments. None of her children survived long, suggesting that some strong tendency toward respiratory illness was prevalent in her family by genetic predisposition.[36]

The level of medical knowledge about respiratory diseases was limited at best during her lifetime. According to researchers, asthma has been documented in cultures dating back to ancient Egypt, where a papyrus contains recipes for hundreds of potentials treatments and was mentioned by name by Greeks of the 5th century BCE. The Greeks are reported to have treated it in some cases with "owl's blood in wine." Chinese doctors treated patients even hundreds of years

---

[35] Woodlief, Ann. "Biography," http://www.vcu.edu/engweb/webtexts/Wheatley/philbio.htm (This entire site is written by Ann Woodlief; please contact at awood@vcu.edu to download or link); Caretta, Vincent. *Phyllis Wheatley: Biography of a Genius in Bondage*. University of Georgia Press, 2011.

[36] See http://www.biography.com/people/phillis-wheatley-9528784; http://www.phillis-wheatley.org/biography-early-life/ and related sites.

ago with an herbal mixture containing ephedrine, a common treatment that has more recently been carefully regulated by the FDA due to its side effects.[37]

Living with asthma is now known to be complicated, sometimes difficult, and in extreme cases, even deadly. In the past, however, it has been frequently been considered in part to be a psychosomatic illness, and one for which the general public had little information or sympathy. Phyllis Wheatley spent part of her life in the care of a relatively affluent, educated family, and therefore had some access to the crude treatments of the day. It is safe to assume that this condition made daily life for her challenging and unpleasant, probably rendering everything from routine laundry chores to international travel anything but routine.

As a black woman, Wheatly did have to endure what can only be called the racist barbs of the times. In spite of her recognized talent, one prominent planter suggested she was no more than a parrot, imitating the speech of more intelligent beings.[38] He was not alone. Yet her example can remind us of the universal experience of disability across identities and across time and serve to prove that history is more than white male hegemony. We simply need to work harder to recover it.

George Washington's Disabled Body Double

Returning to George Washington again, the legendary, supposedly indestructible "man in stone," it is fitting to give consideration to his literal body double, Gouverneur Morris, who provides yet another relevant founding figure disability perspective. Morris (not be mistaken for the more famous Robert Morris) posed for the famous French Sculpture Jean-Antoine Houdon in place of Washington, being of a similar build and Washington not being available at the time when Houdon created his famous statue of Washington. Morris was a native New Yorker who served in the Continental Congress, amongst many other patriotic services, and who also embodied many of the complexities of colonial disability.[39]

---

[37] Crosta, Peter. "Asthma information," Last updated on 5 March 2013. *Medical News Today*, 2007, Accessed February 27, 2014 at http://www.medicalnewstoday.com/info/asthma/asthma-history.php; Ford, M. D., Delaney, K. A., Ling, L. J., & Erickson T. (Eds.), *Clinical Toxicology.* W. B. Saunders, 2001.

[38] Wise, Steven M., *Though the Heavens May Fall*. Cambridge, De Capo Press, 2005, p. 15.

[39] Foster, Thomas A. "Recovering Washington's body-double: Disability and manliness in the life and legacy of a Founding Father," *Disability Studies Quarterly*, Vol. 32, No 1, 2012; Morris, Anne Cary (Ed.). *Gouverneur Morris, The Diary and Letters of Gouverneur Morris, Minister of the United States to France: Member of the Constitutional Convention.* Charles Scribner's Sons, 1888. 2 vols. Accessed from http://oll.libertyfund.org/title/1169/82365 on 2014-02-28 .

Historian Thomas Foster has used Morris's diaries to provide a unique insight into this founder's disability experience. Morris lived with a mobility impairment that was a result of an amputation when he was in his twenties, as well as complications from burn wounds that impacted functions on his right side. Interestingly, some scholars and some of Morris's contemporaries blame Morris for his own disability because the amputation was a result of daredevil stunt during which he broke his leg. Because of his active life as male bachelor, and then later as an energetic husband, his masculinity emerged from his disability experience mostly intact by the standards of the times, although he was never literally and physically whole again after the accident. Unlike Washington who seemed to be beyond the mere mortal physical limitations imposed on others, Morris was with a few exceptions generally admired for persevering in spite of the physical handicaps he faced.

Morris in his own writing presents to us a curious mixture of acceptance of his own physical disability, even using it to his competitive advantage at times—for example, it is a frequent subject of sexual innuendo in his romantic adventures in the Paris salons—but also with a degree of existentialist angst and some bitterness about the social consequences of doing so. His wooden leg was a double-edged curiosity that both made people inquisitive and was also a reminder of his physical deformity.

> My interview with the Minister of Foreign Affairs [May 15th] is very short. I tell him that I have a small favor to ask of the King, which is that he will receive me without a sword, because of my wooden leg. He says there will be no difficulty as to that matter, and adds that I am already acquainted with the King. I reply that I never saw His Majesty but in public, nor ever exchanged a word with him in my life, although some of their gazettes have made of me one of his ministers, and that I am persuaded that he would not know me if he should see me.[40]

Some of Morris's angst came through in his regular criticism of the various artificial limbs he tried: those he had especially designed for himself, or those he heard about in his travels; but almost all of which he rejected out of hand. In some ways, the more elaborate the limb, the more of a reminder it was to him of his physical deficiency. By one account, his preference was to use something far simpler: "A wooden leg, of primitive simplicity, not much more than a rough oak stick with a wooden knob on the end of it."[41]

---

[40] Morris, Gouverneur Morris. *The Diary and Letters of Gouverneur Morris*, vol. 1, CHAPTER XXIV.

[41] Ibid., CHAPTER I.

Foster notes that Morris was not known as a complainer, generally, but he did make remarks in his writings from time to time about the physical discomfort of his disability:

> While I am visiting I am troubled with spasmodic affections of the nervous system which give great pain at times in the stump of my amputated leg, and, in the other leg, an anxious sensation which I conceive to arise from some derangement of the nervous system, and therefore I must expose myself more to the air and take exercise. The wind has blown all night very hard and continues high this morning. I think it is from the southwest, and I fear that many have fallen victims to its rage.[42]

In the end, Morris represents a type of colonial disability identity that, while clearly different, is analogous to a much more complex twenty-first century disability identity in terms of the continuums on which it oscillates: curiosity verses monstrosity; capability verses incapability; important verses irrelevant; and rational verses irrational. One might be surprised to hear Morris's reaction to seeing disabled veterans at the Hotel Royal des Invalides, which was perhaps quite telling: "Poor wretches! They have no hope this side of the grave…" Ironically, some of the same disabled soldiers pitied Morris for his own physical disability, although Morris reported the incidence in his own typical flamboyant fashion, saying that their attentions to him were a result of his gifting them money.[43]

Morris, like every other founding figure (sans Washington) considered in this disability dialogue, ultimately could not fully escape the stigma of his physical difference. He made peace with it in different ways on different days, but it was never completely ameliorated. Morris sometimes found himself devalued and disabled in ways which historians and social scientists like Claire Liachowitz trace in large parts to American Exceptionalism and "conceptions of individualism and responsibility."[44]

> This morning I got a fall in the street which barks my stump a little. Go to sup with Madame de Nadaillac. Tell the Abbé Maury that I expect he will get the hat the Cardinal de Lomenie has sent back. I tell him also that the Holy Father has done wrong in not laying the kingdom under an interdict…[45]

---

[42] Ibid., CHAPTER XI.

[43] As quoted in Foster, p. 9.

[44] Liachowitz, p. 9.

[45] Morris, CHAPTER XVIII.

For Morris, writing about his extra leg became routine; living with a disability, however, was more complicated. His dry humor in his back and forth conversation with people about it belies the existentialist angst and social pressure he likely felt as a result of it and that peeks through in his writings.

A Prosthesis Almost as Famous as the Man

Weight:
31 lbs.

This primitive prosthetic leg was worn by the vital, energetic and outspoken United States founding father Gouverneur Morris who is widely credited with writing the preamble to the U.S. Constitution. He served as a U.S. senator as well as George Washington's minister to Versailles during the turbulent years of the French Revolution. On May 14, 1780, while taking the reins of his phaeton—a four-wheeled carriage—on a Philadelphia street, Morris was dragged and entangled in a wheel when the two horses bolted. His left leg was broken in several places, and doctors quickly amputated it below the knee. For the rest of his life, Morris relied on a series of pegged oak legs that were fitted to his stump, although he briefly tried a copper limb cast from a mold of his right leg. Rumor quickly spread that the unmarried Morris, a notorious ladies man had incurred the injury while leaping from a window in flight from an enraged husband. Hardly deterred by his infirmity, Morris used the wooden leg as an accessory to his carefully cultivated image as a charismatic public man. In one legendary story, which may or may not actually have happened, Morris claimed to have been surrounded by a mob of angry French Revolutionaries who screamed "an aristocrat" as he passed in his coach. Morris took off his wooden leg, thrust it at them and responded to the accusation, "Yes, truly, who lost his leg in the cause of liberty" which quickly won over the angry Parisians. Gouverneur Morris served as President of the New-York Historical Society in 1816, which was also the year of his death. In case you were wondering, Gouverneur was his first name, not a political title. It was actually his mother's maiden name.[46]

Image available and courtesy of the New York Historical Society

---

[46.] This description is verbatim from the New York Historical Society; accessed November 11, 2020 at https://www.nyhistory.org/gouverneur-morris%E2%80%99s-wooden-leg-ca-1780

The founding figures were also unwittingly on the cutting edge of a fledgling argument over consent and custodial rights. On the classic liberal surface of it, the discussion seemed to be about benevolence and basic human rights. Beneath it, however, were deeply entrenched notions of power and gendered dominance that would take decades of social revolutions to finally break loose.

Following the founding of the republic, the coming decades would see a growing codification in subtle and not so subtle ways that continued to reify these power structures, and which were ultimately accompanied by the creation of networks of actual physical institutions and social structures—asylums, home, hospitals, etc.—used to reinforce and protect the status quo, or more bluntly, to keep people disabled—especially people of color and other gendered.

The shift of rights for individuals with disabilities, particularly relating to those with mental health-related issues, would not truly be felt until the late 20th century. But the founders began a process of replacing the family with institutions, the consequences of which we are still dealing with today.

All of the founding figures with disabilities mentioned in this chapter, even spanning gender and race, enjoyed a certain privilege which mitigated a complete loss of autonomy. This would not be the case for many countless others. An example in the legal code would be the increasing codification of laws "protecting" minors, children, and wives who in Enlightenment terms were unable to make decisions for themselves ("A child is free ... by his *father's* understanding," Locke said). This obviously included slaves and less wealthy people with disabilities, as well as women. The continued formalization of this paternalistic "protection" ultimately meant that even adults with disabilities were in essence treated routinely as children, and this would only increase in intensity during the New Republic era.[47]

Although the founding figures generally acted out of benevolence (as they perceived it), their own disability experiences were usually seen as different and apart from many others who were actually "disabled." Their charity and desire for social order meant that they were unwittingly contributing to a disability and illness-focused ontology which actually reinforced persistent historical labels. They did not have a disability agenda by any stretch of the imagination or conceive of a governmentality of the mind and body.[48]

---

[47] Brewer, Holly. *By Birth or Consent: Children, Law & the Anglo-American Revolution in Authority.* The University of North Carolina Press, 2005.

[48] Tremain, Shelley (Ed.). *Foucault and the Government of Disability.* The University of Michigan Press, 2005.

These, then, were men and women who were quite representative in some important ways of the Americans that founded the new republic, and not so much in others, but their influence was measurable. The constitution they designed formalized much of what would be considered "American" for more than two centuries, despite the fact that it was remarkably silent in terms of legislating disability experience. The founding figures experienced disability but did not fully consider themselves "disabled" in the modern sense of the term and as a result of their privileged perspective did not identify with others who were disabled. But their actual lived experiences, coupled with their enlightened desire for a "progressive" form of social justice (one that was obviously imperfect, but arguably well-intentioned), meant that their ideas had the power to persist until modernism ultimately ran its powerful course, followed by a counter reaction, and in that wake a true disability identity did finally push through into a new type of American "cripped" individualism that embraced difference rather than pitying it or studying it as a social problem, or caring for it as a father. The founding figures who lived with disability had no idea that they were constructing a shadowy outline of these types of structural challenges or changes of the future, or in any sense living a life with disability that would have meaning beyond their experience with it…

CHAPTER 3

Deafness, Blindness, and early American Institutional Disablement

Disabilities in early American culture (1780 to 1860), including the New Republic period, ran the gambit from congenital, developmental, and psychological disorders to the random misfortunes of physical accidents. Deafness and blindness, however, had been relatively stable conditions and subcultures within large populations of humans for thousands of years, and in some cases had even formed their own unique and insular communities nested within the macro culture, such as the deaf community in late 18th century Paris, France, or notably in the New World, the community of deaf in Martha's Vineyard, who invented their own sign language that the hearing used as well.

In America, the deaf and the blind were the first disability-specific groups to draw city-wide, state-wide and then nation-wide attention at the beginning of the 19th century. Although what might now be interpreted carelessly as a growing collective spirit of egalitarianism was evidenced, the movement was actually still religious and charity-based, grounded solidly in traditional Enlightenment ideals of paternalism and pity. The growth of institutions in the same time period for the more highly stigmatized mentally ill and individuals with intellectual disabilities also provided glaring warning signs about increasingly oppressive institutional practices, hyper medicalization, and signs of a coming eugenics-driven future.[1]

Part of the move to institutions was a natural function of a rapidly expanding population and a shift from primarily rural to more urban-based communities. All of the great industrial centers in the so-called rust-belt of the late 20th century—Pittsburgh, Buffalo, Cincinnati, Cleveland, Detroit, etc.—were cities that blossomed in the early half of the 19th century at the beginning of the industrial era, and for the first time in the United States there were multiple areas with critical mass to develop schools for the deaf and blind in more than just

---

[1.] *Chilmark Deaf Community Digital Historical Archive*. Chilmark Free Public Library, "Martha's Vineyard Sign language (MVSL) important in development of ASL, etc." Accessed July 20, 2012 at http://catalog.chilmarklibrary.org/pdf/default.html.

one or two major city centers. With enough students in one area, it was much more feasible for parents and interested residents in many urban areas to band together in organizing services, locating the resources for developing specialized schools, founding institutions, securing state funds and charters, and fostering small communities for identity normalization (although at that time it wouldn't have been thought of in those terms).

In spite of the age-old physiognomy of stigma surrounding *any* disability, a unique stigma remained firmly entrenched at the time that was overtly associated with deafness and blindness (unless the disability was encountered through more normalized work-related accidents or military service, which legitimized them). Still, the move toward institutionalization was in one way a critical first step forward in the general direction of a more progressive meta-cultural disability attitude; an attitude necessary in much greater amounts later to foster a modern disability rights movement, and new disability identity. For the first time in the modern era outside of Europe, communities of similar disability identities began to coalesce in North America and form into identifiable groups, even with the shortcomings to shortly be discussed.

Regional Spread of Institutions

The institutional movement began across regions, but arguably more prominently in the Northeast, and generally spreading westward and southward. Examining such newly founded institutions in the American South is particularly revealing, as it was here that progress met head on and collided with more conservative and traditional structural norms and obstacles, including race-based slavery, and therefore stands out in an X-ray type of contrast, where the evidence of ideas slowly changing from superstition and gendered class hierarchy to something inching slowly toward a social justice framework can sometimes be identified. Institutions of all types generally came to the South late, even though some researchers like Gerald Grob argue the South had more of certain types than other regions (related in part perhaps to the regional exceptionalism correlated with slavery and an excessively patriarchal society), but they did come, and they became part of the complicated Jacksonian Era social and political landscape. They were evidence of and contributed to what would also become known as the Great Awakening.[2]

---

[2] Grob, Gerald N. *The Mad Among Us: A History of the Care of America's Mentally Ill*. The Free Press, 1994, pp. 31–39, as quoted in Brown, Alison R. "Reform and Curability in American Insane Asylums of the 1840's: The Conflict of Motivation Between Humanitarian Efforts and the Efforts of the Superintendent Brethren"," *Constructing the Past*, Vol. 11: Issue 1, Article 4. Available at: http://digitalcommons.iwu.edu/constructing/vol11/iss1/4.

By the standards of the disability rights movement in the 1960s, these developments were certainly not changes tantamount to a cultural revolution in any sense. Joseph P. Shapiro, disability scholar and advocate, linked some of the institutions of the period to the Elizabethan tradition organized around poor laws, which tended to focus on lack of functionality and the flaws within the individual, and charity, rather than on a meaningful understanding of the social and ethical context behind creating almshouses for the poor and deficient:

> …The disabled and non-disabled, criminals, and those with retardation, epilepsy, and mental illness were all thrown together. [Dorothea] Dix had found people with mental illness and retardation "in cages, closets, cellars, stalls, pens! Chained, naked, beaten with rods, and lashed into obedience."[3]

In a sense, they were a version of the "feel good" ableism that the 21st century has openly eschewed. The case specifically of deafness, along these similar historical lines, had an extremely long cultural tradition which more often than it should have centered the problem of lack of hearing in the individual, a history of blame that dated back to ancient times. A person who was deaf was cursed; mired in sin; born as punishment meted out on his/her parents; a negative portend; etc. The American Enlightenment fascination with the Greeks and everything in their culture meant that many early American attitudes about deafness mirrored ancient Greek ideas. Aristotle, for example, believed that deaf-mutes were uneducable, and that the loss of any of the five senses resulted in a corresponding loss of knowledge and human capacity (rather than heightening the remaining senses, as the modern theory of twice exceptionality, or 2E, sometimes postulates). Hippocrates "treated" hearing impairments without any true knowledge of the inner ear structures. Plato was reportedly fascinated with the use of hand signals amongst the deaf and hard of hearing but had no "lasting contribution" to make on their behalf in terms of education or equal participation in society.[4]

Early 19th century Americans were a product of Western Enlightenment thinking, visibly illustrated in the long-standing contradictions of a Judeo-Christian tradition which both pitied and feared disability, while also exhibiting and permitting a growing scientific curiosity. It also privileged sight above all of the other senses

---

[3] Shapiro, Joseph P. *No Pity: People with Disabilities Forging a New Civil Rights Movement*. Time Books, 1993, pp. 59–60.

[4] Enerstvedt, R. T. *Legacy of the Past (some aspects of the history of blind education, deaf education, and deaf-blind education with emphasis on the time before 1900)*. Oslo, Norway: PDF manuscript housed with University of Oslo, introduction by Knut Arnesen, 1996, pp. 6–8. Accessed as Chapter 2: The Development of Education for Deaf People from http://folk.uio.no/regie/pdfd/Deaf.pdf.

(again a Greek hallmark: "The eyes are the window on the soul...") The deaf and blind were banned from certain roles in the ancient Hebrew temple hierarchy; later they were miraculously healed by prophets. The disability of blindness in particular was one often positioned both as a divine punishment and as a means of divine deliverance.

Both groups were afforded some special protections in ancient Israel, and both were also groups singled out for their overt physical blemishes which distanced them from God. The metaphor of blindness as a statement about the human condition—Peter Bruegel the Elder's high Renaissance painting of the blind leading the blind was quite well known—was a metaphor not lost on Americans of this period, who struggled on the societal level to accept the blind, while also feeling a quaint dignity they would defend about their charitable efforts to help the less fortunate with disabilities.[5]

Even sexual issues were seen as a "disability" in the Old Testament. In Deuteronomy 23:1 we find that: "No one who has been emasculated by crushing or cutting may enter the assembly of the Lord." Physical disability, commonly seen with blindness and deafness, but also manifesting in myriad other ways, was simply a tattoo indicating second class citizenship.[6]

Institutionalization as a response to deafness and blindness was of course a much wider Western phenomenon that did not originate solely in the New World, reflecting what were seen as progressive Enlightenment ideals—charity, to be sure, but also empirical processes relating to everything from medicine to sanitation—and in North America the movement became unique for a number of important reasons. Beyond the European tradition of institutions, the geographic width and breadth of the continent and the primacy of rural communities (in Canada, as well, and in places like Australia, New Zealand, etc. which had analogous frontiers and subsequent institutional growth) meant that individuals with disabilities experienced more of a "congregational effect" which impacted the availability of resources, treatments, and opportunities, but just as importantly, shaped early notions of an early disability identity. More than one-hundred years later in the U.S. when Ed Roberts and others would lead the Independent Living Movement (ILM) and the push for deinstitutionalization, the very idea that individuals with diverse and unrelated medical conditions and disabilities would share a common, radicalized disability identity in common was possible

---

[5.] Prosper Grech, "Blindness," in Bruce M. Metzger, and Michael D. Coogan (Eds.), *The Oxford Companion to the Bible*, (Oxford: Oxford University Press, 1993), 92.

[6.] Deuteronomy 23:1. Accessed August 9, 2022 at https://biblia.com/bible/niv/deuteronomy/23/1.

in part because of the unique communities and networks that the 19th century institutions initiated, albeit, with many complications and often negative consequences, as well. The idea, for example, of simultaneous disability events in major American cities was not dreamed of, nor feasible in early America, even though technology connected politics and other institutions that way.[7]

The institutions were also important cultural artifacts and metaphors, as well, symbolized overtly by their grandly scaled architecture, which was often in the federal and gothic revival styles, and less overtly by their shared mission. They were physical and metaphysical centers where power clearly was clearly demonstrated, but which also intersected with disability, race, gender and cultural positions. Beyond the politicians who initially founded such institutions, the power was primarily vested in the first wave of positivist disability experts—doctors, teachers, ministers, administrators and later counselors, clinical psychologists, interpreters, social workers, nurses, and therapists—but the very fact that such concentrated resources were aimed at disability and intersecting with it meaningfully (although not always happily) was a significant shift in human affairs, and helped to define the type of charitable social justice associated with classic 19th century liberalism, and the American experience. Although it is far from comparable to the identity politics of the late 20th century, it must be seen as an important bridge. The focus was often on physical disabilities perhaps because people could see the impact of their efforts more readily.

This movement was a post-Enlightenment, Western phenomenon, but was particularly accentuated in the North American European colonies and former colonies which had rapidly changing social environments where cultural imperialism had already leveled some forms of native resistance and temporarily created a power vacuum of sorts. These institutions ultimately included not only schools for students with disabilities and mental asylums, but also orphanages, poor houses, homes for the feeble minded, and even nautical school-ships in some countries (where the separation metaphor is obvious). They also included prisons, which administrators began to run using scientific methods for the first time, congruent with more "benevolent" institutions such as those for the deaf and the blind. They were part of a social justice awakening that mirrored a religious awakening and changed the cultural landscape, even though the norms seem strange and uncomfortable by today's standards.[8]

[7.] See Foucault, Michel. *Madness and Civilization*, for insight into the European tradition of institutions.

[8.] Ramsland, John. "Children's institutions in nineteenth-century Sydney," in *Dictionary of Sydney*. 2011, accessed online March 1, 2014 at http://www.dictionaryofsydney.org.

Foucauldian Governmentality

In the tradition of French philosopher Michel Foucault, the creation of regional and state networks of experts and positivist practices within an even larger network of institutions was a grand but somber development in terms of the influence of the state over the individual, the beginnings of a new governmentality of the mind and body that remains oppressive even in a post-ADA world, where institutions still wield significant cultural, political, and practical power. But it cannot be understated what a significant development such institutions were at this time, both for good and for bad. Like the creation of the new nation itself, institutions came about as part of a wide and growing acceptance that a democratic state, representing the general public good by freely elected mandate, had a moral obligation to address the issues of the general welfare as it intersected with health, wealth and accidental hardship.[9]

Some social commentators go further than the simplistic notion of "progress" and even the Enlightenment desire to cure social ills and suggest that the humanism of this period was more indicative of a quasi-utopian movement, which included amongst its goals the final curing of all disease, the rehabilitation of all psychological disabilities, and even the promotion of institutions as new centers for culture and creativity, rather than ersatz prisons to remove unwanted minorities. Although Benjamin Reiss makes part of this difficult case bravely, he also admits to the key notion that historically institutions were eventually both equal parts good and bad, and even he cannot avoid the contradictions that make a more optimistic position difficult to maintain, citing that even luminaries such as Poe and Emerson "viewed the system alternatively as the fulfillment of a democratic ideal and as a kind of medical enslavement."[10]

In terms of disability history, two specific types of institutions had a disproportionate impact on American disability history. Schools for the deaf and blind created communities of advocacy and brought the tensions over the role of expert verses individual autonomy into the public dialogue, and eventually provided breeding grounds for disability radicalism. Asylums for the mentally ill and profoundly physically disabled, on the other hand, solidified the power of the bureaucracy of expertise, and stunted the growth of cultural acceptance

---

[9] Tremain, Shelley. "Foucault, Governmentality, and Critical Disability Theory," in Tremain, Shelley (Ed.). *Foucault and the Government of Disability.* University of Michigan Press, 2005, pp. 1–44.

[10] Reiss, Benjamin. *Theaters of Madness: Insane Asylums and Nineteen-century American Culture.* University of Chicago Press, 2008, pp. misc., including also several editorial reviews.

of Otherness. Each type of institution was far from monolithic and subject to the whims and nuances of individual communities and administrators, but examined in total, and contrasted with each other, suggest the critically important role that institutionalization in general had in pushing forward, and sometimes holding back, the pre-modern disability rights movement.

Deaf Education

Specialized schools for the deaf began at the state level, with the first being established in Hartford, Connecticut in 1817 as the Connecticut Asylum for the Education of Deaf and Dumb Persons. The movement quickly spread through other Northern states, including next New York and Pennsylvania. Soon thereafter, such schools sprang up in Midwestern frontier areas like Kentucky, and then eventually in the South, in places like Texas and Virginia. Schools for the deaf and blind were often "pioneering" schools, establishing the early educational patterns that eventually helped lead to the founding of broader public school systems, particularly in the South after the Civil War.

Deaf education inevitably brought up the historically complex issue of sign language, or "hand signals" as they were often referred to. The use of hand signals, or an organized sign language, is documented in some ancient sources, and many scholars insist that intuitively and logically various sign language systems must have evolved in both rural and urban deaf communities over time, and across myriad cultures. Linguists note that there are several hundred sign languages in the present period, and there is no reason not to suspect that this has been the case in the long distant past. Plato himself made notes and studied with curiosity the signs that he observed the deaf using to communicate with each other in ancient Greece. In ancient Egypt, the deaf had often been channeled into specific jobs that were useful to the community good and the work of the government bureaucracy and had to use some type of hand gesturing to communicate since very few people outside of scribes were taught to write.[11]

Later, in medieval European cities, such patterns of sign use were common, as well. Coming out of the Dark Ages and into the Enlightenment, superstition competed with rationalism, and the deaf were both an object of pity and charity, as well as an object of curiosity and scientific inquiry. It was a complex and contradictory era. While witch trails took place in one part of the city, church

---

[11.] Trammell, Jack. "Disability in the Ancient World," unpublished paper, IN SUBMISSION, 2022.

officials founded institutes for the mentally ill in another quarter; while some deaf and blind were forced to live in the street homeless and destitute, others were gathered into wealthier homes and the first organized urban institutes for the disabled. Louis XIV in 1670 initiated the founding of the first modern home for disabled veterans in France. The beginnings of a formalized (i.e. published and/or more widely disseminated) sign language evolved in countries like France and Great Britain during this period. The 17th and 18th century European history of deafness was a strange time of the rational and irrational competing daily, side by side, and often with conflicting results.[12]

There was an equally complex history of forcing the deaf to adapt to a hegemonic hearing culture, through reading lips and attempting to speak proper English (French, German, or any native oral tongue). The education of the deaf to speak, or to communicate orally, eventually became known as *oralism*. In the United States, one of the first problems to erupt as schools for the deaf were established and spread was determining which philosophy, *oralism* verses *manual signing* (or communicating through sign language), the school would subscribe to. The deaf were often naturally predisposed to use sign language in their own communities for very obvious practical, social and linguistic reasons.

Two key personalities in the early battle over deaf education were Laurent Clerc and Thomas Gallaudet, who together co-founded the first school for the deaf in Connecticut in 1817. Clerc was born in France in 1785 and was deaf from near birth. He studied at the famous school for the deaf in Paris, the Institution Nationale des Sourds-Muets. Clerc met Gallaudet in England while visiting there, and when Gallaudet returned the favor with a visit to France in 1816, they decided together to bring deaf education to America.[13]

Gallaudet, a Yale graduate who entered the ministry, found his life transformed when he met a nine-year-old deaf girl named Alice Cogswell. He began attempting to teach her, and growing in interest, soon found himself in England consulting with European experts about oral communication with the deaf. Dissatisfied by what oralism experts told him, he later visited France, where he met Clerc and others who demonstrated the manual system or signing. Gallaudet was won over. Clerc and Gallaudet's partnership and hard work resulted in the founding of the first school for the deaf in Connecticut, the first of its kind in the U.S.[14]

---

[12] Frazier, James George. *The golden bough: A study in magic and religion.* The MacMillan Company, 1942; Smith, C.; Lentz, E. M.; & Mikos, K. *Signing Naturally: Student Workbook Units 1–6.* San Diego: Dawnsignpress, 2008, pp. vi-vii, etc.

[13] Lane, Harlan. *When the Mind Hears: A History of the Deaf.* Vintage, 1989.

[14] Ibid.

The Connecticut school was groundbreaking, and an instance of institutionalism that accelerated social justice, brought preeminent experts together, and promoted an independent and pride-based disability identity for deaf students. It was also reportedly the first school in the U.S. of any type, public or private, to receive significant federal money for its support. It remains a disability landmark site in the present time, preserving in its museum and archival records an invaluable resource to all students of education and disability. Today it is known as the American School for the Deaf.[15]

Clerc was, without any doubt, ahead of his time as he hinted at notions of twice exceptionality (2E). In 1818 he is recorded as saying: "Every creature, every work of God, is admirably well made; but if any one appears imperfect in our eyes, it does not belong to us to criticize it. Perhaps that which we do not find right in its kind, turns to our advantage, without our being able to perceive it..." He could not have stated the case for twice exceptionality, or the co-existence of disability and giftedness, any clearer.[16]

Clerc outlined the nature of signing itself, which he believed "reflect[ed] the movements of the soul." Although institutionalization in other settings would mean the tyranny of oralism, a cultural hegemony that forced generations of deaf students to speak a language they could not hear, and did not love, and had great difficulty mastering, Clerc remains a seminal figure in the history of American Sign Language (ASL) and treated it as a rich language, culturally viable, and worthy of a place with other mainstream languages. His famous fallacies debunked about ASL include many misconceptions about signing: sign language is [not] pictorial; sign language is [not] universal; sign language is [not] concrete; sign language is [not] primitive. Clerc and Gallaudet believed that the mental energy devoted to the painstaking task of learning to lip-read and form sounds that could not be heard (oralism) was a usurpation of human energy that was unethical in any progressive educational system. They believed that ASL was a rich, abstract, unique human language.[17]

"It is only through language we enter fully into our human estate and culture," Harlan Lane, historian of deaf culture wrote. "If we cannot do this, we will be bizarrely disabled and cut off."[18]

[15.] Gallaudet, Edward M. "History of the education of the deaf in the United States," *American Annals of the Deaf and Dumb*, 31 (2), 1886, pp. 130–47.

[16.] Clerc, Laurent. *An address...* [for governor and legislature]. Hartford, CT: Hudson and Co., 1818.

[17.] Lane, pp. 210–213, etc.

[18.] Ibid, p. 8.

Native Americans and Sign Language

As has already been mentioned, anthropologists and historians believe that the use of hand signals and sign language amongst the deaf are long-standing traditions that cross cultures and historical epochs. The data to confirm that, however, is sometimes difficult to document.

In North America, Europeans immediately noticed and continued to report on the unique use of signs by natives. William Tomkins, author of *Indian Sign Language*, has written that the language transcended tribe and crossed regions:

"Every record of the landing of Columbus tells of how they communicated with the Indians by signs. The records of all early explorers have information of this nature."

Many of the tribes across North America, but particularly those in the Great Plains region, had legends and traditions that suggested that "signs" had originally come north from the area that is now Mexico. Every trapper and mountain man west of the Mississippi presumably had to learn the signs in order to survive. Most likely, the use of native signs evolved not to accommodate the deaf or hearing impaired but to facilitate communication across language barriers.

For critics who later would argue that American Sign Language (ASL) did not constitute a true language, the example from native cultures might actually be used to argue the opposite—that sign language is more universal than any single other spoken and written language.[19]

[19.] Tomkins, William. *Indian Sign Language*. Dover, 1969, p. 1; Tomkins, William. "Sign History," accessed August 19, 2015 at http://www.inquiry.net/outdoor/native/sign/history.htm

In Virginia, as in other parts of the South, the process to establish a school for the deaf and blind predictably moved forward in fits and starts, and later than in other regions. An early attempt by several individuals to establish an institution around 1812 in Petersburg and Goochland failed for lack of critical mass; others were not enthusiastic in supporting the cause. Two separate governors in the 1820s asked the General Assembly to establish a school for the deaf and also made no headway. Finally, a bill was pushed forward by two prominent citizens in the Richmond area, and on March 31, 1838, Virginia legislators finally passed a bill to formally establish the Virginia School for the Deaf and Blind. The first student was a female, Elizabeth Baker, who came in the fall term of 1839 when the school officially opened; the first teacher was the Reverend Job Turner.[20]

Schools for deaf and blind came to the South more quickly in the late Antebellum Era. The Texas Deaf and Dumb Asylum (now known as the Texas School for the Deaf) was founded in 1856 in Austin, established by the Sixth Legislature, and is the oldest "continuously operating public school" in the state. In this case, the inspiration for the founding of the school came directly from a deaf citizen of North Texas named Matthew Clark, who "inquired of the Legislators if there was a school for the deaf in this State. They answered, 'none' and then determined that there should be an institution opened at once." A board that was appointed sent Mr. Clark into the nearby counties to take an informal census of how many deaf children were living there in preparation for the opening of the school. By 1857, there were seven boys in residence when the first superintendent arrived from New York. It was not uncommon for the first wave of Southern administrators or teachers to come from Northern schools that had already been in operation for some time.[21]

America developed over the course of time its own pantheon of deaf celebrities, including in the early eras such personalities as: James "Deaf" Burke (British born, but boxed in the U.S.); John Brewster, Jr. (Federalist period artist); and William Elsworth "Dummy" Hoy (an early baseball player, whom some now believe belongs in the Baseball Hall of Fame). Erastus Smith, known as "Deaf Smith" (and many of these terms or nicknames were not considered pejorative at the time, although they obviously are now), was an iconic deaf figure in Texas during the first half of the 19th century, and a ranger contributing to the Texas Revolution.[22]

Like schools for the deaf, the growth of institutions for the blind followed similar antebellum pathways. The earliest was founded in 1829 in Massachusetts, today known as the Perkins School for the Blind. Dr. John Fisher was a medical school student traveling in Paris when he visited a school for the blind there and was so intrigued by it, that he returned home and organized support to

---

[20] *History of V.S.D.B. in the 1800s.* Accessed January 20, 2014 at http://nathanbullock.tripod.com/vsdbhistoryinthe_1800_s.html, directly linked from the VSDB site.

[21] Lewis, Emily. "A Brief History of the Texas School for the Deaf," accessed online May 11, 2013: http://www.tsd.state.tx.us; Reprinted from October 1, 1909 issue of *The Lone Star, Texas School for the Deaf.*

[22] *Deaf Digest.* "Honoring USA's most famous deaf military fighter." January 9th, 2014.

start such a school in the U.S. The first director when the doors opened in 1832 was the later famous Samuel Gridley Howe. Howe devoted a great deal of effort to embossing books for blind students, even attracting the attention of Charles Dickens, who later wrote about his visit to the school and a student named Laura Bridgman, a young deaf/blind girl.

This school is also known for its firsts: the first blind kindergarten in the U.S. (1887), and first school to prove with testing that intelligence and blindness were not inherently correlated (using the relatively new Hayes-Binet IQ test). In more recent times, the school has expanded to offer education to students with disabilities other than blindness, a controversial decision, but one consistent with a late 20th century overarching disability rights movement and universal design in education paradigm.[23]

Schools for the blind slowly spread westward and southward. The Texas School for the Blind and Visually Impaired, originally called the Blind Institute, was founded in 1856 by the same Sixth Texas Legislature that formed the school for the deaf already discussed. A local resident and friend of Governor Elisha M. Pease leased his residence to the school initially, which the following year had three students in attendance. The school changed locations several times during its history, and ultimately stayed on a seventy-three-acre site between Burnet and Lamar roads. The initial curricular focus was functionally oriented, and by 1888 roughly 54% of returning alums reported being self-supporting (a much higher rate than the present day employment rate for many segments of Americans with disabilities, for comparison).[24]

In 1965, the Texas school for the Deaf, Blind and Orphans merged with the school for the blind. Such mergers were not only forged to save money and pool resources; they also reflected the radical sixties social realignment which encouraged the conjoining of disability identities that was fundamental to a basic human rights-based framework consistent with the disability rights movement. This movement suggested that people with disabilities had more in common with each other than might be assumed and that labels were in large part socially constructed, rather than a result of a specific physical deformity of deficiency. Institutionalization in the Jacksonian Era, in its own way, began the long process of coalition that would not fully bear fruit until nearly one hundred years or more later.

[23.] "Perkins History." Perkins School for the Blind. Accessed March 4, 2014 at http://www.perkins.org/about-us/history/.

[24.] "A Brief History of the Texas School for the Blind and Visually ImpairEd." Accessed January 10, 2014, http://www.tsbvi.edu/general-information-and-services/197-a-brief-history-of-the-texas-school-for-the-blind-and-visually-impaired.

Insane Asylums

Institutions for the mentally ill, or psychologically disabled, had a much longer and more controversial history than schools for the deaf and blind, even though both were re-born in an era of intellectual optimism and modernistic expansion. The stigma of mental illness, as Michel Foucault and others have argued, might be the ultimate form of human Otherness. To be mad is to lose something much more profound than losing something physical, such as Gouverneur Morris losing his leg—it is to lose what philosophers sometimes say makes us different from other animals—our ability to reason and behave rationally; the agency to decide for ourselves.

In the three major North American nation-states—Mexico, the United States, and Canada—the 19th century represented a major transition. The Jacksonian Era in the U.S. was characterized by a physical and geographical expansion of mental health institutionalization, as well as a political and intellectual expansion of cultural progress, a manufactured idea that sought rational solutions to many persistent social problems.[25]

Although it is difficult to place schools for the deaf and blind side by side in comparison with institutions for the mentally ill, or the profoundly physically handicapped, it is instructive to do so during this period of American history. The good and bad that comingled in each are not without significant overlaps, and the same cost benefit analysis lies at the heart of present-day conversations about education in the *Least Restrictive Environment*, universal access to higher education, healthcare, and integration into the mainstream. Institutions in the antebellum period served both constructive and destructive processes, and that is in part why some institutions remain today and others have mercifully closed their doors. Many institutions were a mixture of the best thinking and ideas of the time, as well as the attitudes and shortcomings that seem all too readily apparent to us today, and cannot be fully judged by the standards and identity politics of the present time.

In fact, this period of U.S. history provides unique insight into the repeating themes of conflict that later became the most familiar battlegrounds for the modern disability rights movement. Institutionalization reflected the best human motives of the day: a desire to ensure public welfare, recognize concern for the well-being of families, a need to practice charity, a classical liberal

---

[25] Foucault, Michel. *Madness and Civilization*. Vintage, 1965.

interest in social justice, and a positive curiosity and commitment to advancing medicine, science, and preventive care. Institutions also came over time to represent cultural structures associated with some of the worst of human motives, or governmentalities: blaming the victim for the disorder; limiting individual choice about major life possibilities for those thought to be less than fully human; centering control in experts who often were not accountable to anyone, and who often didn't fully see the consequences of their work; and characterizing abject human Otherness as an individual rather than a societal or community problem.

Because institutions for the deaf and blind were cloaked in the terminology and semantics of "education," and evolved simultaneously with a more general movement toward public education, they often represented the more of the positive aspects of institutionalization. Unlike asylums, friends and families had more immediate access to students at such schools (and they normally weren't called "patients"). The outcomes were more normalized: graduation, "gainful" employment, and some type of life in the mainstream. Because institutions for the mentally ill, profoundly physically disabled, and intellectually disabled were not seen by mission as "educating" individuals, but rather "housing," "treating," or even intentionally isolating or even punishing individuals, they quickly began to reflect many of the darker aspects of institutionalization, becoming in some cases not much different from prisons for the criminally convicted.

For all of the success stories and "progress," and accounting for the many challenges and unintended consequences, the first half of the 19th century in North America remains an important historical dialogue about how people processed Otherness. It's no coincidence that this era corresponded almost exactly with the evolution and popularity of the American circus and freak show network. It's no coincidence that this era overlapped with the zenith of the original American sin: race-based slavery. Americans remained curious and frightened of the Other, as Rosemarie Garland-Thomson notes in her outline of a visual rhetoric, but were never fully unaware of the meaningful consequences of staring or "beholding." They took satisfaction in the charitable outcomes they pursued (educating those who might be perceived to be more difficult to educate) but were often uncomfortable confronting the Darwinian implications of faulty genetics and social engineering.

There is also in the present time a serious difficulty in recovering these early historical experiences—records in the second half of the 19th century are extensive; those from the first half are often missing, without detail, or were never made at all. Records from successful institutions are carefully kept for posterity; those from places and experiences people wish to forget are often missing or gone, quite intentionally.[26]

> ### Techniques and Treatments in Early Asylums
>
> The early Enlightenment science and medicine practiced in association with asylums is sometimes horrifying, often fascinating, and usually quite difficult to frame in the context of 21st century norms. A list of some of the common techniques, with minimal interpretation, allows for both positive and negative imagery to easily come to mind:
>
> - Restraint (chains; straightjackets; bed binders; etc.)
> - Isolation (sometimes actual cells)
> - Restricted diet
> - Untrained attendants
> - Unpaid manual labor
> - Discussion-based or talk therapy
> - Cultivation of rationality (although what constituted the definition varied)
> - Emphasis on moral character (again subject to interpretation)
> - Reward or punishment for behavior
> - Medical aids: bleeding, cold water treatments, various pills
>
> As medicine advanced in the larger world, treatment within asylums evolved. However, by their nature, such institutions were isolated, private, and a breeding ground for potential abuses. In the century before web cams and phone cameras, testimony turned on eyewitness accounts, and a patient's word seldom carried the same weight that the account of a physician or attendant did.[27]
>
> ---
> [27.] Porter, Roy. *Madmen: A Social History of Madhouses, Mad-Doctors & Lunatic.* Tempus, 2004; Foucault, *Madness*.

[26.] Garland-Thomson, Rosemarie. "Integrating Disability, Transforming Feminist Theory," in Davis, Lennard (Ed.). *Disability Studies Reader, 4th edition*. Routledge, 2013, pp. 333–353; Nickell, Joe. *Secrets of the sideshows*. University of Kentucky Press, 2008.

Philosopher Richard Kearney, who believes that we as humans may be neurologically hard-wired for noticing differences in spite of our benevolent wishes to the contrary, suggests that the law of hospitality should govern our curiosity and fear of Otherness. Gerald Grob puts it in slightly different, perhaps more positive, and succinct terms:

> The treatment of the insane, has ever varied with the philosophy and intelligence of the age. That they are treated better in modern times, more kindly and judiciously, is not owing to any increase of benevolence, but to an increase of knowledge.[28]

Knowledge in the present, however, is always predicated upon knowledge of the past. Researchers at Mississippi State University have used archeology to unearth the unmarked graves of hundreds of patients, as well as primary source material to uncover part of the above-ground past of the Mississippi State Asylum, which was first proposed in 1846 by Mississippi Governor A. G. Brown. Brown encountered opposition to his proposal in spite of the fact that outside observers like Dorothea Dix found individuals with intellectual and psychological disabilities living in squalor, sometimes "chained in closets and attics." None-the-less, he managed to secure an appropriation by legislative act in 1848.[29]

Although it is believed that this was actually the sixth such institution to be built in the U.S., it was the first in the South following what was known as the Kirkbride Plan. The Kirkbride system was based on a template created by Philadelphia moral physician (psychiatrist) Thomas Story Kirkbride, and eventually several hundred institutions would bear some imprint from his work, including institutions in Canada and Australia. Kirkbride's premise was that the building and grounds themselves were to have an inherent curative effect, in addition to the physician-based treatments that were taking place within the inner walls. In his seminal work, *On the Construction, Organization, and General Arrangements of Hospitals for the Insane*, he laid out in precise fashion everything from how hallways in the grand buildings were to be laid out, to the neighborhood (on the edge of the city, sometimes facing pastoral scenery) in which the asylum should reside. His work influenced all types of institutional construction and design for the next century; arguably, the impact is still felt today.[30]

---

[28] Grob, as in Brown. Kearney, Richard. *Strangers, Gods and Monsters: Interpreting Otherness*. Routledge, 2003.

[29] "History of the Mississippi State Asylum." Mississippi State University. Accessed February 17, 2014 at http://msacp.cobb.msstate.edu/history.html.

[30] Yanni, Carla. *The Architecture of Madness: Insane Asylums in the United States*. Minneapolis, MN: Minnesota University Press, 2007; Kirkbride, Thomas. *On the Construction, Organization and General Arrangements of Hospitals for the Insane*. Philadelphia, 1854.

Regardless of what actually happened in many institutions then and later, Kirkbride made clear in his own work that intentional abuse and cruelty were not part of the Kirkbride design:

> An insane member of a family, wherever he may be, has really a claim for everything that will contribute to his comfort and gratification, far beyond those who are in health and have so many other resources; and the justice or morality of a different course, as occasionally observed, cannot for a single moment bear examination.[31]

Like schools for the deaf and blind, the spread of asylums for the insane moved initially from the Northeast to the Mid-west, and then South, often following pre-organized plans and patterns like Kirkbride's. Over one hundred years later, a similar geographic pattern would emerge within the modern disability rights movement, which began on both coasts, slowly spreading to the heartland, with the South picking up speed at the very last. Although some psychiatric hospitals in the South were remarkably early in formation—the first being at Williamsburg in colonial Virginia in 1771—the more general pattern, ultimately involving hundreds of institutions, big and small, followed the same geographic patterns the schools had, as the following table illustrates.

Table of Major Antebellum Southern Lunatic Assylums

Name of Institution	Date of Opening	State
Public Hospital for Persons of Insane and Disordered Minds	1773	VA
Spring Grove	1797	MD
Lunatic Asylum	1824	KY
South Carolina State Hospital	1828	SC
Tennessee Lunatic Asylum	1840	TN
Central State Hospital	1842	GA
The Insane Asylum of the State of Louisiana	1848	LA
Mississippi State Lunatic Asylum	1855	MS
Insane Asylum of North Carolina	1856	NC

(Continued)

---

[31] Ibid, p. 5.

Name of Institution	Date of Opening	State
Alabama Insane Hospital	1861	AL
State Lunatic Asylum	1861	TX
Trans-Alleghany Lunatic Asylum	1864	WV/VA
Florida State Hospital for the Insane	1876	FL
Arkansas State Lunatic Asylum	1883	AK

The Mississippi State Lunatic Asylum, after some machinations, finally opened in 1855, and over time, represented both the best and the worst of the consequences of institutionalization. While some doctors practiced relatively rational forms of study and the humane treatment of patients, drinking water came from a nearby muddy pond. While patients often had more resources available to them than their families could have provided, the only light was provided by crude coal oil lamps almost into the early 20th century. Like almost all institutions for the insane of the period, it represented both a step forward and a step backwards, and in hindsight it's not always easy to distinguish which was which. (There are more than 7,000 bodies identified buried in the MSLA area).[32]

The human stories that come out of such institutions remain mostly hidden, and almost exclusively penned by the experts who maintained the power over daily life, and who also crafted the perspective that the public should have about such places. Although it would be an overgeneralization to say that such institutions attracted employees and administrators who were unusually cruel, sadistic, or inhumane, it would also be unfair to suggest that this factor did not have a significant impact on many patients' lives. Most of the institutions were constructed in such a way that those on the outside had very little opportunity to see what happened on the inside; those inside had no easy access to the outside world, and only limited means of communicating even with family members. Such a combination of factors, combined with the tremendous power handed over to doctors and other "experts," made abuse much more likely.

Even new superintendents coming in to administer were often taken aback by what they found, as Dr. Thomas J. Mitchell found in Mississippi in 1878,

---

[32.] "History of the Mississippi State Asylum;" Accessed May 19, 2022, at https://allthatsinteresting.com/mississippi-state-asylum

with conditions "verging on what the original Bedlam must have been like." It was, as Foucault might have put it, an illustration of the governmentality of the mind and body that was connected to powerful but often invisible external social and political forces; structures of power that would not end with the closing of many such institutions.[33]

Gender and Race Intersect

The experiences in such institutions were highly gendered, and racialized. Wendy Moore, discussing the situation of Mary Eleanor Bowes, Countess of Strathmore, outlined just how terribly women were treated in Georgian England. In America, the situation was quite analogous. Even President Abraham Lincoln reportedly pointed out to his spouse Mary Todd Lincoln that he might have to place her in an asylum if she couldn't control her violent emotions, evidently with great regrets. In Virginia, in spite of the VSDB success, the first school for deaf and blind *negro* students would not be established until roughly eighty years after the original VSDB, even though prisons for negroes were regularly overcrowded and had existed all the way back to the founding of the nation. The twin issues of race and gender intersected and entwined with disability in ways which would later fuel the identity rights movements in 1960s and inspire social scientists to continue building on the work of intersectionality begun by sociological pioneers like C. Wright Mills, W.E.B. DuBois, Proudhon, and others.[34]

There can be little doubt that women suffered disproportionately more greatly than male patients in many institutions. The categories used to label them became the foundation of a brand-new medical science, *psychology*, and read like a list of conditions that no sane person would want to have: furious mania, erotomania, dementia, hallucinations, raving mania, melancholy, delirium of grandeur, imbecility, religious mania, puerperal mania, etc. In as many as half

---

[33] "History of the Mississippi State Asylum" for more see: https://asylumhillproject.org/Asylum_Hill/History/Mississippi-State-Hospital-for-the-Insane.html; History of the VSDB, Deaf History Museum; Foucault, *Madness;* Tremain, Shelley, (Ed). *Foucault and the Government of Disability*. The University of Michigan Press, 2005.

[34] Moore, Wendy. "18th century domestic violence," accessed on March 1, 2014 at http://www.wondersandmarvels.com, and as published in her book, *Wedlock: The true story of the disastrous marriage and remarkable divorce of Mary Eleanor Bowes, Countess of Strathmore*. Random House, 2009; McNamara, Robert. "Elizabeth Keckly: Dressmaker and former slave became a trusted friend of Mary Todd Lincoln." *19th Century History Newsletter*, accessed March 2, 2014 at http://history1800s.about.com/od/Lincoln-Family; Mills, C. W. *The Sociological Imagination*. Oxford University Press, 1959; Barnes, Colin; Mercer, Geof; & Shakespeare, Tom. E*xploring Disability: A Sociological Introduction*. Cambridge UK: Polity Press. 1999.

the cases, records suggest that husbands and fathers were the primary agent of the commitment. It is also alarming how many patient notes have appended a death notice that occurred while the patient was housed in the asylum. Although some asylums, like the Boston Female Asylum, made rigorous efforts to maintain ethical standards for behavior and treatment interactions between patients and doctors, *many did not*.[35]

Mary Huestis Pengilly, writing in the decades after the Civil War, captured with great accuracy and through first-hand experiences the emotions and abuses of institutional care that begin to become more widespread before the war. Her diary, published in 1885 and entitled *Diary Written in the Provincial Lunatic Asylum*, was shocking in its time, yet represents the almost complete lack of public awareness about conditions in some institutions that dated back to well before the Civil War.

> Massachusetts, by one who has had so sad an experience in this, the sixty-second year of her age, that she feels it to be her imperative duty to lay it before the public in such a manner as shall reach the hearts of the people in this her native Province, as also the people of Massachusetts, with whom she had a refuge since driven from her own home by the St. John fire of 1877. She sincerely hopes it may be read in every State of the Union, as well as throughout the Dominion of Canada, that it may help to show the inner workings of their Hospitals and Asylums, and prompt them to search out better methods of conducting them, as well for the benefit of the superintendent as the patient.[36]

Pengilly's account is particularly important because her experience spanned two countries, Canada and the United States, and demonstrates the parallel processes taking place in each country. Although she wrote after the period in question in this chapter, her experience clearly points to the problems that some institutions, particularly asylums and prisons, were predisposed to suffer from.

> They will not allow me to go home, and I must write these things down for fear I forget. It will help to pass the time away. It is very hard to endure this prison life, and know that my sons think me insane when I am not.[37]

---

[35] City Archives. New Orleans Public Library. "New Orleans (La.) City Insane Asylum," Record of Patients, 1882–1884; 1888–1882 (1–50)—Transcription; Lainhart, Ann S. (Ed.). *Records of the Boston Female Asylum*. University of Massachusetts, 2013.

[36] Pengilly, Mary Huestis. *Diary Written in the Provincial Lunatic Asylum*. Self-published, 1885.

[37] Ibid.

Pengilly was remarkably tolerant considering what she endured; her joy upon release, was quite understandable:

> At last I am free! Seated in my own room at the hotel, I look back at that prison on the hill. I had won a little interest in the hearts of the nurses in our ward; they expressed regret at my leaving. Ellen Regan, who was the first to volunteer me any kindness, said, "We shall miss you, Mrs. Pengilly, for you always had a cheerful word for everyone." I did not bid all the patients good-bye, for I hope soon to return and stay with them. I would like so much to look after these poor women, who are so neglected. I will ask the Commissioners to allow me to remain with them, if only one year, to superintend the female department, not under the jurisdiction of the present Superintendent, but with the assistance of the Junior Physician and the nurses, who each understand the work of their own departments, and will be willing to follow my instructions. I will teach them to think theirs is no common servitude—merely working for pay—but a higher responsibility is attached to this work, of making comfortable those poor unfortunates entrusted to their care, and they will learn to know they are working for a purpose worth living for; and they will be worthy of the title, "Sisters of Mercy."[38]

According to Michael Stephenson, who has helped make extensive Canadian institutional asylum admissions records dating back to 1841 available to the public, "The aberrances deemed most disturbing, even if not violent (most in fact not), were those seen linked to sex/gender. Of women locked up at the Toronto Queen Street Asylum prior to 1900, a quarter were in for 'female trouble' – 'childbirth, lactation, miscarriage, menstrual disorders, uterine disorders' and other natural conditions seen as 'the predisposing cause of insanity.'" In other words, by modern medical standards there was likely nothing psychologically wrong with many of these women.[39]

Because there was a greater stigma attached to intellectual disability, and especially mental illness, families were much less likely to visit and routinely check on the care of family members who were moved to and essentially lived in insane asylums. Schools for the deaf and blind generally benefited from being "schools" which by mission focused on education and often encouraged travel and engagement; asylums were essentially prisons, holding areas for the unwanted

---

[38.] Ibid. Penned upon her release.

[39.] Stephenson, Michael, "Upper Canada (Ontario) Insane Asylum Inmates," (2010) accessed on February 28, 2014 at http://www.ontariogenealogy.com/insaneasylum/insaneasylum_part1.html.

and stigmatized, and ultimately a laboratory with experimental guinea pigs used to further the causes of pseudo-science and social progress, particularly in the eugenics period between 1880 and 1930. There were even "mysterious" epidemics in such institutions that aroused great scientific interest, which conspiracy theorists today wonder about being engineered intentionally, all while patients suffered the unintended and often unpredictable consequences.[40]

Whether institutions ultimately did more harm or good is an unanswered question, and one that implies that the good can be separated easily from the harm. Postmodern advocates for deinstitutionalization, like Ed Roberts and Justin Dart, for example, lived in an era where the resources available to the disabled—transportation, education, employment, technology—made some of the good that institutions originally served much less relevant. After all, many of the institutions had been founded before or immediately after the Civil War in a period when cities were becoming central collection points for resources usually well beyond the means of individuals or their families; eighty percent of America was rural.

It is also dangerous to overgeneralize about institutions of this period. It is true that some families either chose not to visit or did not find it easy to visit their family members who were in some types of institutions. But exceptions are to be found to almost everything. In 1850, the administration at the Boston Female Asylum reported that:

> The committee reported favorably of the house and school. Also that Mr. Zoeller, who had, since the admission of his three children been exceedingly *troublesome by frequent visiting* and interfering in little particulars respecting them, had now withdrawn them from the Asylum not being willing to conform to its regulations... (italics author's)[41]

Many institutions that still are open after long histories dating back to the 19th century, like the Virginia School for Blind and Deaf, have mostly embraced their history, and accept that their past is as complicated as their future. They embrace the progress that has been made, and celebrate the human efforts that come from what were often benevolent motives, ranging from the land that was given free by James Bell on which to start constructing the school buildings in

---

[40] Foutoura, Paulo. "The 'Ajuda Paralyses': History of a neuropsychiatric debate in mid-19th-century Portugal," *Brain: A Journal of Neurology*, 133, 2010, pp. 3141–3152.

[41] Lainhart, p. 373.

1839, to a celebration of graduates who went on to general success, like Fred Yates, Jr. who after attending Gallaudet returned to the VSDB as principal and teacher, and a disability activist.[42]

Language from the original VSDB charter, passed in the Virginia General Assembly, read in part:

> Be it enacted by the general assembly, That there shall be established on a site, at such place as the legislature may, by joint resolution select, an institution to be called "The Virginia institution for the education of the deaf and dumb and of the blind," which shall be under the government of seven visitors, to be appointed annually by the president and directors of the literary fund, who shall notify them of their appointment, and prescribe a day for their first meeting, or in the event of failure, for a subsequent one. The said visitors, or a majority, shall appoint from their own body, a president to preside at their meetings, and a secretary to record, attest and preserve their proceedings. In the said institution, there shall be two schools, each separate and distinct from the other in all respects whatsoever. In one of them, such deaf mutes, and in the other, such blind pupils as may be placed in said institution, as hereinafter provided, shall be exclusively educated under so many professors, instructors and assistants as may be deemed necessary and expedient by the board of visitors.[43]

So, how is one to make peace with such a movement? It began both formally and informally, out of the determined efforts of interested individuals and the collective interest of the states, and with grand intentions and sometimes surprisingly modest expectations. It was powered by American industrialization, wealth, and technology. It is a history filled with contradictions.

The institutional movement during the antebellum period was ultimately quite important to the coming disability rights movement in the next century. It was a major intellectual leap, a newly created common space where the industrial and technical might of modernism could be brought to bear a sharp focus on medical and psychological problems, like mental illness, that humans had confronted since the dawn of civilization. Yet it arguably had no true conscience yet, and was largely unregulated, and its own semantics and definitions of progress were ill-defined in ways that would sometimes encourage abuses and excesses.

---

[42] "Yates recalled as champion of VSDB cause." *The News Leader*, Staunton, VA. August 9, 2007.

[43] *Acts of the General Assembly of Virginia, passed at the session of 1838*. University of Virginia.

Although one may argue that institutions were successful and progressive in the cases of schools for the deaf and the blind, one may equally argue they failed in other important cases, as with asylums (and prisons, which operated along remarkably similar lines).

Therefore this period remains enigmatic, and troubling. It was a crystal ball allowing a glimpse into the future of America that allowed only a hazy view into the next century, a startling time to come which would be characterized ultimately by genocide, a rejection of modernity, and an explosion of identity rights movements. The protests on the campus at Gallaudet would look remarkably similar to marches in the Civil Rights Movement, and the aftermath of World War II and the Holocaust would leave 19th century Social Darwinism with much that it couldn't possibly explain scientifically. Some institutions with a foundation on human dignity, and that master science to ethical ends, remain still; others are literally in ruins and a laboratory for ghost hunters and history buffs, and often are seen as unfortunate cultural markers that still highlight the need for an ongoing Disability Rights Movement.

CHAPTER 4

Civil War Veterans with Disabilities and the Roots of the Modern Disability Rights Movement

The American experience with disability prior to the Civil War had been largely defined by the three major factors treated in the previous chapters: a new world, with a wide-open frontier experience; the "enlightened" leadership of a classically educated liberal cadre of men and women who adapted to that frontier and enforced a limited vision of ableness (that included "disablement" through race-based slavery); and the growth of institutions which represented the confluence of scientific advancement, economic prosperity, and urbanization. The American Civil War which erupted in 1861 had many complicated factors behind it (primarily race-based slavery), but the larger effect it had on the American disability experience, and what it now means to be American, was transformative. Hundreds of thousands of disabled veterans returned home, and due to the sheer numbers involved relative to the country's population, it was in many ways the first true, albeit nascent, American disability rights movement as the soldiers and their advocates tried to cope with a massive human services crisis.

The economic and physical impact of the war on America has been well documented historically, although some scholars or critics of culture also remark on the lack of a great defining fictional literature coming out of the time period, or the temporary stagnation of the arts, and a seeming halt to some forms of social progress (such as the public schools movement, particularly in the South). Perhaps this was due in part to the enormous shock and dissonance of the divisive war-time experience, which still sends continuing ripples through race relations and politics even in the present day. The war did, however, transform disability.

For all of the thousands of historical books and articles written about the war, very few until recently deal directly with disabilities or disability experience.[1]

---

[1] This is changing as the writing of the book is being completed...

Ironically, it is sometimes in the rare but important creative writing genre that some disability philosophy pieces do come out of the period, such as those produced by Union soldier Ambrose Bierce, where emphasis can be found on the alienation from self that characterizes not only the shock of the war, but also the historical plight faced by those with disabilities. Bierce's writings emphasized the terror, the violent death and disablement of men in battle, and the dark shadow that the war threw over the grand hopes of the prior era, and the ideals of the frontier and founders. The shock of death and the mass disablement that was often portrayed as worse than death was part of the Civil War story that still remains partially untold.[2]

The particular Antebellum situation of the male gender identity and its relationship to physical wholeness was also one with profound implications for the coming conflict. Men were expected to exhibit a kind of bodily normality, in order to enjoy the full fruits of their privileged status. A perfect case in point is an 1859 article in which the Freemasons declined to let a man with only one ear become a pledge for membership:

> What constitutes a physical disability? The question has arisen this year, and may arise again. I have had to decide the question; but, perhaps my decision will not be in accordance with the Grand Lodge. My decision was that a candidate with but one ear constituted such a defect or malformation as to preclude him from enjoying the privileges of the Order.[3]

Soldiers have historically been a privileged class, especially so in warrior-centered cultures, and disabled soldiers have often received forms of charity, compensation, and social leverage that other individuals with disabilities did not. Dating back to the Roman Empire and many other ancient cultures, soldiers often received land, pension payments at the end of their service, and in some cases, a form of what would today be considered disability compensation for wounds or sickness incurred in the line of duty. While a relatively rare privileged disability class in terms of social compensation, wounded soldiers were also the first group of disabled individuals to crystalize in a public fashion the long-held view of many that disability was centered in the person, rather than situated environmentally

---

[2.] Trammell, Jack. "Civil War Literature." in Inge, Thomas M.; & Wilson, Charles Reagan (Eds.). *The New Encyclopedia of Southern Culture: Volume 9*. University of North Carolina Press, 2008.

[3.] "PHYSICAL DISABILITY." *The American Freemason*. Louisville, 1 May 1859, p. 394 etc. American Historical Periodicals, accessed August 23, 2019 at https://link-gale-com.msm.idm.oclc.org/apps/doc/LRUMIH822248224/AAHP?u=msmu_gvrl&sid=AAHP&xid=008c2b0d.

or socially—one soldier couldn't share another soldier's wound. In other words, their service in essence "proved" their right to a disability status.

This was reflected most in early forms of certification and validation that much later in the modern era placed very specific monetary values on various parts of the body, and generated rehabilitative processes that aimed at restoring the body rather than accepting it as it was. When in the 20th century social welfare programs were expanded beyond soldiers to a larger public in Western nations, this lingering assumption dating back centuries that disability was centered in the person would have very dramatic importance.[4]

Ancient Traditions

The fair treatment of the nobly disabled soldier is a stereotypical Western motif, as well as a firmly entrenched American tradition. Dating back to ancient stories—Longinus, the blind Roman soldier who pierced Christ with his lance; a traumatized Odysseus returning home; the medieval fisher king, who spent his later days fishing due to his battle-disabled condition—Americans inherited this Western tradition and were from the beginning of their North American history predisposed to decorate and commemorate their own battle heroes, many of them disabled in service. George Washington remains perhaps the most commemorated soldier of all-time, still appearing on the one-dollar bill, the quarter, postage stamps, and countless American objects and cultural icons. Perhaps ironically, this most decorated soldier was also one who firmly resisted the very idea of disability as something normal and socially acceptable (see earlier chapter on founders).

Commemoration is not the same as integration, and memory is not always interrogation. Despite earlier efforts to help disabled vets in the Revolutionary era, the Civil War first created in America a human landscape of suffering and disability that had never been imagined, and one where some type of acceptance and reintegration became the key post-war story.[5]

Many current histories of the Disability Rights Movement (DRM) trace the origins of disability activism, Section 504 of the Rehabilitation Act, and the Americans with Disabilities Act (ADA) to vocational rehabilitation efforts for

---

[4] Trammell, Jack. "Disability in the Ancient World."

[5] Littleton, C. Scott; & Malcor, Linda A.. *From Scythia to Camelot*. New York, Garland Publishing, 2000. P. 263, etc.; Shay, Jonathan. *Achilles in Vietnam: Combat Trauma and the Undoing of Character*. Simon & Schuster, 1995; Shay, Jonathan. *Odysseus in America: Combat Trauma and the Trails of Homecoming*. Scribner, 2003.

vets following World War I and later initiatives like the 1944 G.I. Bill for World War II veterans. What is often overlooked, however, is the reintegration of hundreds of thousands of disabled Civil War veterans and the eventually dramatic changes that became part of American cultural and political fabric in the decades following. Civil War veterans were (and remain) the largest group of disabled veterans or Americans ever to re-enter civilian life during any single era, mostly in one massive influx, and the efforts to accommodate and re-assimilate them (or the lack of such effort, in many cases) laid important groundwork for a general disability rights movement one hundred years later that would emphasize shared civil responsibility for reintegration, a belated but important connection between mental and physical health, and a unique American flavor of liberal democracy with equal access at the base of its best intentions. Before the turn of the century brought new wars and a new overarching progressive paradigm, Civil War vets were at the center of a new American dialogue about issues ranging from financial compensation for disability to new definitions of disability itself, and also included the widespread use of new technology to define, treat, or mitigate the effects of disability on a scale previously unknown.

The types of disablement that took place during the war were particularly horrific, in part because technology had leapt so far ahead of battlefield medicine and even the unspoken rules of civilized war, and in part because Americans had simply not anticipated the violence or the longevity of the conflict. The unique combination of factors meant that tens of thousands of soldiers could be killed or disabled in a single day, or even a few hours. Four years of war meant more than a million soldiers were killed and wounded.

Although this chapter will not focus on this particular aspect of the war, the conflict also wreaked havoc on the very institutions in which Americans had invested so much in during prior decades to mitigate disability, particularly in the war-torn south where most of the war's destruction took place. In Jackson, Mississippi, for example, the state asylum was ransacked by troops commanded by General William T. Sherman in 1863, practically shutting the operation down. In Baton Rouge, the school for the deaf and blind became a geographic pawn in the back-and-forth chess game of battle, and served as an evacuation center for terrified civilians. Needless to say, civilians with disabilities, most particularly in the south, suffered in ways during the war that are now often overlooked, and the disruption to the Southern arm of the institutionalization movement was not insignificant.[6]

[6.] "History of the Mississippi State Asylum." Mississippi State University, accessed February 17, 2014 at http://msacp.cobb.msstate.edu/history.html; Morgan, Sarah. *Civil War Quilts: Dixie Diary 4: Asylum*, the diary of Sarah Morgan, accessed March 2, 2014, at http://civilwarquilts.blogspot.com/2013/04/dixie-diary-4-asylum.html.

Carnage of Industrialized War

The firsthand accounts from the war frequently exhibit the difficulty soldiers and officers had trying to rationalize the sheer carnage, and often led them to experience constant anxiety about the future, where the social and lived consequences of mental and physical disablement were a literal unknown. There are countless, letters, reports, and memoirs that reveal very consistent themes of horror, depression, anxiety, and fear. "If I survive this war," many said over and over again when penning a note home, with a sense of fatalism that ran throughout their letters. Many others wrote that it would be better to die gloriously than to survive maimed. Survivor guilt is evident in the medical records.

There were even examples of twice compounded disability stigma when already disabled soldiers, having sacrificed their physical and mental wellness in battle once, were discriminated against a second time by being drafted and then immediately rejected due to their war-related disability. This case occurred in Confederate Florida:

> I know three men who resided in the same neighborhood. Two of them were among the first to volunteer; one of the two was killed in battle; the other wounded and his health became so much impaired that he was honorably discharged. The third man refused to volunteer; remained at home an advocate and braggart of States' rights and liberty. When the conscript act passed there was no clause in it exempting wounded soldiers who were disabled in battle and had been discharged as inefficient for military service. Such soldiers should have been exempted-at all events, should have been saved the painful necessity of being forced as conscripts into camps of instructions to be there again discharged. The wounded soldier, not yet able to perform the duties, but anxious to render service to the county and avoid the reproach to which conscripts by the thoughtless are subjected, hired a substitute to go into the ranks. The braggart, healthy, able-bodied, and wealthy, and in time past known as a rampant secessionist, has neither volunteered nor sent a substitute, but has hitherto avoided the enrolling officer by resorting to the coast under the pretense of making salt. Shall the skulking coward be favored by a legal exemption, while wounded and discharged soldiers shall be forced as conscripts into camps of instruction?[7]

---

[7] *The War of the Rebellion: A Compilation of the Official Records of the Union and Confederate Armies.* Accessed through Ohio State University. Series 4, vol. 2, Part 1 (Blockade Runners). Letter from Governor Milton of Florida to the Floridian Confederate Congressional Delegation, September 11, 1862. Referred to hereafter as OWR.

It is evident that many generals and commissioned officers, who also witnessed the technologically advanced horrors of modern war, shared with the enlisted men the existentialist angst that such carnage and random disabling produced. In an open letter to his men during the Atlanta Campaign, Union Major General Oliver Howard discussed this quite frankly:

> To mourning friends and to all the disabled in battle, you extend a soldier's sympathy. My first intimate acquaintance with you dates from the 28th of July. I never beheld fiercer assaults than the enemy then made, and I never saw troops more steady and self-possessed in action than your divisions which were there engaged. I have learned that for cheerfulness, obedience, rapidity of movement, and confidence in battle, the Army of the Tennessee is not to be surpassed, and it shall be my study that your fair record shall continue, and my purpose to assist you to move steadily forward and plant the old flag in every proud city of the rebellion.[8]

When men were wounded, they were often disfigured to the point that they could not be recognized, or in the case of death, could not be identified for burial or return home. Some brave surgeons, notably on the Federal side, attempted reconstructive surgeries (in fact, the science of such did advance). But often the challenges were too much. At Cold Harbor in 1864, Union soldiers about to engage in a hopeless charge pinned slips of paper with their names written on it to portions of their body the least likely to be struck by lead in the coming storm (often their backs). Even those who survived knew that as wounded men they might never be able to lead the life they had once been accustomed to living. Men were terrified that they might die and never be identified, leaving their families and friends in permanent limbo, a type of final disablement and stripping of identity. Union Colonel Robert West wrote in his report outlining the attack along Darbytown Road late in the war not far from Charles City, Virginia:

> The reports show the losses in this brigade to have been 13 killed, 34 wounded, and 111 missing. These must be inaccurate, since 16 dead bodies of our men were found by us afterward where they had fallen at the works. They had been partially buried by the enemy, and were so disfigured by their wounds and dirt that some of them could not be recognized. Ten of the missing are

---

[8] OWR. Series 1, vol. 38, Part 3 (The Atlanta Campaign). Letter from O. O. Howard, September 10, 1864.

known by their comrades to have been wounded before they were left upon the field. The reports embracing lists of casualties of regimental commanders are enclosed.[9]

West goes on to lament, to the extent an official report allows such emotionalism, the terrible casualties his unit suffered:

> First Lieutenant Herman, E. Smith, Third New York Cavalry, acting as my aide, was very seriously wounded in this fight, and, as I have since learned, died in Richmond after his arrival there. Lieutenant Smith was in the prime of his life and usefulness when he fell. He was an earnest, brave and faithful officer. First Lieutenant George C. Gibbs, Third New York Cavalry, acting assistant inspector-general of the brigade, and serving on my staff at the time, was severely wounded in the leg.[10]

Men sometimes feared an anonymous death more than they did permanent disablement, although fear of disablement was so prominent that many refused medical treatment which was perceived to be permanently disabling in and of itself (amputation is a common example). In the official return of casualties in the First Brigade, First Division, Second Corps, at the battle of Cedar Mountain, August 9, 1862, the returns add this note which makes cogent the fears:

> The greater proportion of those reported missing are supposed to be killed. The bodies found on the field were so much disfigured that recognition was impossible. This report embodies positive information only.[11]

In 1865, the shock of the war remained even after the military surrender at Appomattox. An exhausted temporary relief at peace was present, to be sure, but it was coupled with myriad complex issues related to officially dismantling slavery and immediate attention was not focused on disability. Approximately three million soldiers and sailors served in the combined armed forces of both sides during the American Civil War, and tens of thousands of them returned to their communities permanently disabled—blind, mobility impaired, missing limbs, or with other deformities—and just as often psychologically scarred in

---

[9.] OWR. Series 1, vol. 42, Part 1 (Richmond-Fort Fisher). Report by Colonel Robert West.

[10.] Ibid.

[11.] OWR. Series 1, vol. 12, Part 2 (Second Manassas). Report by Union General S. W. Crawford.

addition to any permanent physical wounds. Their assimilation back into the mainstream represented an influx more powerful in sheer numbers than the total number of foreign immigrants entering the country in 1865—more than 200,000 according to the Bureau of Citizenship and Immigration—and challenged many long-held perceptions about disability and society. In fact, parallels between the soon to be implemented pension programs for Civil War veterans and modern disabilities legislation like the 1990 Americans with Disabilities Act suggest that important changes were occurring in 19th century American social perceptions long before a formal disability rights movement existed in the 20th century. But it was certainly not obvious in 1865.[12]

A Disabled President: Lincoln the Melancholic

Abraham Lincoln was a well-known melancholic, a personality archetype noted by postmodern French philosopher Michel Foucault as one characterized by great intelligence, prudence and sometimes an overt shunning of human companionship. Foucault called the melancholic effect "madness at the limits of its powerlessness," a paradoxical mixture of ability and disability that some in the 21st century might refer to as twice exceptionality, or 2E. Depression is the nearest modern medical/psychiatric analog, although the DSM-V definition of clinical depression does not capture the richness and complexity of the melancholic experience the way a Foucault, or before him, an Aristotle could. The social utility of madness, however, for centuries has mostly escaped doctors, although philosophers and prophets often embraced it.[13]

Lincoln's melancholy was arguably a primary source of his greatness, perhaps the most important one. More recently, authors like Joshua Wolf Shenk have suggested that it "fostered empathy and tenacity," or perhaps more practically, it "enhanced his political realism."[14]

---

[12] The United States Civil War Center. "Statistical summary America's major wars." 2001. Retrieved May 27, 2003 from http://www.cwc.lsu.edu/cwc/other/stats/warcost.htm; *Bureau of Citizenship and Immigration, Statistical yearbook of the Immigration and Naturalization Service.* Washington: U. S. Department of Homeland Security, 2001; Blanck, P.; & Song, C.. "Civil war pension attorneys and disability politics." *University of Michigan Journal of Law Reform*, 35, 2002, pp. 1 & 2.

> Lincoln's leadership included a kind of unspoken moral authority, perhaps best characterized as a power in his personality itself that was palpable to those around him and was even felt on the battlefield by soldiers who were not in direct contact with him. It stirred confidence, promoted patience, and rewarded intellectual diligence. Some scholars and historians look back on Lincoln now and suggest that his own battles with fatigue and depression cultivated within him those traits that he so famously engendered in others.
>
> "How miserably things seem to be arranged in this world," he once wrote to his friend Joshua Speed. "If we have no friends, we have no pleasure, and if we have them we are sure to lose them, and be doubly pained by the loss."[15]
>
> ---
>
> [13] Foucault, Michel. *Madness and Civilization.* Vintage Books, 1973, p. 122.
>
> [14] Ghaemi, Nassir. *A First-Rate Madness: Uncovering the Links Between Leadership and Mental Illness.* The Penguin Press, 2011, p. 68, etc.
>
> [15] "Turning Depression into Wisdom." Accessed May 7, 2014 at http://collegepubs.com/turning_depression_into_wisdom.

Many wounded soldiers were at higher risk of being captured by the enemy, as their wounding slowed their attempts down to keep up with or rejoin a home unit or prevented their immediate evacuation. Although it is natural in warfare to treat your own wounded first, both Union and Confederate doctors and orderlies, to their credit, almost always treated whoever showed up on their operating table with equal care. The same cannot always be said of prisoner of war camps, both North and South. At notorious Andersonville, in Georgia, or Camp Douglass in Illinois, soldiers on both sides suffered miserably, even when better resources for their care were readily or reasonably available. Countless thousands of veterans returned home (if they were lucky enough to survive) more disabled by the conditions of their captivity than by battlefield wounds.[16]

---

[16] Trammell, Jack. "Voices from the past: Letters detail camp life, POW miseries." *The World and I Online*. June 2009; Trammell, Jack. "Richmond's Belle Isle a Rival to Andersonville." *Washington Times*, August 31, 2002, p. B3; Hesseltine, William B.. *Civil War Prisons*. Kent, OH: The Kent State University Press, 1972.

This criminal negligence on both sides is typified by this letter from Confederate Surgeon, Provisional Army, Isaiah H. White:

> Having been ordered to this post, I am lending my aid to the surgeon which charge in the construction of hospital accommodations. Temporary sheds are being constructed sufficient in number and capacity to accommodate 2,000 sick. Great difficulty is experienced in procuring from the Quartermaster's Department the necessary tools for the advancement of the work. Any number of laborers can be obtained among the prisoners, and with the necessary tools the work could soon be completed. The law of Congress creating a hospital fund to provide for the comfort of sick and wounded is completely abrogated by the Commissary Department failing to fill requisitions for funds.[17]

In other words, he was making sure his superiors knew that the terrible conditions for Federal prisoners were not his fault. The history of prisoner of war camps in the Civil War is rampant with such blame.

Complicating the terrors of battle, long-standing stereotypes about the disabled person (*Other*) being lazy, unwilling to work, or leeching off the able-bodied were perpetuated by war-time propaganda about deserters and shirkers. Both sides formed invalid corps, units of walking wounded and those hopefully recovering from surgeries and more serious wounds, who could serve in light duty positions and that would keep them from becoming a burden on civilian resources. Many became hospital orderlies.[18] An official report by a Maine provost officer addressed this issue in typical fashion, trying to sort out who was worthy of accommodation and who was not:

> Bvt. Lieutenant Colonel R. M. Littler, acting assistant provost-marshal-general for Maine, August 12, 1865, forwards a communication from Captain Elijah Low, provost-marshal, Fourth District of Maine, representing that his district is overrun with deserters from the Army and draft; that they are insolent and abusive too [sic] soldiers who have endured the hardships and perils of war, and *many of whom are crippled by wounds or disease and are entitled to protection.* He fears that as the only disability put upon deserters is disfranchisement by the United States Government, and as each state regulates the qualification of its

---

[17] OWR. Series 2, vol. 7, Part 1 (Prisoners of War). Report from Isaiah H. White.

[18] Numerous accounts in the archives at the National Museum for Civil War Medicine, Frederick, MD.

own voters, they will have the right to vote under existing State laws. He asks permission to appoint suitable persons as deputy marshals to assist in executing the laws in his district. (italics author's)[19]

It was common on both sides for the deserters and the walking wounded to be mingling everywhere behind the lines. By some formal estimates, there were as many as 400,000 disabled veterans (counting both sides) by the time the war ended. As many as 100,000 (probably many more) of them were amputees, while the rest suffered from a variety of ailments contracted or incubated during service that ranged from rheumatism to blindness. If we account for psychological disabilities, like post-traumatic stress disorder (PTSD), called "soldier's heart" or "shell shock" at the time, and which remained remarkably underappreciated in spite of being documented since ancient times, it is more likely that 600,000 wounded warriors returning home is still a conservative estimate. In fact, the evidence on hand suggests that almost all officers and soldiers who saw any combat at all came back significantly changed in ways that would make civilian reintegration difficult.[20]

Some were lucky to get out when they did. Henry S. George, a Union sergeant wounded and residing in a hospital in Alexandria, Virginia, in August of 1864 sent a personal letter to Abraham Lincoln, asking that he be allowed to leave the army due to being "unfit for Cavalry duty for at least sixty days" according to a doctor's disability certificate, and wanting to pursue entering politics. Many were discharged for reasons far more obtuse than entering politics, but most who were disabled found reintegration difficult either way.[21]

Surgeon Alfred Hasbrook, a Union doctor, was typical in recording dozens of permanent cases of disability, each with a slight variation in its formulaic medical chart: "Pain in wrist resulting from gunshot wound, disability 7/8, probably permanent; gun shot [sic] wound left arm near shoulder, total disability, permanent, left arm has been amputated; consumption, total disability, permanent (was never sick before); musket ball right shoulder, right arm hangs paralyzed and useless,

---

[19] OWR. Series 3, vol 5, Part 1 (Union Letters, Orders, Reports). Report from Bvt. Lieutenant Colonel R. M. Littler.

[20] Gilder Lehrman History Online. "Casualties and cost of the Civil War," 2003, retrieved May 27, 2003 from http://www.gliah.uh.edu/historyonline/us20.cfm; Clarke, F. "Honorable scars: Northern amputees and the meaning of Civil War injuries." In Cimbala, P. C.; & Miller, R. M. (Eds.). *Union soldiers and the northern home front: Wartime experiences, postwar adjustments*. New York: Fordham University Press, 2002, pp. 361–394; Kolb, R. K.. "Thin gray line: Confederate veterans in the new south." Kansas City, MO: Veterans of Foreign Wars of the United States, 2000, retrieved May 27, 2003 from http://www.vfw.org.

[21] George, Henry S.. "Letter to Abraham Lincoln," August 20, 1864. From manuscript division, Library of Congress.

disability total, duration uncertain; etc., etc." A completely new lexicon, medical records system, and professional terminology had to be created to even catalog the destruction and disablement.[22]

The Ancient Stigma

Disability was an occurrence that did not respect rank, age, or class status. Roughly one-hundred fifty generals died in the conflict, and many more were temporarily or permanently disabled. Confederate General John B. Hood, who trained at the U.S. Military Academy, was wounded multiple times while leading soldiers in Robert E. Lee's Army of Northern Virginia. Hood lost the use of his left arm at Gettysburg, and later had his right leg amputated after Chickamauga. As with so many of the wounded and permanently disabled, his war wounds were a badge of honor having come during valiant military service, but they were also an ancient tattoo carrying a centuries old stigma—he failed at high command later in the war, and after the war he failed at various businesses and perhaps not coincidentally struggled with his disability and personal identity. Historian Ralph Henry wrote of him after his multiple woundings and command failures:

> Poor brave, devoted Hood was cast in a part beyond his capacity. He was suffering from the disabling of an arm and the loss of a leg by battle wounds, and no doubt was mentally worn and impaired by his physical state...[23]

Henry's assessment was perhaps unfair, but typical of the times. Even when "legitimately" earned on the field of battle, physical disabilities became human liabilities by the common thinking of the day. People assumed, rightly or wrongly, that once disabled a man was simply not capable of doing as much physically, accomplishing as much, or even of thinking as clearly (i.e., intelligent). In Hood's case, like many others, the pity associated with it may have been the worst stigma of all.

Another example comes from the ordinary rank and file. Union private Ephraim Miner served in the 142nd Pennsylvania Infantry and 22nd Veteran's Reserve Corps, although he mainly saw inaction, due to frequent sickness and luck of the draw.

---

[22] Hasbrook, AlfrEd. "Dr. Alfred Hasbrook's record of disabilities for Civil War veterans, 1863–1866." 1866, retrieved May 20, 2003 from http://www.valstar.net/~jcraig/docnotes.htm.

[23] Henry, Robert Selph. *First with the Most: Forrest*. New York: Mallard Press, 1991, p. 395.

Miner spent a great deal of time in convalescent camp (much to his consternation due to the boredom associated with it), but moreover, the exposure to bacteria and illness in the hospital left him with chronic health issues that persisted even after the war and to the end of his life. The very camps designed to treat disability actually created more in some cases. Miner also knew the challenge of disability in his personal family life, as he had several children after the war born with "significant mental disabilities." Although he never was shot in battle, Miner spent the remainder of his life confronting war-related disabilities and caring for those around him with significant disabilities. When considering sheer numbers of disabled soldiers, those like Minor not otherwise accounted for in the records may number in the additional tens of thousands.[24]

Lieutenant J. R. Boyle, 12th South Carolina Volunteers, recorded his own wounding at Gettysburg:

> I received a grape shot in my right leg below the knee, which shattered the bone into splinters, the shoe on that foot flying off some distance; within a radius of a yard and a half two members of my company also fell -- John A. Robertson and Jim Williamson; I could not move, but plainly saw what was going on; our brigade was wavering and about to fall back, when Col. Perrin, in command, still on horseback with drawn sword, dashed to the front, telling the men to follow him, this action gave new life to the brigade, who charged and dislodged the enemy from behind a stone wall.[25]

Editor Alethea D. Sayers notes that Boyle's future as a disabled person was far from optimistic: "Upon returning home, Boyle found himself of little use to the Confederate Government as a cripple, and immediately went to work learning to serve as a telegraphic operator." Once again, the impact of the tattoo already was marking against Boyle.[26]

Franklin Eldredge was discharged due to disabilities from the 7th Infantry, Ohio Volunteers in 1864. He recorded simply in his diary: "I got a bullet through my right thigh." Later, he added more details about the subsequent disabling

---

[24.] Miner, Mark A.. *The Civil War Diaries & Army Convalescence Sage of Farmboy Ephraim Miner*. Beaver, PA: Minerd.com Publishing, 2011, pp. 18, 134, 139, etc.

[25.] Boyle, Lieutenant J. R. (12th South Carolina Volunteers). *Diary*, accessed online March 6, 2014 at http://ehistory. osu.edu/uscw/features/articles/0006/boyle.cfm. Note: *Reminiscences of The Civil War* by Lieut. J. R. Boyle of company "C," 12th S. C. V., Gregg's Brigade Afterwards McGowan's, can be found in the State Archives of South Carolina.

[26.] Ibid.

experience: "had my leg dressed at barn we go 6 miles in ambulances ... many of the boys visit me; Bill Horner made me a crutch & cane; Cronk makes some for the Oberlin boys." In his matter-of-fact way, he was accepting his new mobility impairment that would likely be with him for the rest of his life. It also foreshadowed the booming postwar industry for prosthetics and other assistive devices.[27]

Camps for the Disabled and Hospital Networks

The war created an immediate, systemic demand for some type of unified military health system in both regions of the country that simply did not exist prior to 1861, the closest thing perhaps being the hospitals associated with the standing army and navy, which even then, were relatively small facilities/networks. In the South, where there was a relative paucity of transportation, medical infrastructure, and trained physicians this lack was felt with a particular keenness. In fact, many wounded and disabled Southern soldiers were furloughed to recover at their actual homes, simply because the fragile hospital system was overwhelmed with the more seriously wounded and sick.

Richmond Virginia, as the Confederate capitol for the vast majority of the war, eventually boasted a complex of dozens of buildings, small and large, that comprised the most prominent military hospital network in the Confederate system, the most famous of which was Chimborazo. Similar hospital complexes were created in other major Southern cities, or at railheads where it was easy to bring the wounded by train. There were, in some cases, specific camps for the disabled with a practical emphasis on rehabilitation for service behind the lines, or even a return to active duty in many cases.

In the North, where there were considerably more resources that could be brought to bear, large hospitals were built or modified to deal with the thousands of wounded coming in. Poet Walt Whitman famously visited wounded soldiers in such settings. In spite of the relatively better material care in the North, few

---

[27] Eldredge, Frank. *Civil War Diary*. Accessed March 6, 2014 at http://ehistory.osu.edu/osu/sources/letters/eldredge/default.cfm.

> soldiers on either side were sad to leave the crowded rooms where they were lucky to have an individual bed. Many never did leave.
>
> "Everything wet and no place to lie down and I got so bad off till they started me to the hospital through the rain and I got as far as Mr. Lemmons. I just felt like I was going to die so I went in and just told them I must stay there. They soon fixed my bed and done all they could for me." Eli Landers, a Confederate, was one who never left the hospital in Rome, Georgia.[28]
>
> ---
> [28.] Landers, Eli. "Letters." Available at http://www.gacivilwar.org/story/the-personal-story-of-life-as-a-confederate-soldier

Each man (and more than a few women who secretly fought disguised as men and were sometimes only exposed on the surgeon's table) who returned home disabled faced potential physical barriers to gainful work in a time when almost all labor was physical in nature, requiring two hands and two legs. In some communities, North and South, as much as eighty percent of the labor performed in the community generally required two hands and two legs, whether standing behind a two-horse plow, or working in a blacksmith's shop. It usually required being able to see with relative efficiency, as well. As a result, many disabled vets (including those blinded) attempted to change careers, perhaps selling insurance, for example, or working as clerks in office positions. Moreover, the psychological mindsets in communities that had long privileged able-bodied, propertied white males, presented an invisible but highly impermeable barrier to resuming a normal life in the community. Worse yet, conversation about such barriers facing those with disabilities was not yet part of the normal American discourse (although over the coming decades vets would force such a dialogue). In fact, the Official Records of the war demonstrate the use of the term "cripple" just as often to describe the wounding of a horse, or an aborted military action, as to talk about the serious wounding or disablement of a man.[29]

[29.] OWR.

Sometimes soldiers used wry humor and irony to process their disability, as this poem composed by an amputee testifies:

> I look at this, the feeble thing before me—
> The piteous wreck of what was once an arm—
> And can you wonder, if a cloud comes o'er me?
> If smiles are vain, and kind words cease to charm.
> The cloud does come at times, but does not tarry;
> It passes over, and again 'tis fair;
> Ungrateful I, to murmer, or to carry
> A heavy burden, which I need not bear
> What matters is, one arm its task has ended?
> 'Tis well, it may be, why should I repine?
> For Life's stern conflicts I am still defended,
> While, true and faithful, one stout arm is mine.
> With that, and Heaven to aid me, let me labor
> With cheerful heart, whate'er my lot may be;
> And though may rust the rifle and the sabre,
> May that lone arm a final "victory" see![30]

Contemporary sociologists and psychologists draw very obvious historical connections between the physical soundness of a man's body, and the total "wholeness" or humanity of the man, especially in male-dominated, patriarchal cultures. At the conclusion of the Civil War, many disabled veterans were only temporarily insulated from the normal social stigma attached to lack of physical completeness, due to the fact that citizens viewed their immediate past-service as a distinct honor and privilege. The end of the war provided temporary relief and distraction to practically everyone. But the lack of wholeness for soldiers with disabilities—a missing limb, chronic limp, or scarred face, or what we call PTSD—which served as a visible badge of such service and sacrifice, only remained so for a time as normality quickly returned.

Soldiers themselves tended to have evolving views of their disabilities in a similar way, at first, as a temporary inconvenience or circumstance that presumably (hopefully?) wouldn't be permanent. In fact, many amputees during the war chose to remain in active service with the Invalid Corps in a patriotic spirit that belied their now severely impaired abilities. This often changed after they had been home for a time, and the normal attitudes prevailed again. Soldiers would

---

[30] Whitehouse, in Clarke.

eventually begin to lobby for themselves, but not before seeing this discriminatory return to "normality."

Disability scholars frequently note that disabled veterans in the 20th century have often been given preferential treatment that ordinary citizens with disabilities were not granted, and thus were arguably spared some of the usual social stigma and prejudice in civilian life. But this "grace period" so to speak in the Civil War era, rapidly began to dissolve within six months to a year after the war, when the reality of a difficult and large-scale human transition set in.[31]

The general prevailing view of the day continued to blame those who were disabled or in poverty for their own plight. Heroes or not, attitudes about any disability then (and unfortunately all too frequently in the present) remained stubbornly entrenched in a negative ontology, and charity often took the form of "helping the needy to help themselves" (a negative twist on the concept of rehabilitation). As modern scholars like James Charlton (1998) have pointed out, disability was "rooted in the political-economic and cultural dimensions of everyday life," and to overcome the prevailing stigma would involve what would have often seemed a Sisyphean-like task, and even if tens of thousands of returning disabled soldiers could organize and advocate, which eventually they did, the hurdles remained. Soldiers by and large contented themselves with finding a job and trying to return to a family of some sort; when that failed to address their larger needs, they began to organize.

Fitness, as has been mentioned, was largely equated with ability and willingness to work. Whether a soldier in the North or the South, the loss of control over one's own body was potentially catastrophic. Sarah Handley Cousins explains that "The ability to command one's body and use it in labor to maintain independence was a value shared across boundaries." It was, in an ironic way, a shared American value that transcended regionalism.[32]

Civil War veterans were contemporaries with people of the same social fabric that were fascinated by Victor Hugo's Quasimodo, circuses and freak shows, and Herman Melville's one-legged Captain Ahab. Disability equated a glaring lack of wholeness and was still widely attributed to divine judgment or punishment for sin. The seeming randomness of the bullet's victim was in contrast with Darwin's theories of logical evolution which were appearing widely in public debate, and the implications of "survival of the fittest" which were now quite uncomfortable

---

[31.] Houck, D. W.; & Kiewe, A.. *FDR's Body Politics: The Rhetoric of Disability*. College Station, TX: Texas A&M Press, 2003; Garland-Thomson, Rosemarie. *Extraordinary Bodies: Figuring Physical Disability in American Culture and Literature*. Columbia University Press, 1997; Zames Fleisher, Doris; & Zames, Frieda. *The Disability Rights Movement: From Charity to Confrontation*. Temple University Press, 2001.

[32.] Handley-Cousins, Sarah. *Bodies in Blue: Disability in the Civil War North*. The University of Georgia Press, 2019, p. 3.

to those whom society had up to now labeled as fit and dominant, and who were now suddenly switching identity from abled to disabled. It is no wonder that many soldiers expressed the idea that death was easier to contemplate than permanent disability. To be killed dramatically in battle meant glorious immortality; to be maimed and left behind to mostly fend for oneself in a world ill-equipped to help or understand was depressing. The idea of the *normate*, pioneered more recently by Rosemarie Garland-Thomson, was in full evidence by the end of the war.[33]

To restore "wholeness," many Northern and Southern communities offered free prosthetic limbs to returning vets, a visible attempt to restore men to the status quo and transition soldiers back into gainful employment, although in some cases, some men chose to not take advantage of the offer as a matter of pride or a desire to be independent. Many post-war portraits of disabled soldiers intentionally display their "noble" missing limb.

This was in partial contradiction to the traditional European experience, where soldier amputees often received a license to beg. Many disabled Federal veterans did not bother, at first, to apply for pensions or other types of aide at the end of the war because of a general cultural aversion to government handouts (Confederate veterans, of course, did not even qualify for Federal aid). Rugged individualism was still in 1865 a long-held and firmly entrenched America ideal. A rational consideration of a soldier's "wholeness" at this time also did not usually include psychological wellness or possible mental disorders; Blanck and Song even found that veterans with more visible, obvious physical disabilities generally received higher pensions and were granted pensions more often than those with "invisible" disorders.[34]

Further complicating matters, America's dominant normative identity of white, non-disabled, propertied male, framed all attempts at reintegration in a complex network of contradictions. According to Rosemarie Thomson, America's 19th century fascination with freak shows which highlighted human oddities was a de facto affirmation of the white, male norm, and rejection of the incomplete or malformed Other. The terrible, exaggerated and deformed figures were a clear indication of what America did *not* perceive itself to be. Thomson calls this perception an "aristocracy of the body," with an ideal self that was "self-governed and self-made." This aristocracy transcended any regionalism of the North and South. A veteran with a disability could easily find himself

---

[33] Covey, Herbert. *Social Perceptions of People with Disabilities in History*. Springfield, IL: Charles C. Thomas, 1998; Smith, J. David Smith. *Minds Made Feeble*. Austin, TX: Pro-Ed, 1985; Garland-Thomson, Rosemarie. "Integrating Disability, Transforming Feminist Theory," in Davis, Lennard (Ed.). *Disability Studies Reader* 4th Edition. Routledge, 2013.

[34] Clarke; Blanck and Song.

outside the normative identity (as did growing numbers of victims of industrial accidents, too). While the country progressed economically after the war and steadily grew in population, the lingering contradictions first highlighted by Civil War vets would become much more glaring problems for many other Americans in coming decade.[35]

Left-handed Penmanship

No story illustrates these contradictions better than William Oland Bourne's initiative to reward off-hand penmanship skills of veterans missing their original writing hand due to war injury. Bourne, the editor of *Soldier's Friend*, a monthly periodical, advertised seeking "the best specimen of their left-handed penmanship" (another long tyranny of the norm is the assumption of right-handedness), requiring soldiers to send in a hand-written letter demonstrating their new offhand writing skills. To the postmodern mind, it is also interesting to note that since almost everyone in the 19th century penned with the right hand, a greater cultural and literal physical value was attached to this hand than to the left. Even disability payments to soldiers were higher dollar values for the loss of a right hand than for a left. A perceived mini tragedy within the larger drama of all war maiming was the group of men who lost their right hand, rather than their left hand, or even a leg, etc.[36]

All of the retrained letter writers uniformly demonstrated remarkable new-hand calligraphy and penmanship skills (although just as typically none of them were especially good spellers), especially noteworthy in light of what some perceive to be the cultural downgrading of such penmanship skills in the 21st century landscape, when superior handwriting has largely been supplanted by practical keyboarding skills and texting adeptness. Bourne's efforts unintentionally highlighted one small, minor aspect of an overall disability drama about to be played out by thousands back in their own hometowns.

Some of the soldiers told their story matter-of-factly, simply relaying facts for the sole purpose of demonstrating penmanship, like Orderly Sergeant Lyman E. Brown of the 98th New York Volunteers, who glibly related his

---

[35.] Garland-Thomson.

[36.] "Letters from Union war veterans." Manuscript Collection, U.S. Civil War, Bancroft-10579E, Bancroft-10576E, Bancroft-15667E, Bancroft-10575E, and Bancroft-10580E. Columbia University Rare Book and Manuscripts. Hereafter referred to as BL (Bourne Letters).

terrible wounding during the assault on Fort Harrison in 1864: "In the above assault I was shot through the right arm which resulted in amputation above the elbow." Other soldiers, however, hinted at the more dramatic changes the physical loss would ultimately mean, such as James Green Cunliffe, Company E in the 51st New York Volunteers, who came from Great Britain to New York City and received a bounty to join the Union Army. Cunliffe, like Brown, was wounded near Petersburg in 1864, and knew he would need help after the war:

> I was wounded in my right arm as I was loading my musket... A few of us [Union wounded] got two rebels to take us to the nearest doctor... The doctor said it would have to come off... Though it could I think have been saved... [After parole] I stayed at the Soldier's Home in Howard Street [New York City]. I put in my claim for a [disability] pension...but I have not got the papers as yet through...[37]

Other soldiers like Martin B. Goule, wounded at Gettysburg, moved from the future expectation of physical labor into the possibilities of a life of the mind. In 1865: "I was attending lectures at the Law University," he wrote to Bourne. Although not anything like World War II under the G.I. Bill, disability also sent many disabled vets back to school, or into education, an environment where something like a missing leg was much less relevant.[38]

Another foreign soldier, Theodore B. Guenther, was born in the Kingdom of Hanover, Germany, where he served five years in the Hanoverian Army. But "when the great rebellion in this country broke out, and the existence of this government depended entirely upon the patriotism of its citizens, I at once concluded to immigrate, and shoulder the musket to fight for right, justice and liberty." Guenther would give an arm to the Union cause: "At last in the battle of Bull Run, where I lost my right hand by a cannon ball on the 30th day of August, 1862."[39]

It was not unusual for vets to remember the exact day and circumstances of their fateful wounding, or the surgery, and many of the details about it, even years later. It was clearly a marker for them of a sea shift in their human experience.

---

[37] BL.

[38] Ibid.

[39] Ibid.

Civil War Odyssey

In spite of an exterior bravado, and a genuine patriotic appreciation from the public, disabled Civil War vets were ultimately marginalized like others with disabilities. "We lose in a great measure our place in society," said John Thompson, wounded in both arms and legs. The return of thousands of men missing limbs or otherwise disabled, eventually threw American attitudes about obligations to the disabled and poor into a new flux. Similar to the modern Vietnam experience, soldiers came home bearing burdens that affected all of those they came into contact with for years to come. Yet outside of friends and family, there was not much public sympathy for disability. President Grover Cleveland would later summarize the prevailing social skepticism regarding disability in defense of an 1887 pension veto: "There can be no doubt that the race after the pensions ... would not only stimulate weakness and pretended incapacity for labor, but put a further premium on dishonesty and mendacity." Civil War soldiers returned home as heroes, but as heroes who were expected to work and not demand too much of society in repayment. "If there remains a spark of that patriotism that prompted you to seize the musket ... seek at once ... honorable employment," Phinicas Whitehouse advised soldiers with disabilities. Although change was in the air as a static electric potential due to the sheer number of disabled vets and their real needs, old attitudes were also firmly entrenched in ways that challenged the few advocates of a new paradigm.[40]

Of course, the war had impacted civilians, as well. During the siege of Petersburg, for example, William Banister was killed as a direct result of being deaf. He did not hear Union soldiers calling upon him and other civilians to surrender, and as a result was shot down. Civilians suffered mightily during various battles and army movements across the South, many becoming disabled, or finding their previous disabilities to now be more profound. The civilian disability experience during the war is vastly understudied.[41]

Nevertheless, a growing body of scholarship suggests that it was soldiers in the aftermath of the Civil War who "changed conceptions of disabled persons in American society." For the first time in American history, serious consideration was given to the long-term effects, visible and invisible, on men serving as soldiers, and then returning home disabled. When Union veterans finally

---

[40.] Blanck and Song; Clarke.

[41.] Trudeau, Noah Andre. *The Last Citadel: Petersburg*. El Dorado Hills, CA: Savas Beatie, 2014, p. 9.

organized themselves and applied political pressure, attitudes slowly began to shift. A here-to-fore unparalleled political and social movement grew in tandem with swelling pension plans for Union veterans, despite presidential vetoes and continuing public resistance. Even the soldiers themselves began to overcome stereotypes and verbally ask for help, applying for pensions in record numbers. A cottage industry for lawyers grew up around lawsuits related to pensions (and some skeptics date the reputation lawyers currently enjoy to this period).[42]

In 1866 national homes for disabled *volunteer* soldiers were established (*regular* army vets already in theory had access to army hospitals and doctors, as well as to an army or navy home depending on the type of service). These homes ultimately numbered twelve, and served tens of thousands of disabled Union veterans, many of whom lived out the last of their days there. Originally called the National Asylum for Disabled Volunteer Soldiers, the name was changed in 1873 to the National Home for Disabled Volunteer soldiers, and it is an interesting footnote in the evolution of the term asylum, which by the 20th century had a very negative association with it. According to researcher Trevor Plante, people "came to see many of the one-armed and one-legged veterans parading around in their blue uniforms." Of note in terms of gender and racial effects, benefits were extended to women in 1928; only 2.5 percent of the veterans assisted were black, while roughly 10 percent of the war-time Union army had been black.[43]

In the defeated South it was a remarkably different story. Soldiers were paroled or simply left to return home as fast as the devastated transportation network would allow (a few immigrated to other countries like Brazil).

"I was sick; cold; wet; hungry; and sleepy; picture as bad as you can and we were in worse condition," one Captain remembered. "His was the retreat of a wounded stag," historian Paul Buck (1937) wrote about returning Confederates. A few diehards held out beyond Appomattox, or left the country, but the vast majority returned to their farms, families and small businesses, many of them permanently disabled. In most southern communities, according to one source, about one in every three returning Confederate soldiers at the end of the war was missing at least one limb. Of the more than 200,000 estimated wounded Confederate soldiers in the war (the number was probably greater), roughly one-quarter of them at least were amputees. The loss of a limb (or limbs, in many cases)

---

[42] Ibid; McConnell, S. C. *Glorious Contentment: The Grand Army of the Republic, 1865 – 1900.* The University of North Carolina Press, 1992.

[43] Plante, Trevor K.. "Genealogy notes: The National Home for Disabled Volunteer Soldiers," *Prologue*, Vol. 36, No. 1, 2004.

was a disability of no small import in an era and region where the vast majority of men in the South made their living as agricultural laborers or farmers, and in essence the war wounded them afterwards into "economic incompetency."[44]

Charitable organizations sprang up all over the South to provide artificial limbs for returning Confederate veterans, and in Mississippi the state spent one fifth of its entire revenue in 1866 on artificial limbs. Under Reconstruction and the 14th Amendment, federal pensions were only granted to Union veterans, and Ex-Confederate states were temporarily prevented from providing any substantive state benefits. During the immediate post-war years, Confederate veterans relied almost totally on the care and charity of local communities, families and friends. It was not until 1958 that Congress symbolically granted the last surviving Confederate a federal pension.[45]

When Reconstruction ended in 1877, former Confederate states began to establish their own state pensions, as well as state run homes for disabled vets, and widow's and orphan's homes or charities. Georgia, to take one example, allotted payments to disabled veterans and those veterans unable to work, or their widows. Like the federal government, southern state governments tended to become more generous as time went on, especially since indigent and disabled veterans were increasingly visible in the public eye. The growth of the Lost Cause, which through literature and iconography reframed the war experience as a glorious libertarian fight against tyranny, fueled greater concern about vets. By the time the last Confederate veteran or dependent was dead in 1962, Southern states had spent more than five hundred million in real dollars on pensions and soldiers' homes.

Demographically, Confederate veterans had larger families on average, were more likely to live on a farm (70% were farmers) and had a 6% lower literacy rate than their Union counterparts. A disabled Confederate veteran with a family to feed often found himself in a very difficult position. In some cases, they were forced to sell farms and look for work in cities that were being rebuilt. Sometimes, they were forced to migrate or move north or west to find a new life. The disability aftermath of the war radically and permanently altered the southern landscape.[46]

[44.] Tennessee State Library and Archives, *Tennessee Civil War Veteran's Questionnaires*, 2000, retrieved May 19, 2003 from http://www.state.tn.us/sos/statelib/pubsvs/quest.htm; Buck, P. H., *The Road to Reunion: 1865 – 1900*. Boston: Little, Brown and Company, 1937; Kolb.

[45.] Kolb; Department of Veterans Affairs, *Veterans Benefits Administration annual benefits report fiscal year 2000*, retrieved June 25, 2003 from http://www.vba.va.gov/bln/dmo/reports/fy2000_abr_v3.pdf.

[46.] Georgia Department of Veterans Service, "History," 2003, retrieved May 20, 2003 from http://sdva.georgia.gov/01/article/0,2201,1264696,00.html: Kolb.

Union veterans returned home with generally little fanfare after initial celebrations, and usually experienced fewer immediate economic problems than their Confederate counterparts. The war had hardly touched the vast agricultural and industrial resources of the North and had in fact fostered tremendous economic growth. After the Grand Review of both major Union armies in Washington D.C., most soldiers moved to a dispersal camp, received discharge papers, and then used a train pass to get somewhere close to home. Demographically, the average Union veteran was 26 years old, a former farmer, mechanic or laborer, and from a small town. During the war, the army had actually intentionally made some efforts at preparing to transition men out of service. Less than one year after the close of the war, however, the army had closed its rehabilitation hospitals and employment offices, and veterans were left mainly to fend for themselves.[47]

Especially in the case of soldiers with disabilities, America at the end of the Civil War seemed to increasingly forget the need to reintegrate her wounded warriors. It was ultimately veterans themselves who carried the cause into the mainstream. Concerned citizens like the aforementioned editor William Bourne sporadically took up their cause. To set an example, Bourne even hired disabled soldiers as salesmen and marketers in his business. Still, many soldiers found it difficult to find work of any kind. Pension records reveal many examples of soldiers who had pre-war physical occupations (such as mechanic), who were disabled during the war and took up post-war, non-physical occupations (such as salesman). Many soldiers with disabilities who couldn't find work subsisted solely on charity. Benefits held in large cities like the "Left-handed Penmanship Competition" in New York raised money for those who had lost a hand, but significant numbers of soldiers still found themselves destitute or struggling. When disabled Confederate General John B. Hood died, he left behind ten children and a widow in abject poverty, practically homeless.[48]

The federal government provided benefits under the pension act of 1862 for those who had lost a limb or had otherwise become disabled during active military service. But Union veterans quickly found the system inadequate to meet their needs, increasing the large disabled and even homeless population. Jacob Erb of Angelica, Wisconsin was typical: for the loss of two fingers and one hand, he received eight dollars a month, or roughly the equivalent of ¼ of a subsistence laborer's monthly wages. This was hardly the kind of "benefit" that a man unable

---

[47] McConnell.

[48] Clarke; McConnell; BL.

to find work could feed himself on, let alone care for a family. The tradition of soldiers receiving half pay after becoming disabled persisted into the Civil War, perpetuating the stereotype of the disabled as less than human and less valuable to the economy. Over time, post-war reforms to the Civil War era pension system began to improve benefits and access.[49]

The American Civil War—like all wars—created its share of psychological scars. Men who had been bonded together in the heat of combat, often found the transition to quiet, sometimes solitary civilian life, difficult and unexpectedly complicated. Those who had not fought, or had not even been in the service, couldn't fully understand what the experience meant. Like soldiers of all generations, their choice was often to remain silent, or to patiently begin an advocacy that would without their consent single them out for comparison to others with profound disabilities.

Ultimately, the collective response to this situation was the formation of the Grand Army of the Republic (GAR) and numerous smaller veterans' associations. The GAR was founded in 1866 by Benjamin Stephenson and reflected a desire for both camaraderie and political power to legislate relief as well as increase public awareness. Organized like the former Union armies, each "post" had a "commander" and an annual "encampment." The GAR eventually boasted more than 400,000 members and contributed millions of dollars to the relief of disabled and needy Union veterans. More importantly, the GAR harnessed political power and aimed it straight at the politics of the pension issue. The pension debate framed a wider cultural acceptance of shared responsibility for returning vets and became a hot perennial issue in national and state elections ("Waving the bloody flag").[50]

The evolution of dual pension plans after the war—one strictly for war-related disability passed by Congress in 1862, and the other for general service enacted in 1890 that allowed coverage of post-service illnesses or disabilities—was later considered by many to be a very liberal development (particularly the 1890 law) compared to previous wars, and was only possible because of the strong and unified lobby the veterans maintained, most specifically through the GAR. Veterans with severe disabilities dating back to war service tended to stay within the first system, while those who could

---

[49.] Blanck & Song; Shawano County Civil War Page, "Pensioners on the role: Residing in Shawano County, Wisconsin as of January 1, 1883," 2003, retrieved May 27, 2003 from http://lonestar.texas.net/~gdalum/shawano/1883_pensioners.html.

[50.] Knight, G. B. Knight. *Brief history of the Grand Army of the Republic*. 2003, retrieved June 3, 2003 from http://suvcw.org/gar.htm; McConnell.

still generate income in other ways or had disabilities or illnesses that did not date to the war could utilize the second system. By 1910, over 90% of Union Army veterans were recipients of one plan or the other, and payments under the pension acts totaled more than one billion dollars for the years immediately before and after the turn of the century. In 1893, for example, there were 966,012 pensioners.[51]

Many veterans were troubled by the monetary supports, as they seemed like charity, even as significant numbers of them reached out with the encouragement of pension lawyers to accept them. In a similar vein, the GAR fed into the contradiction by trumpeting the manly virtues of selfless soldierly sacrifice at the same time that they were lobbying for a more liberal disability pension coverage. The GAR was also criticized for its' rituals, internal politicking, and "bloody shirt" mentality, which some thought held politicians hostage to the patriotic sacrifices of veterans. None-the-less, the GAR made disability a national issue, gave America the 30th of May as Memorial Day, and lightened the suffering of many disabled and indigent Union veterans.[52]

In fact, the modern U.S. Disability Rights Movement (DRM) traces its 20th century origins to the treatment of disabled veterans after the Civil War. By World War I and World War II, following the example of the GAR and building on subsequent political developments spurred by Civil War veterans, 20th century veterans with disabilities were able to integrate back into society with relatively fewer obstacles than those faced by soldiers in the past. Part of this was (and remains) a natural and understandable desire to pay back the men and women who had so bravely risked their lives and limbs for the safety of the country. In addition, the efforts of veterans also sparked important civilian reform, and contributed to a public shift in attitudes. The growth of the field of psychology was closely related to the re-integration of war veterans and also led to an increasing sensitivity to invisible disabilities caused by war.[53]

The GAR wrestled with the same macro issues that the country at large was forced to deal with: inequality of opportunity in a competitive industrial age; the shift from a largely rural to a largely urban population; and the question of charity and entitlement. Many veterans died years after the war from injuries and illnesses related to their war service, and their children and spouses, while awarded with limited monetary pensions, still were left to deal with a society

---

[51] McConnell; Blank and Song.

[52] Ibid.

[53] Shay.

that struggled to assimilate and accommodate any people with disabilities. Whether they realized it or not, their struggles helped America experience significant change.[54]

Disability scholar Lennard Davis talks broadly of the models that American society has historically used to explain and rationalize disability. In the early 19th century, the charity model was a major mindset for dealing with disabilities. After the Civil War and during the early 20th century, advances in technology led to a more medicalized model, which explained disability in terms of physical limitations, and empirical, rational explanations. In the second half of the 20th century, the return of Vietnam vets with disabilities (concurrent with the Civil Rights Movement) led eventually to the adoption of the Civil Rights Model, identity-based, where those with disabilities (both physical and psychological) began to demand equal treatment under the law and legal accommodations. Civil War veterans with disabilities were directly involved in the slow shift from the charity model to the medical model of viewing disability, and ultimately toward a civil rights and identity-based model.[55]

The shift in attitudes that Civil War veterans sparked later allowed psychologists and doctors during World War II to initiate another paradigm shift. They began to see that advances in medicine were saving many more lives than had previously been possible, but that very little was being done to ensure the quality of those disabled lives when they returned to civilian life.[56]

The outcome of the lessons from the Civil War era was a 20th century that saw the creation of the Veteran's Administration in 1930, the G. I. Bill of 1944 which some historians and intellectuals consider possibly the most important single piece of legislation of the 20th century in terms of its social implications, and the passage of the 1990 Americans with Disabilities Act (ADA), which opened doors for all people with disabilities.

Some modern disabilities scholars note in the last twenty-five years a remarkable worldwide change in attitudes about people with disabilities, away from the historical "perception of disability as a sick, abnormal, and pathetic condition," to one that is increasingly normal, and "demands self-determination." Not enough credit, however, is given to veterans of the American Civil War, who went

---

[54] McConnell; Glatthart, J. T.. "Afterward." In Cimbala, P. C., & Miller, R. M. Miller (Eds.). *Union Soldiers and the Northern Home Front: Wartime Experiences, Postwar Adjustments.* Fordham University Press, 2002, pp. 486–487.

[55] Davis, Lennard J.. *Bending over Backwards: Disability, Dismodernism & other Difficult Positions.* New York University Press, 2002.

[56] Meyerson, L.. "The social psychology of physical disability: 1948 and 1988." In Nagler, M. (Ed.). *Perspectives in Disability.* Palo Alto, CA: Health Markets Research, 1988, pp. 13–23.

back to work when they could, organized themselves into a powerful political advocacy, and utilized the legal system to gain additional rights and privileges. Perhaps some of the typical Victorian veneer in a banner that read, "The arm and body you may sever, but our glorious Union never," was penetrated by real men, with real disabilities, who fought to regain rights that had been granted without question before they became disabled. It's very possible that they brought about more social change than is generally realized.[57]

Jonathan Shay brought PTSD and reintegration of disabled vets into the public eye following the Vietnam War era. In many ways, his work could have just as easily focused on the Civil War, where an equally large numbers of wounded vets came back to try and live a civilian life in tandem with their disabilities. Shay had the benefit of immediacy, and myriad media sources as well as living witnesses. It is now up to social historians and archeological ethnographers to capture that vital experience of vets after the Civil War, but there can be little doubt that it redefined the American disability experience. To borrow with deference from Shay, it was the original American disability Odyssey.

During the end of the siege of Petersburg in the spring of 1865, Confederate "convalescent camps" were filled with disabled patients. "There," according to historian Noah Andre Trudeau, "the 'quiet surroundings enabled many to obtain the much-needed renovating sleep.'" Civil War veterans both during and after the war paved the way through sheer human mass for the coming leaps in disability rights in the 20th century and beyond.[58]

---

[57] Charlton, J. I.. *Nothing About Us with Us: Disability Oppression and Empowerment.* University of California Press, 1998.

[58] Trudeau, Noah. *The Last Citadel: Petersburg.* El Dorado Hills, CA: Savas Beatie, 2014, p. 291.

CHAPTER 5

Hiding Disability: Presidents, Disease, and the Globalization of Disability

Between the late 19th century decades of accommodating Civil War veterans and the end of the Second World War in the mid-20th century, America as a nation transformed into a modern superpower, and the notion of personal identity and disability experience charted new territory. The enormity of the transformation of Western life during this period cannot be understated and has been examined extensively in every major academic field of inquiry from literature to anthropology. This period saw the zenith of positivism, social Darwinism, and eugenics (a term introduced by Francis Dalton); it also saw the ashes of genocide, the epic failures of monolithic institutions, and the painful shortcomings of grand civic initiatives. It was a period characterized by globalization, American Exceptionalism, shifting definitions of progress, and a struggle between the sciences and humanities to claim intellectual space in the voids modernism ultimately created. No issue or human experience highlighted the contradictions of this period better than disability.[1]

Many of the contradictory experiences people had with disability and disease during the 20th century were framed by a gradual transformation that took place over many decades semantically. The change began with a generally static understanding of disease as something to be cured, and not necessarily synonymous with physical or mental handicap (disability), which was presumably more permanent, and most importantly, impacted work and social position in the capitalist stratification negatively. Over time, however, as an appreciation for the social consequences of both disease and disability grew, the line between disease and disability began to blur. In the early 21st century, in fact, many temporary disabilities are covered under the ADA. The nascent social science of sociology which was born into this transformative time contributed to this blurring, by

---

[1.] Peyser, Thomas. *Utopia and Cosmopolis: Globalization in the Era of American Literary Realism*. Duke University Press, 1998; Smith, J. David. *Minds Made Feeble: The Myth and Legacy of the Kallikaks*. Austin: Pro-Ed, 1995, p. 2.

redefining social facts, and opening a window into the inner workings of grand-scaled social structures which we today take for granted as part of the cultural landscape (ex. structural racism; physiognomy; etc.).

For example, the diagnosis of attention-deficit disorder (ADD/ADHD) in the later part of the 20th century (first seriously studied as a brain defect at the beginning of the 20th century) showed the fruit of that process, where there now was both pathology (brain differences; genetic components; medical/pharmaceutical interventions; etc.) and social consequence (difficulty in school; higher rates of auto accidents; social stigma; etc.) that could be distinguished from one another and understood better in context. The "disease" become normalized to a point that the conversation shifted in the direction of accommodation, acceptance, and sociological/cultural understandings, rather than purely medical or psychological explanations. The shift is, of course, ongoing as old paradigms remain persistent.

This transformation did not happen all at once, and it is important to remember that it remains an evolutionary process. It also did not usually happen publicly. The evolving relationship between disease and disability today can be witnessed in the vast health data keep by institutions, hospitals, asylums, and agencies from that era—not always digitized and easily accessible—but still there to be found in some cases as disability historian Douglas Baynton reminds students and scholars (once you start looking, "disability is everywhere"). In North Carolina, for example, great efforts and resources were spent treating and preventing tuberculosis (TB), which was then treated as a disease, and largely ignored as a disabling condition in the neomodern sense.

The era was also framed by two deeply flawed presidents with disabilities whose complicated personal and political legacies helped define the substance in the primordial ooze of the coming Disability Rights Movement (DRM). President Wilson was a dyslexic, yet also a brilliant and tireless academic (he was also a racist and an elitist); President Franklin Roosevelt was a wheelchair user and behind-the-scenes disability advocate, yet went to great lengths to keep his disability sheltered from the public view and portrayed himself instead as a powerful, capable (non-disabled) man. Together, these two very imperfect figures captured and embodied the contradictions, dilemmas, and failures of early modernism and its aftermath, the struggle to progress and improve the world for everyone without compromising on individualism (even though that individualism benefited a very specific class of Americans), and the bumpy road that would also, ultimately, forward collective, national disability-oriented social justice late in the 20th century.

These two figures were bookends of a cultural and medical shift of tremendous import, but this narrative is not intended to portray either as a naturally heroic figure, or a good human being. Wilson, in fact, is in historical "jail" for his racist and elitist views. Instead, their position of authority and influence, and their very flaws, are an important mechanism to give us insight into what constituted a disability, and how it impacted social status. Their accomplishments (or the damages their beliefs inflicted on people) are very much open to a longer conversation.

To cite one example, the relatively new field of DisCrit (the combination of Disability Studies and Critical Race Theory) postulates that the similarities between race and disability can make a distinction between the two difficult to define, or that their differences are less important than their similarities in a conversation about "normality." In the same sense that ableism assumes "normal," racism assumes "whiteness." The tyranny of the norm could be seen as a metaphorical white male with an ideal body and mind. This intersectionality can perhaps be seen in Wilson's equally negative attitudes about both race and disability. For Wilson, to be black was to be disabled. To be disabled, was to be black (or a lesser citizen).

America's transformation during this time involved shifts from a rural to a largely urban demography, from an agrarian to an industrial economy, from a state and local citizen's focus to a polarized and in some ways compulsory nationalism, and from an expanding frontier outlook to a more sophisticated inward-focusing social infrastructure that developed alongside a wealth-dominated cultural mindset. The modern mindset impacted art, architecture, literature, and even spawned new sciences like psychology and sociology. As science and medicine provided one spectacular discovery or invention one right after the other, disability and chronic illness moved out of the shadows of superstition and the narrow focus of religious judgment, and into a positivist ontological light. Although the semantics and public perception of disability remained largely negative and charity based, there was suddenly the possibility of cure and a world that could potentially be rid of non-accidental disability.

Labels began to proliferate, particularly in medicine and psychology. The use of measurement became highly sophisticated.

Perhaps predictably, given the modernist proclivity for labels, is the fact that negative stereotypes about disability remained doggedly persistent throughout this period, even in the bright light of science, and individuals often remained convinced of older popular wisdom and outdated attitudes even in the face of overwhelming empirical medical evidence to the contrary. In fact, on rare occasions science/medicine were made to bend over backwards in order to support outdated popular wisdom and stigmas.[2]

Disability as tragedy—a motif that had dominated Western thought for thousands of years—for a short while existed side by side in a world where leaps in medicine and technology promised to abolish monsters to the darkness. But attitudes that were part of powerful social norms were not changed so easily. The disability discourse in academia and science in this period moved forward through a rational process that mirrored the attitudes of the times. Eventually, through a sometimes ponderous and inevitable dialectical march that ended with the Holocaust and Hiroshima, the disability discourse encouraged a radical questioning of the status quo, but not before continuing to confront and sometimes even embrace misconceptions and primitive attitudes.

The result is a time period that seems now strange and dissonant, resulting in many unhappy but at the time seemingly logical marriages like eugenics and social engineering with the ideas of progress and medical advancement. Such marriages resulted in institutions that both cared for and abused individuals; roughly 30 states had sterilization laws, some of which remained in effect well into the 1960s and the modern DRM.[3]

Another complication—perhaps even an important element of American Exceptionalism—is the notable diversity of policy and practice centered around disability as it varied from state to state, and locale to locale. Even scholars of the time in the late 19th century remarked on the lack of uniformity in areas like education for individuals with disabilities. Although all fifty states had somewhat similar initiatives for the deaf and blind, practically none of them had uniformity in laws or provisions for those with mental disabilities. The persistent rationalism and quest for uniformity championed by science was in stark contrast with the reality of state policy and actual cultural practice.[4]

The overall historical and cultural shift between Civil War disabled veterans care and the G.I-dominated prosperity and scientific boom of the 1950s is one upon which multiple volumes have been and will continue to be written. Veterans in America (and Canada on a smaller scale) have always paved the way for all individuals with disabilities. In addition to making note of specific legislation and landmark events, which must be mentioned, this period was so rich in change that one must sample representatively to not lost track of the larger paradigm shifts taking place.

---

[2] Smith.

[3] Smith, p. 3.

[4] Giordano, Gerard. *American Special Education: A History of Early Political Advocacy*. New York: Peter Lang, 2007, p. 172–173.

Inventions and Improvements 1870 – 1950 (adapted from the National Consortium on Leadership and Disability for Youth Disability History Timeline, and Bancroft Library Collections, UC Berkeley)[5]

- 1872 Alexander Graham Bell develops the telephone to "make speech visible"
- 1883 Sir Francis Galton coins the term *Eugenics*, related to social Darwinism; much of U.S. disability policy and Western European social policy is guided by it throughout the 20th century culminating in the Holocaust
- 1907 First eugenic sterilization law in Indiana; several dozen states follow suit
- 1917 U.S. enters World War I; disabled vets return to the political discourse
- 1918 Smith-Sears Veterans Vocational Rehabilitation Act
- 1920 Fess-Smith Civilian Vocational Rehabilitation Act
- 1921 American Foundation for the Blind (AFB) founded
- 1935 League of the Physically Handicapped founded; disability protests lead to additional WPA jobs
- 1946 Hospital Survey and Construction Act passed in Congress; targets individuals with disabilities for access to services
- 1949 First wheelchair basketball tournament, Galesburg, Illinois

---

[5.] NCLD Youth. *Disability History Timeline: Resource and Discussion Guide.* Accessed at www.ncld-youth.info/Downloads/disability_history_timeline.pdf; "The Disability Rights and Independent Living Movement Project," *Timeline.* Accessed at bancroft.berkeley.edu/collections/drilm/resources/timeline.html.

A President with Dyslexia

President Woodrow Wilson exhibited dyslexic traits in his early childhood reading patterns and later became a central figure in the politics of disability and rehabilitation in America at the national level, as well as a (now controversial) luminary in a nascent international globalization movement that would eventually, roughly seventy-five years later, define disability access as a basic human right (although he didn't intend that). He is a curious and controversial figure around which to begin to organize a phase of American disability history—he was, for example, the only president who was also a true academic, having earned a Ph.D. and served as a university president; he is also considered a racist by 21st century standards—his leadership and his own imperfections coupled with the dramatic changes taking place in America and around the world suggest in hindsight that he represented a swirling mix of traits and attitudes typical of the times.

Wilson is quite controversial in the present time. His attitudes about race and acceptance of aspects of eugenics make him enigmatic at best, and at worse a discredited historical figure that some writers will avoid all-together. None-theless, he was a figure who can serve the neomodern reader as a rhetorical lever, and his own disability story was unique, both early in his life, and near the end of it, where the politics surrounding his disability became of tantamount importance to the safety of the entire world.

Wilson was a human who can be defined by the unique historical bookends of his lifespan—he was born into an era with horse-drawn plows and no indoor plumbing, and served as president when the automobile, motion picture, and airplane were common. His childhood struggles with dyslexia serve as a fascinating experience with which to pry at the modern and progressive notion of disability because, in spite of so many changes in the American cultural and physical landscape, the impact of a cognitive-based reading disorder in a relatively well-to-do family was no less impactful amongst the literate at one end of the era than at the other end of the spectrum, perhaps. Without literacy (and maleness, whiteness, perception of ableness, etc.), Wilson and others could not rise to the levels of ultimate influence.

Wilson seldom wrote or spoke about his early reading difficulties, and obviously learned to compensate for it in ways that did not prevent him from eventually moving through the loftiest social corridors and halls of academia, and then actually becoming an icon for the intelligentsia at that time. The metaphor of hidden disability within Wilson's success and rise to prominence is equaled by the hidden disability at the end of his life. His attitudes and even policies he crafted reveal a great deal of the contradictions of disability ever-present at the times.[6]

Wilson, like Franklin Delano Roosevelt, did not consider himself disabled (and today we are left mainly with records of others to tell us how disabled he probably was). He apparently "overcame" (a term of the times; not a 21st century accolade in the DRM) his reading difficulties through dogged practice and determination, although it is generally understood in the present that no one actually "overcomes"

[6.] Trammell, Jack. "Woodrow Wilson and the classic era of U.S. numismatics: Presided over changes to U.S. money, now gets his own dollar coin." *Coin World*, December 30, pp. 50–53.

dyslexia as much as they learn to compensate for it, or rewire; current research is focusing on white matter in the brain, and stealth dyslexics, who do appear to "overcome" it. By the time Wilson was President, he obviously had secretaries, aides and assistants who could also help mitigate any persistent reading challenges, although he obviously read a great deal for himself. Disability was not (apparently) a personal identity for him; he didn't talk about it; he acted as if it did not exist. As a lecturer at Princeton, few would have suspected him of having what in today's terminology would be called a classic learning disability (LD).[7]

Ironically, much later in life a physical disability in the form of a stroke did intersect with Wilson's day to day living at the very time he was pushing forward the most ambitious plans of his career, that of creating and growing an international community of nations that would work together to prevent anything like World War I, the Great War, from ever occurring again. Wilson's rejection of nationalism and his vision for the way nations could work together in an international community was as revolutionary in some ways as the Russian Revolution in 1917, and even mirrored themes that would reappear in the 1960s when disability activists promoted the universality of disability experience as evidence that collectively humans could be more effective in creating an accessible world for everyone. Although Wilson certainly didn't envision that, he did see value in America leading a global community for the betterment of all.

The identity rights movements of the 1960s became increasingly reliant on international support. Malcom X called it "Internationalism" to forward the freedom of people of color. Ed Roberts argued for a shared disability perspective, a concept that is now coupled with technology and termed Universal Design (UD). Although Wilson was far from a activist for minorities, his attempt at globalization eventually led others to do the same with much more sophistication and attention to human dignity (the United Nations has disability charters).

Wilson had other health issues during his term as President. But he eventually lived with a physical disability that could not be "overcome," and his political dreams were not to bear the immediate fruit he hoped for, largely as a result of his physical incapacitation/disability, and the shifting fortunes of world politics. Sadly, even his ability to lecture and communicate effectively—the academic and intellectual gifts that had taken him so far in his career—also escaped him late in his life due to the effects of the stroke that he suffered in 1919.[8]

---

[7] Konnikova, Maria. "How children learn to read." *The New Yorker*, February 11, 2015.

[8] Berg, A. Scott. As reviewed by Wawro, Geoffrey. "The definitive portrait of a political icon," *History Book Club*, Fall 2013, pp. 2–3.

Those closest to him went to great lengths to conceal the degree to which he was disabled, or before that, physically ill, a theme that would be repeated in an ironically similar pattern with Franklin Delano Roosevelt in the 1930s and 1940s. White House Physician, Cary T. Grayson, was a firsthand witness to this and some his related correspondence has recently been highlighted by the Woodrow Wilson Presidential Library. Before Wilson's stroke, he suffered from other medical problems, including trouble breathing, as Grayson reported:

> The patient is progressing most satisfactorily, so far, and I have good reasons to hope for a most beneficial result. It has been a big undertaking... ...No one knows anything about it except Ms. E., Miss Harkins, Hoover – It is one secret that has been kept quiet, so far, and I think it is safe all right now.[9]

Before the debilitating stroke, Grayson also wrote about Wilson contracting influenza:

> The president was suddenly taken violently sick with the influenza at a time when the whole of civilization seemed to be in the balance. And without him and his guidance Europe would certainly have turned to Bolshevism and anarchy. From your side of the water you can not realize on what thin ice European civilization has been skating.[10]

Grayson, who spent many years close to Wilson, would also watch with "great anxiety" as the president suffered from the life-threatening stroke in 1919, and was part of the closest family members and advisors who were the only ones who knew the president's truly fragile and compromised condition. The public did not know. In fact, researchers have uncovered some evidence that photos of a disabled Wilson were even doctored to conceal his fragility.[11]

Moreover, it's not easy to discern how Wilson himself felt about his condition(s). What is clear is that those around him were gravely concerned about his ability to function as president, and just as importantly, the public need for him to appear strong and presidential regardless of how he was functioning in private life. The

---

[9] Grayson, Cary T.. "Telegram to Alice Grayson," July 16, as quoted from the Woodrow Wilson Presidential Library at http://www.woodrowwilson.org/about/president; originally written about by Chandler, Michael Alison. "A President's illness kept under wraps: Woodrow Wilson's deteriorating health detailed in doctor's correspondence." *Washington Post*, February 3, 2007.

[10] Grayson.

[11] Chandler.

side effects of stroke are, and were in 1919, well-known: loss of balance, aphasia, vision problems, cognitive impairment, spasticity, fatigue, etc. For Wilson, the worst possible side effects would have been those that impacted his intellectual capacity and processing speed. Where dyslexia had not ultimately stopped him from learning to read, or communicating effectively, stroke took away the very life of the mind that he valued almost above all else.[12]

Wilson remains a fascinating, tragic, and controversially figure who embodies some of the complexities of disability, identity, and science in the early 20th century. Acknowledging again the terrible legacy of his racism which taints his legacy, Wilson, from the information available, did not see himself as a figure of disablement, just as the founding figures who had disability experiences did not generally, either. The timing of his experience, in the context of the Progressive Movement, modernism, and the scientific revolution (and its specters of eugenics, genocide, and persecution), combined with the authority with which he governed an international community, mean that Woodrow Wilson and later FDR as elites represented many of the conundrums that the DRM would later attempt to resolve—were disability rights and healthcare for everyone or just a wealthy elite? Who ultimately was responsible for equal access?

Wilson is representative of a period where Americans felt a tension to both reveal (treat/cure) and to conceal disability; to solve it; and sometimes, occasionally, to accept it; but more often to continue to hide it or ignore it.

Wilson, as an elite, had many advantages disability-wise that most other Americans did not—few dyslexic students received the educational support they needed; few could afford the kind of healthcare the president could—but he did have a disability experience, and it tells us much about the misconceptions, the hopes, the tensions and the potentially forthcoming changes, and he made decisions that would impact the coming DRM whether he realized it or not.

World War I Veterans

In the grand outline of Western history, World War I represented a jarring disruption to modernism, progressivism, and even the Greek tradition of physiognomic beauty and wholeness. The horrific carnage, industrialized on a scale never before imagined—the British lost twenty thousand soldiers killed in a single day at the Somme—was brought into stark relief by the lack of sophisticated medical

---

[12.] List of symptoms from a more complete list at: http://www.stroke-rehab.com/effects-of-stroke.html.

preparation for the first weapons of mass destruction like artillery, machine guns, and tanks. Similar to the American Civil War, but on a much grander scale, the Great War was the end of an innocence. As medical science struggled to deal with the human carnage, those soldiers lucky enough to survive disfiguring and disabling injuries found themselves in a depressed Europe and America unprepared to comfort or accommodate them.

The flower of European youth, and the optimism of the modern age, both came to a cataclysmic bump within a four-year period (1914–1918). The result for the history of disability and disability identity was profound, suddenly ushering in of an era of fierce dialectical conflict between modernism (science, eugenics, medicine, and the notion of social progress) and social confusion that had to reconcile the lived reality of mental and/or physical disability (disfigurement, loss of occupational ability, loss of wholeness; loss of life). World War I literally, "overwhelmed all conventional strategies for dealing with trauma to body, mind and soul."[13]

Surgeons originally trained to mend small scars, or fix minor deformities, suddenly were confronted by men missing half of a face, or large portions of their limbs or other body parts. The necessity of this unexpected crisis resulted in a strange collaboration between doctors and artists, the latter of which attempted to reconstruct what a man's face formerly looked like, and the former who attempted to reconstruct the actual new face through surgery.

Anna Coleman Ladd has recently been rediscovered as one of the artists who contributed her talents to the challenge of war wounds and facial disfigurement, through the creation of personalized World War I facial masks. The jarring disconnection between the iron technology of machine guns and artillery, and the horrific wounds they produced, and the corps of artists that attempted to inspire disfigured veterans to create a new identity and wholeness, with literally a new prosthetic face, is a fitting metaphor for the disruption to Western culture that the war produced, and exposes the persistent tension between old and new views of disability that it brought into focus.

Ladd, who was later recognized as Chevalier of the French Legion of Honor, was not the only artist employed in such work in Europe. British soldiers called the mask department "The Tin Nose Shop." Several parallel operations were ongoing in France (under the *Office National des Mutiles et Reformes la Guerre*). The artists were tasked with recreating the original likeness of a man's

---

[13] Alexander, Caroline Alexander. "Faces of War: Amid the horrors of World War I, a corps of artists brought hope to soldiers disfigured in the trenches." *Smithsonian*, February 2007, p. 1.

face—drawing on their skilled portraiture training and artistic experience—so that the new mask would be as much like the former man physically as possible. It is not too much of an exaggeration to call these masks visual prosthetics. A literal "corps" of artists was involved in the work of creating a new part of each man, both in Europe and in America, one that would often go to the grave with them, still in place.[14]

World War I also brought other types of traumatic wounds back into the American cultural landscape, almost always with jarring results. Shell shock, or PTSD patients, who returned by the thousands, brought invisible disabilities back into the forefront for the first time since the Civil War. Referred to as "le cafard" in France, or the disability of the brain due to concussion, it was in reality as we know today a psychological dysfunction due to shock and stress, a reaction to being subjected to repeated trauma. According to some sources, as many as one hundred and fifty thousand or more American soldiers suffered from what would today be called PTSD. There were over five thousand cases reported in neighboring Canada.[15]

Many men suffered both psychological *and* physical wounds. Conditions at the front, and even safely behind the lines or after the Armistice, were so terrible and unsanitary as to compound simple wounds and sometimes transform them into permanent disabilities.[16]

"The realities of trench warfare were horrifying and nauseating," David Gosoroski wrote recently. "Cold and wet produced trench foot and respiratory illnesses. Rats, flies, and nits carried all manner of potentially fatal diseases."[17]

Soldier letters from the time seldom use the term "disability" but cogently reveal a discourse on gender, wholeness, and physiognomy that was poignant, individualized, and remarkably authentic coming as these soldiers did out of the recent Victorian era. It was a discourse that could not take place with complete public honesty in the wider American progressive cultural landscape; people simply weren't ready or equipped for it. But as increasing numbers of wounded and disfigured vets returned home, it was a discourse that eventually compelled action, and couldn't be ignored.

[14.] Ibid.; McMurtie, Douglas Crawford. *The Evolution of National Systems of Vocational Reeducation for disabled Soldiers and Sailors*. Washington DC: Federal Board for Vocational Education, 1918, p. 29.

[15.] McLaren, Angus. "The creation of a haven for 'Human Thoroughbreds': The sterilization of the feeble-minded and the mentally ill in British Columbia." *Canadian Historical Review*, No. 2, 1986, p. 132; Gosoroski, David M.. "Brotherhood of the damned: Doughboys return from the World War." *VFW Magazine*, September 1997. Accessed online at http://www.worldwar1.com.

[16.] Douglas, John. "Letter from John Douglas, Mayenne, France, December 24, 1918." Accessed at http://www.historychannekl.com/letters/john_douglas2.html.

[17.] Gosoroski.

One national action involved the creation of dozens of additional hospitals to deal with the returning sick and wounded. Over the decade following the war, many of these new military hospitals or repurposed hospitals began to transition into offering public health aimed at helping veterans more smoothly re-enter society. In 1921, a National Home for Disabled Volunteer Soldiers was approved, as well.[18]

A sampling of the personal letters from the time reveals much that gives insight into the motivations that soldiers—now civilians—with disabilities would try to articulate to the public several decades later. "Nurse's Mail," is now a collectible genre for philatelists (stamp collectors), due to the special markings related to military hospitals and healthcare. The bitter reality for many disabled soldiers was that they could not physically write letters home themselves due to their injuries.[19]

W.B. "Scufs" Scripture wrote home from Europe to his parents claiming that practically everyone in his division had been sent home disabled:

> Now you needn't worry if I get sick, I will let you know. I don't know when I will get home but it looks like spring. So cheer up, it's almost here. See you can't hurry it until peace is signed. All the troops coming now are wounded. There is no fighting division. Yes I am in the same old 82 division…[20]

Some of the most horrifying wounds were caused by mustard gas and other chemical attacks. Scripture felt lucky to have escaped that:

> Who has brought Paul Peakes out(?) This mustard gasses that the fellow got it burn just like hot water but worse. I had a friend had got some but is alright. You let it come in the night and it lay on the ground and then the (sic) seem to come out well rise. I have been through some. But never got first with it.[21]

Benjamin Edgar Cruzan kept a diary that chronicled some of the disabling injuries he witnessed, and he sometimes went to pains to make sure his reader would know the soldier would not suffer permanent disablement as a result of

---

[18] Ibid.

[19] The National Postal Museum (NPM). "Mail Call: Morale, mail matters." Accessed at http://postalmuseum.si.edu/mailcall/3.html.

[20] W.B. Scriptures, *War Letter* (from Genevenies, France, January 14, 1919). http://www.war-letters.com/0019/0005.html Jan 14, 1919

[21] Scriptures, April 8, 1919.

his wounds: "Jake had been wounded by a Bomb dropped out of a Dutch plane not bad he get all Right Soon he got one piece in the ankle one in the Left Wrist one in the chin..."[22]

Cruzan later voiced the question at the end of the war that many permanently disabled soldiers experienced in a quite different way: "OH Joy Oh boy where do we go from here. 'That's the question.'" Many of those wounded, particularly those who were wounded by poison gas, had no realistic idea of how long-term the health effects would be on them. "I suppose you have heard before this that I have been in hospital gassed," Will Wasson wrote to a friend, "but I am better now and in a con[valescent] camp."[23]

For soldiers who were wounded so badly as to be permanently disabled, prospects back home were not promising. America in 1918 remained a blue-collar labor force, and the loss of a limb or a mobility impairment of almost any nature automatically excluded the possibility of a factory job or similar type of physical labor. The eugenics of the time also was layered with racism and gendered notions of cultural value. Black soldiers wounded in World War I confronted a particularly complex set of barriers, twice-disabled as Dr. King would later describe.

Some mistakenly thought that the opportunity to serve in the war would lift black males up, and present new social opportunities. Paul Lawrie argues that many black leaders such as W.E.B. Du Bois were convinced of this. The reality turned out quite differently, and when black soldiers became disabled, the equation became even more complicated. In a foreshadowing of letters Dr. Martin Luther King would receive from wounded black servicemen in the 1960s, black soldiers returning home wounded from World War I faced a double barrier.[24]

In a similar way, the women who served in various capacities during World War II, and became disabled as a result, generally found disappointment in the treatment they received as individuals with disabilities. Their double-stigmatized identity resulted in additional cultural barriers and was a stark contradiction to the other forms of "progressivism" of the early 20th century in America and Great Britain.[25]

---

[22] Cruzan, Benjamin Edgar. *The Diary of Bugler Benjamin Edgar Cruzan*. The Kansas Collection: Accessed at http://www.kancoll.org/articles/cruzan/c_diary2.htm.

[23] Wasson, Will. "Letter to Leonard Turner, France, November 19, 1918." Accessed http://website.nbm-mnb.ca/MOP/english/ww1/dosearch.asp?browse=9&results=50&all=true.

[24] Lawrie, Paul R. D.. "*Salvaging the Negro:*" *Race, Rehabilitation, and the Body Politic in World War I America, 1917–1924.*" In Burch, Susan, & Rembis, Michael (Eds.). *Disability Histories*. University of Illinois Press, 2014, pp. 324, etc.

[25] Anderson, Julie. "British Women, Disability, and the Second World War." *Contemporary British History* 20, no. 1, 2006, pp. 37–53.

None-the-less, soldiers—specifically disabled veterans—became the central figures in moving a disability discourse forward during the period, just as after the Civil War. This was most visible in two pieces of related legislation: the 1917 Smith-Hughes Vocational Education Act, and the 1918 Smith-Sears Veterans Rehabilitation Act (both of which replaced the 1914 War Risk Insurance Act). These two acts set a course that eventually allowed individuals without military-related disabilities to enter into similar national conversations.[26]

There were two key elements in the legislation that were significant departures from previous efforts. First, the payments that disabled vets received were not to be determined by privilege—i.e., by military rank—but rather would be scaled by only the actual amount of disablement they were experiencing. Second, efforts to help vets gain employment upon returning would focus on training and "rehabilitation," or the use of resources that would either alleviate their condition or mitigate it in terms of finding work.[27]

The double-edged sword of Western Modernity is quite evident in these landmark pieces of legislation. On the one hand, the capitalist system which was driven by the value of labor and at that time a male-dominated labor force, demanded that men work in order to maintain their privileged status. Wounded vets therefore—particularly those most permanently disabled—moved in cultural and economic terms from the most secure and privileged positions prior to the war, to ones synonymous with the most highly stigmatized identities (non-white, non-male, non-working). If occurring in large enough numbers without being addressed, such a shift was a threat to the system status quo.

On the other hand, the general benevolence and charity-driven desires embedded in the Progressive Movement meant that such men (patriot/warriors) absolutely had to be cared for, and moreover, reintegrated into something approximating their former privilege and status, which meant resuming meaningful (or profitable) work and (one might say cynically) reinforcing the white, male-dominated, capitalist driven economics of prosperity.

The legislation was a parsimonious way to address all of the variables in play, without benevolence being the *only* ingredient. Rehabilitation—the term, the industry, the concept—blossomed into a booming new business, government, scientific

---

[26] Zames & Fleischer, pp. 170–172.

[27] Ibid; Foreman, Michael L., et al. *Sharing the Dream: Is the ADA Accommodating All?* U.S. Commission on Civil Rights, 1998.

and cultural entity. The wonders of science could mend and retrain broken men so that they might resume their required/expected roles in an ordered capitalist/democratic society.

The unintended outcome of this effort, however, was an unseemly exposure of just how badly individuals with disabilities who were *not* solder heroes (or white, educated, middle class, employed, etc.) were actually treated and culturally positioned. The counter-reaction took two forms: one direction headed toward a more stringent eugenics and social Darwinism, including a redoubled effort to define the science of deformity and abnormality and that ultimately led to most unfortunate events (outlined elsewhere in this chapter) ranging from forced sterilization to life-time internment/institutionalization, or worse; the other direction headed toward a broader civil and human rights, globalization, and the increasing public assimilation of all individuals with disabilities (this trend was admittedly more hazy than the prior).

As after the Civil War, disabled vets from World War I inadvertently led the way for all people with disabilities. Although people at the time viewed the legislation as the debt owed to vets, a debt made particularly heart-wrenching due to the heinous nature of many wounds, it contributed significantly to the inevitability of a much broader Disability Rights Movement down the road.

Eugenics

The differences in terms of semantics between disability, addiction, medical condition, disease, physical impairment, intellectual impairment, and illness or sickness shifted constantly during the Progressive Era (as they had in earlier eras examined in previous chapters). The common thread that held them together and confounded any overlaps was a positivist, progressive medical mindset that saw all of them as flawed but scientifically correctible conditions. They were viewed as stable but not meaningful human identities. They were unwanted liabilities mired in a negative ontology. The "devil in the details" can often be seen in the semantics.

1929, for example, saw the establishment of two "Narcotics Farms" that were to specialize in the treatment of individuals who were sentenced for violating federal narcotics laws, one in Kentucky and one in Texas. At this time, too, there was a clear distinction between the alcoholic—who was seen as reformable—and the narcotics addict who was generally "sequestered." Similar to arguments later occurring under the ADA, doctors, psychologists and social scientists used eugenics to determine who was worthy of a second chance, verses those who needed others to make that decision for them.[28]

Much earlier than that states individually embarked on a program of expanding institutions from serving just the mentally ill and criminally convicted to a much wider social network that included the so-called "feeble-minded" and others medically unfit (ex. epileptics). These definitions, too, were grounded in the eugenic science of the day, but varied widely in practice from state to state. New York, for example, established such an institution in 1907 and shortly thereafter named it Letchworth Village. Letchworth Village, named after progressive William Pryor Letchworth, was intended to be a positive, caring response to disablement. It was quite typical of the corresponding efforts made in many states—it was considered forward-thinking, humane, and based firmly in a work-valued model for social rehabilitation.

For example, in this case, "inmates" were individuals and children with developmental disabilities (some called mental retardation at the time) who worked on the agricultural lands that were part of the facility, and thus received the best of what was considered humane care, while they also learned agricultural tasks and other skills which resulted in the production of more than a million dollars' worth of crops. It was a state-of-the-art example of rehabilitation—the "inmates" were also non-consensual subjects of passive and coercive research; a scientist working there using such subjects discovered the cause of one form of mental retardation, Phenylketonuria.[29]

But many good intentions did not survive the first few years of an institution's existence. The science behind much decision-making in this era was also typified by the work of Henry Goddard, a pioneering, award-winning, social Darwinist and psychologist, who famously (now infamously) studied the Kallikak (pseudonym) family. The goal of eugenics, dating back to its erstwhile founder Sir Francis Galton, was to eliminate undesirable human characteristics, at least in part through practices directly affecting hereditary traits. Family degeneracy, for example, was considered linked to physical and inherited traits. Unfortunately for many individuals with disabilities, the focus on "human pedigrees" meant that disabilities like mental illness were exclusively blamed on genetics, or lifestyle choice (with the already mentioned exception of the noble wounding of soldiers,

---

[28] White, William L., *Slaying the Dragon: The History of Addiction Treatment and Recovery in America*. Bloomington, IL: Chestnut Health Systems, 2014, pp. 158–165.

[29] "*Letchworth Village Papers.*" Rare Book & Manuscript Library Collections, Columbia University, summary accessed at http://findingaids.cul.columbia.edu/ead/nnc-rb/lbpd_5475441/summary.

who sacrificed their physical wholeness in a way that was exempt from some of the harshest forms of social judgment).[30]

Sterilization was a key component in many North American eugenics programs. Angus McLaren, speaking specifically about the similar sterilization acts passed in Alberta and British Columbia in 1933 in Canada that mirrored those in the U.S., characterizes such acts as supported by a large number of scientists and health professionals at the time, but which by today's standards essentially created a dramatic, legalized interference in the private lives of the disabled. Such laws were passed out of concerns for social control and to solve perceived societal problems, rather than formulated as a medical response to a purely medical problem, in spite of what scientists at the time repeatedly claimed.[31]

Science was a double-edged sword, with a darker side that was used to justify eugenics, but a much more positive side, as well, where technology made an immediate and impactful difference in the world of disability in countless ways. This era saw an explosion of assistive devices, cures, and medical advancements that mitigated many of small inconveniences that individuals with disabilities might encounter in daily life. In this way science and medicine (and capitalism) also strangely increasingly, slowly reified the worth of people with disabilities, intentionally or not. Later, this would become even more important when proponents of disability rights harnessed the power of media and capitalism for their own cause (and which not surprisingly was sometimes openly hostile toward "science" and the medical profession).

Wheelchairs provide a good example. Although devices that functioned as wheelchairs had been around for thousands of years—images of wheelchairs exist in 6th BCE century Chinese drawings, for example, or on Greek vases, and during the renaissance we know that some members of royalty used wheelchairs—it was the modern industrial age that brought the wheelchair into widespread popular use. Like many other assistive devices, wheelchairs saw an explosion of improvements, innovations, and reductions in cost for basic models between 1850 and 1950. With the advent of computers in the last half of the 20th century, some wheelchairs have become as sophisticated (and sometimes just as expensive or more so) as automobiles. Some wheelchairs are now "smart" devices linked to phones and wireless networks.[32]

---

[30] Smith.

[31] McLaren, Angus. "The creation of a haven." *Canadian Historical Review*, Vol. 67, No. 2, DOI: 10.3138/CHR-067-02-01149.

[32] "The History of Wheelchairs," Access at http://www.wheelchairnet.net; note other print resources on the history of wheelchairs are also listed here.

The first wheelchair basketball game is thought to have occurred in the U.S. just after the Second World War; the first Paralympic games were held in Tokyo, Japan in 1964. By the start of the 21st century, there were more than three million wheelchair users in the United States alone. The wheelchair revolution began to gain steam in the interwar period, 1918 to 1940, and later would be a key part of the 1960s Disability Rights Movement.[33]

Guide dogs provide another illustrative example from this period. According to an unofficial history, even though dogs had been trained to do countless tasks for humans since time immemorial, the first formal school to train dogs for the blind was established in Potsdam, Germany after World War I resulted in countless German soldiers returning home from war with visual impairments. An America living overseas brought the idea back to the states and wrote about it:

> Morris frank, a young blind man living in Nashville, Tennessee heard the article And wrote to Ms. Eustis asking her to train a dog for him. Morris Frank had lost the use of his eyes in two separate accidents and did not like depending on others. He asked Ms. Eustis to train a dog for him and, in return, he would teach others who were blind so that they, too, could become independent. Ms. Eustis replied that if he could come to Switzerland for the training, she would accommodate his request. Morris Frank became the first American to use a dog guide and Buddy, a female German shepherd, became the pioneer dog guide in America.[34]

Dogs were a natural choice to be service animals for three very distinct reasons: their intelligence; their size; and their ten-thousand-year historical relationship with humans. Elephants are also highly intelligent and have enjoyed a long history of interaction with humans, but their size precludes them from fitting easily into human spaces. Primates are intelligent, and do fit easily in human spaces, but don't enjoy the rich, historical cultural and emotional relationship with humans. It is unlikely even in the current time that any other types of animal will supplant dogs as service animals until robotic aid completely takes over (noting that the ADA does in fact also protect miniature horses as service animals in court cases and guidelines).

The Progressive Era provided "firsts" in a number of important disability advances that today are taken for granted. They also, however, must be situated in the contradictory science and philosophies of time, which operated on altruistic,

---

[33] Ibid.; http://www.newdisability.com/wheelchairstatistics.htm.

[34] "History of Dog Guides," made available through Muhlenberg University online at http://www.muhlenberg.edu/studorgs/companion/ccfaqhistory.html and cited as information originally from Seeing Eye, a non-profit organization.

charity-driven levels that objectified and focused on return to meaningful work, rather than restoration and acceptance of the imperfect soul and body. Progress came at a price, but generally moved the dialogue forward.

> Important Early 20th Century Legislation Pushing America Closer to a DRM
>
> 1914 War Risk Insurance Act
> 1917 War Risk Insurance Act Amendments (option for veterans disability coverage)
> 1918 Smith-Sears Veterans Rehabilitation Act
> 1920 Smith-Fess Vocational Rehabilitation Act
> 1921 U.S. Veterans Bureau established, which becomes the Department of Veterans Affairs
> 1930 The World War Service Disability Act (compensated non-service disabilities)

FDR—a President with a visible (invisible) Disability

Almost everyone today knows that Franklin Delano Roosevelt (FDR) was a president who was also a wheelchair user. What they don't know or generally realize is the extent to which he intentionally hid his situation from the public eye and presented a strong physical appearance purely for political purposes. In FDR, we have the other bookend president of modernity—one who denied his own disability identity in important ways, yet also was a frequent advocate behind the scenes for individuals with disabilities. FDR, in short, embodies the complexities of disability in the unique setting of the modern era.

FDR became disabled through illness, and the best science of the day had no answer for the Polio that he contracted. Prior to that, he had lived a very active life, with few if any physical limitations. The myth of the "cured cripple" is famously associated with FDR, since he appeared to be "overcoming" his situation, although he seemed to struggle privately in accepting himself as anything other than the image he projected. Some of those around him who knew him best thought that maybe his physical challenges resulted in bringing about or crystalizing some of his best leadership traits as a result of the paradigm shift. Even his wife, Eleanor, referred to it as a "blessing in disguise."[35]

---

[35] Zames, p. 2.

One of the more fascinating elements of FDR's adulthood disablement is the extent to which he himself accepted (or didn't accept) himself as an individual with a profound disability. He was brilliant as a politician, and his team masterfully manipulated his physical appearances (choreographed his fitness) and political identity, which included limiting the public's exposure to his wheelchair use, and not allowing the media to witness his mobility impairment in any visible form.

Scholars like Houck and Kiewe have conducted insightful research into what they call FDR's "body politics," and concluded that part of Roosevelt's genius was his ability to divert attention away from his own disablement through a political rhetoric of wholeness and fitness, and even using the semantics of ableism to literally recreate himself as someone less disabled than he really was. He referred to his opponents as weak, unhealthy, and unfit, and claimed for himself the rhetoric of strength, unity, and wholeness, making himself a candidate fit for the potential greatness of America. Interestingly, his political opponents often were unsuccessful in employing the same tactics against him in reverse, as relayed by Kim Phillips-Fein:

> Hoover's circle had been eager to see their man face the New York governor in the election of 1932, believing that FDR's partial paralysis rendered him obviously incapable of fulfilling the duties of the presidency. "What is he, himself, thinking about when he allows himself to aspire to that office?" Hoover's congressional liaison, James MacLafferty, mused about Roosevelt. "When I see a man of Hoover's physical and mental power almost groggy from the blows that rain upon him I cannot make myself believe otherwise than that the election of Roosevelt to the presidency would be a crime against the nation."[36]

He remained, too, a man who never gave up on being active in ways he could, or lost his energetic approach to everything, regardless of the loss his disability forcefully brought upon his body. Journalist John Gunther, who followed FDR's career, had this to say, as documented by Nassir Ghaemi:

> His vitality was, as everybody knows, practically unlimited... ...In one campaign he Traveled 13,000 miles in about seven weeks, and made 16 major and 67 second-string speeches... In thirteen years of presidency, he made 399 trips by

---

[36] Phillips-Fein, Kim. "The Bitter Origins of the Fight Over Big Government: What the battle between Herbert Hoover and FDR can teach us." *The Atlantic*, March 2019.

rail, covering about 545,000 miles. In 1936, the strenuous campaign exhausted the physically healthy Republican candidate...[37]

Yet Roosevelt was profoundly disabled, to the point where it impacted his health and probably shortened his life. The contradiction he presented was thus one that created and perpetuated a timeless stereotype—that of the cripple who overcomes through sheer persistence and mental energy—and he also inadvertently tore down the biggest stereotype of them all—if a man in a wheelchair can become president of the world's foremost superpower, then the corollary is that people with disabilities can do anything.

Like Woodrow Wilson, FDR benefited from his position in an affluent, powerful, family. When he initially needed braces in 1926, the bill was for $135.00, well beyond the means of the average person who might need a similar accommodation to continue working. The average worker made something around three dollars or so per day. One must be careful not to draw the conclusions too broadly about the era relying just on FDR's case.[38]

Although critics like Ghaemi have focused more on FDR's hyperthymic personality, it is FDR's physical disability that brings the contradictions of his time, and his own experience, into a historical focus that seems most relevant to the coming Disability Rights Movement in a few decades. This is true even in spite of what some might consider to be an over-romanticizing of FDR's hidden disability, which everyone seemed to know about in spite of the lack of press photos of him in a wheelchair, to give one example (and which was very intentional on the part of FDR and his advisors). Some leaders from other parts of the world claimed later to not know about his physical disability.

FDR over time became profoundly physically disabled, and there are many who think today such an individual would have more trouble getting elected, rather than less, given the demands we place on our leaders to conform to irrational social norms and visual imagery. However, as of this writing, we have had the first black U.S. President elected, and almost the first female president in 2016, so perhaps (and hopefully) this assessment is becoming more out of date.

The contradiction he represented at the time, however, and his absolute disregard for or lack of public acknowledgement of it, was a pathos that arguably made

---

[37.] Ghaemi, Nassir. *A First-Rate Madness: Uncovering the Links between Leadership and Mental Illness*. The Penguin Press, 2011, p. 132.

[38.] Prescription from Dr. Linder Inc. for leg braces; Berish, Amy. "Polio." Accessed at https://www.fdrlibrary.org/polio June 30, 2020; United States. Bureau of Labor Statistics. *Handbook of Labor Statistics*. Washington: U.S. G.P.O., 19271990.

him the perfect figure to bring the early modern, progressive, pre-DRM era to a close in its contradictions, and in spite of the dissonance to still be a figure quite relevant to the politics of it, as well.[39]

Much happened in the realm of policy and disability legislation during FDR's time, and much of it bears his direct imprint. According to the Roosevelt Institute:

> FDR was one of the first American leaders who tried to address the needs of the nation's disabled. But his legislative accomplishments in this field were limited by the prevailing prejudices of the period toward the handicapped. Nevertheless, the principles he set forth in seeking the legislation were bold. In 1929 as Governor of New York State, Roosevelt said 'I conceive it to be the duty of the state to give the same care to removing the physical handicaps of its citizens as it now gives to their mental development.'[40]

FDR himself spoke of his physical status publicly only rarely, and apparently never at international meetings. In spite of that, a study of White House correspondence reveals many individuals with disabilities, including children, reaching out to him and in essence suggesting that they shared a common social and physical camaraderie. A Polio letter from Jimmy Stone typifies them:

> Dear Mr. President, I am 6 years old. My birthday is January 30, too. When I was Little [I] had infantile paralysis. My right arm is in a brace. My left foot is better since my operation. I like to see your pictures. I like to hear stories about you.[41]

FDR seemingly was comfortable with being a national figure, and certainly enjoyed being a hero to many for various reasons, but he was not a hero with a publicly shared disability. Joseph Delph of Lynch, Kentucky, like Jimmy Stone, tried to make common ground with the president's disability identity:

> My Dear Mr. President: Information has come to me that you are in possession of a collection of canes far in excess of your personal requirements. I am a cripple, a Veteran of the Spanish-American War and Father of three boys in the Armed

---

[39] Pressman, Matthew. "Presidency: The Myth of FDR's Secret Disability: The press sometimes described his condition in great detail, and LIFE even published a picture of him in a wheelchair." Accessed July 12, 2013 at http://ideas.time.com/2013/07/12/the-myth-of-fdrs-secret-disability/; Zames and Fleisher.

[40] Roosevelt Institute. Accessed September 4, 2015 at http://rooseveltinstitute.org/policy-and-ideasroosevelt-historyfdr/disability-advocate

[41] Polio Letters to FDR. Accessed at http://www.fdrlibrary.marist.edu/aboutfdr/images/polio_letterstoFDR.jpg.

> Forces. I have a feeling that the pride engendered by carrying one of your canes, a cane from your collection, preferably one you had carried and discarded, would vastly improve my stride.[42]

Delph added important information at the end of his letter, indicating that he was a rare bird of sorts: "A lifelong Democrat…a rare article coming from the mountains of Clay County…" But the more interesting message in Delph's request is his absolute confidence that just having a disabled president had made the world an easier place to walk around in for individuals with disabilities, and beyond that, if one might actually have one his walking sticks—"I prefer one with a crooked handle"—then his own disability would likely be mitigated even further, literally.

Roosevelt, however, let slip very little sentimentalism about his own disability, and only displayed it about others' disabilities usually when it suited him politically or socially. He knew of these letters, of course, and no doubt read a number of them, and responded, but his own replies were more formal and talked of disability usually only in the abstract, as in this letter to a pastor:

> I am particularly anxious that the new Social Security Legislation just enacted, for which we have worked so long, providing for old age pensions, aid for crippled children, and unemployment insurance, shall be carried out in keeping with the high purposes with which it was enacted…May I have your counsel and your help?[43]

Roosevelt was beyond needing charity for himself (in spite of his increasingly high degree of personal disablement) but often tirelessly advocated for it on behalf of others; he thought of himself as strong and enabled, even as he allowed for and cared for those who were weak or unable, and even as he criticized and characterized his enemies as weak, less capable, and feeble. He orchestrated his own pre-Internet and social media-like Hollywood-style ableism, with the collusion of the press, and the active help of those around him. In some ways, it was a boost to a coming postmodernism and the DRM if you chose to interpret it as a strong leader showing that his disability didn't matter (a stereotype with its own baggage); in other ways, it relied on a putative charity model that suggested that disability was to be hidden and not talked about.

[42.] FDR Library files. Accessed June 2, 2015 at http://fdrlibrary.files.wordpress.com/2011/05/50d-p2-sm.jpg.

[43.] Social Security Administration records. Accessed March 4, 2015 at http://www.ssa.gov/history/pics/fdrtoclergy.jpg.

Overall, FDR represented and fought for some of the best aspects of American progressivism, even while he also provided an abject case study in personal, and psychological denial. He was in many ways unique to his time, place, and disability experience, and remains a polarizing figure inseparable from the coming Disability Rights Movement after the Second World War, and today in its aftermath.

On a personal note, the author's grandfather had this to say:

> We all knew FDR was a cripple. We all knew it. But we didn't talk about it.[44]

Disability Verses Disease

This period of time—at the height of modernity—highlighted a tension that had been present in disability thinking ever since the Enlightenment between disease and disability. On the surface, it would seem to be simply that disease is an illness, a temporary and typically treatable or preventable condition, and one over which medicine has a legitimate claim to seek complete victory. Disability, on the other hand, is a circumstance, a sometimes unpredictable and unpreventable event that comes along with many unforeseen social consequences and one for which medicine cannot seek complete victory, as the most important circumstances attendant to it often aren't medical in nature, and often are permanent. If it were this simple, the conversation would be easy, but the reality is that disease and disability are not dichotomous, they can sometimes be the same thing and other times be complete opposites, but more often vacillate in tandem with each other, with one sometimes presuming more temporal importance than the other depending on the moment and circumstance.

Interestingly, the postmodern identity rights movements which included disability attempted (perhaps inadvertently sometimes, but often intentionally) to disengage disability from a medicalized model where disease primarily resided. As a result, people with a disease such as AIDs, found themselves privy without as much question to medical space, but not to disability space or social space (or accommodations). The unintended consequence of this aspect of the DRM is that it has left disease in a liminal space where it is sometimes a disability and sometimes it is not. The question is asked in the definition used in some

---

[44] Trammell, FrEd. Personal interview with author in 2001.

undergraduate disability courses: "When does a difference (ex. diabetes) make a meaningful difference (ex. result in social consequences, or impact major life activities)?"[45]

A case study of a North Carolina woman institutionalized in the 1940s in North Carolina for Tuberculosis (TB) will serve as a case in point. She was institutionalized due to a diagnosed disease; but her life changed drastically because of the disablement her disease brought about in her life circumstances. Sometimes the disease and the disability were synonymous; sometimes they were distinct (a doctor might treat one and not the other). Although it is often difficult to move beyond the frustrations of language, some like Doug Farley, Director of the Museum of Disability History, suggest that we must ultimately do so, in order to forward the DRM and "evolve in our language beyond singular terms."[46]

In the case of Amy Weston (name changed) in North Carolina, her contraction of Tuberculosis in 1943 might not seem to equate "becoming disabled."[47] Yet the life she describes during her stay in an institution for those with consumption was one with severe limitations, hardships, and both physical and mental challenges synonymous with disability. Her "difference" clearly made a difference, as her own writing while there indicates. She experienced social as well as medical consequences and was by today's definitions at a minimum temporarily disabled, with all of the negative consequences potentially associated with it.

The State of North Carolina's legislation that placed the TB sanatorium under the overall administration of the State Board of Health provides direct evidence of a number of such negative assumptions about disability.[48] On the arguably more benign side, it was a state-wide modernization initiative intended to streamline resources, centralize and coordinate research, and insure a degree of equity in determining who received TB services. It did, in fact, achieve some of those practical and administrative goals. Far more troubling, however, were the underlying elements of eugenics and dehumanizing thinking that informed much of the policy in the "improved" system.

The stated goal was not just to treat the physical illness of patients while they were there, but to teach them, "by personal contact, by illustrated lectures, and

---

[45] Taken from my SOC 327 class at MSMU entitled "Sociology of Disability." 2019.

[46] Farley, Doug. In *The Museum of Disability History* (film). Produced by PeopleInc and Hand, Jon R.. 2019.

[47] Personal letter in author's collection, dated September 9, 1943. Postmarked the same evening at Sanatorium post office and mailed to a relative in Goldsboro, NC.

[48] *The North Carolina Sanatorium for the Treatment of Tuberculosis*, Under the Management of The North Carolina State Board of Health, 1913.

by the rules of the institution how to readjust their lives to Nature's laws... ... and how to live with others without infecting them." The directors called this need to protect others an "obligation" that superseded their own personal desires to lead a normal life again. They made it clear that those advanced in the disease should not even be admitted to the institution, and instead left to their own devices: "[those] who have already practically lost their chance to live should not be allowed to occupy the few beds the State now has. ...The reasonableness and the economic considerations...are too evident for comment."[49]

It is only fair to say that the initiative in North Carolina, and many others like it, was based on what were considered at the time the most humane methods of the day. But it also fair and even critical to point out that they were flawed in terms of our post-ADA thinking and based on some forms of pseudo-science that are now officially discredited.

Importantly, however, we can be informed by their history—since disability is everywhere, we must confront it everywhere[50]—but we should do so with caution, and with detailed mindfulness of the differences between ways of thinking about disability across time and space.

Amy's letter of September 9th, 1943, indicates many of the small things that worried her beyond TB medical treatments, x-rays, and diagnoses. She came in with few clothes, and as a "dressed meal" approached (patients wore civilian clothing rather than hospital gowns), she fretted over what to wear:

> I just don't know what to do about clothes. I can wear the same size, I guess, but hadn't had any clothes in a long time when I got sick. And I haven't got any money. I'll have to wait for my C.P. & L. check before I can pay my next bill, and it worries me to try to think what to do.[51]

Amy knew about the war that was burning across the globe by this time and embroiling young women and men she knew in its turmoil, but the disabling aspects of her condition prevented her from fulling knowing everything that was going on:

> The paratroopers have jumped three times since I started this [letter]. Some are supply chutes—the colored ones I think—and the white ones are men. But I

---

[49] Ibid.

[50] Bayton, Douglas. In Lennard Davis (Ed.) *Disability Studies Reader.* 4th Edition.

[51] Letter of 09/09/1943 in author's collection. Mailed from Sanatorium, N.C., 5:30 pm to her mother.

haven't seen the plane yet. These awnings are in the way. I can just lie here in bed and see them dropping down...[52]

Amy was remarkably optimistic, given her taxing medical situation. There is, however, a tinge of depression and negativity over time in her responses, and one can imagine other patients who didn't confront their circumstance so positively. For social creatures, like humans, forced separation is the ultimate form of alienation. Even in the post-war 1940s in modern America, physical, social, and political separation was still a common and alienating experience for people with disabilities.

The concept of modernity is a sweeping ontological (basic framework for reality) paradigm, that has hundreds of different meanings and interpretations (see Appendix A). By the late 1940s the cracks and fissures in modernity were becoming very difficult to ignore.

The World Wars combined with the horrors of the Holocaust had successfully dismantled much of the perceived "progress" that science had made prior to that, and ultimately provided an opening for those who rejected aspects of naturalism, materialism and modernism, to begin deconstructing and reconstructing what it meant to be disabled and have a disability identity in the neomodern world. This questioning took place early on in academia, typified by intellectuals like Erving Goffman and Michel Foucault, and would ultimately contribute to a postmodern disability rights movement with disability identity as a more accepted psychological and human form, and a new field of social science termed disability studies would be birthed, and which is now growing across academia and even within K12 curriculums.

The Holocaust and disability

The modern science of eugenics reached a dubious zenith during the rule of the Nazis in World War II Germany (who not coincidentally built on the award-winning scientific and genetic work of many contemporarily respected Western scientists from the U.K. and the U.S.) Although the Final

---

[52.] Ibid.

Solution was aimed primarily at Europe's Jewish population, individuals with disabilities were also prominent amongst the other groups targeted for sterilization (as many as 375,000) or elimination (as many as 300,000). As the following table shows, Germany's (and subsequently Europe's) population of profoundly disabled was decimated by the actions of the totalitarian regime.

Disability Deaths in the Holocaust

Table Category	Number	Years
T-4 Euthanasia Program	200,000	1939–1945
14f13 Program	20,000	1944–1945
Total Victims with Disabilities	270,000 to 300,000	1934–1945[53]

Numbers cannot be exact due to the incomplete extant records, but it is clear that the Third Reich discriminated against all types of disabilities, excepting those that were incurred in the "noble" vocation of military service. Even groups traditionally accommodated to a degree in Germany, such as the deaf, were increasingly and vigorously discriminated against as a result of Nazi eugenics programs, propaganda, and philosophy. Needless to say, the disabled in occupied countries under German military rule fared little or no better.[54]

Part of the success of the neomodern DRM in the West was built on a collective global shock over the excesses of the Holocaust and Nazi Germany, which forced people to confront the limits of science, intolerance and racist thinking. Although racism and intolerance obviously still exist in the present time, the events of this historical era still represent an extreme that most people will not challenge as being completely unethical and inhumane, beyond the pale, and which has lost none of its capacity to horrify.

[53.] These are the author's estimates—see next note.
[54.] There are widely varying numbers reported from various sources. For the general purposes, several good references are https://www.jewishvirtuallibrary.org/jsource/Holocaust/disablEd.html and http://www.ushmm.org/research/research-in-collections/search-the-collections/bibliography/people-with-disabilities. Accessed September 12, 2015.

Similar to the aftermath of the Civil War, the return of millions of disabled vets at the end of World War II signaled a crisis and an opportunity on a national scale that forced disability into the overall dialogue about military personnel reintegration. Disabled vets were not necessarily intentionally starting a disability rights movement, but soon many became advocates for others with disabilities, and their sheer human weight by numbers meant that American culture and businesses were forced to pay attention to their needs and issues. Non-military individuals with disabilities increasingly were not far behind, benefiting from the opening for a new disability dialogue, and soon benefitting from advocacy from vets for their cause.

World War II veterans were well-aware on some level of the evils that science and rationalism could play on the international political stage—they had fought to defeat the perpetrators of the Holocaust, and the Rape of Nanking—and they knew instinctively, especially by the end of the war, that the provincialism and unjustified optimism of the late 19th century could not survive their integration back into American society. The world would forever be changed by their experience, just as they were changed. The booming Cold War economy coupled with their admission into colleges and universities, or employment into mid-level management and industrial positions, meant that they were in a unique position to impact the wider American culture even without consciously realizing it or planning it.

At the end of World War II, the overall American disability experience was at a crossroads that awkwardly brought together a number of important dichotomous tensions: the different social values and stigmas placed on visible verses invisible disabilities; the triumph of modern medicine juxtaposed with the failures of eugenics and unbridled science; the carte blanche wounded veterans were offered in comparison to the paucity of resources for the poor and elderly non-military disabled, or blacks; the imperative for a universally educated work force verses the unwillingness to educate young people with disabilities (or blacks) equally.

In spite of these tensions, or perhaps while they played out, servicemen and women pioneered many practical elements of the coming disability rights movement which would aim its goals at everyone, military or not. Veterans, in hindsight, clearly had an impact on disability rights greatly out of proportion to their actual numbers in the general population, as they had in several previous periods in American history.[55]

[55.] Zames, pp. 7, 170–171.

An important event leading up the 1960s and 1970s DRM was the establishment of an executive level committee to examine disability and employment. The somewhat convoluted history of the committee early on is best explained by the Library of Congress:

> In 1947 President Truman established the "President's Committee on National Employ the Physically Handicapped Week." This Committee assumed the responsibility of coordinating events and generating publicity for the week. Subsequently in 1949, Congress authorized an annual appropriation for the committee, and in 1954 in the Amendments to the Vocational Rehabilitation Act, ch. 655, 68 Stat. 652, Congress directed the Committee to work with state and local authorities to promote job opportunities for the physically handicapped. In 1955 President Eisenhower issued Executive Order No. 10640, which established the committee as a permanent organization and renamed it the "President's Committee on Employment of the Physically Handicapped."[56]

In the 1960s this committee would be re-invented by President Kennedy; Under President Bush senior the successor committee would play a key role in bringing about the ultimate passage of the ADA. Like many slow changes in America, disability acceptance and accommodation have a long, winding, complicated series of causes and effects that are never confined to a single generation. As WWII veterans finished college and sent their own children to college, a new wave of disabled vets would be ready to make their own impact very soon.

---

[56] https://www.loc.gov/law/help/commemorative-observations/disability-awareness.php; also see Executive Orders 10555 and 10640.

CHAPTER 6

The 1960s and the Blossoming of the Disability Rights Movement

There is a modest debate about when the Disability Rights Movement (DRM) as a social phenomenon actually began. Many believe it should be situated firmly in the 1970s when many important landmark events occurred. History makes it less simple. In 1607 at Jamestown it is now obvious that disabled or non-disabled was not a commonly recognized dichotomy of identity; in the present it is so engrained as an identity that laws, education, and social media constantly orbit around it. Court cases abound that attempt to prove (or disprove) disability identity, and hence deepen and widen the definition constantly. Yet the DRM also remains like the other identity rights movements an ongoing venture, a work in progress, so incomplete and still sometimes ignored in isolated pockets of America as to occasionally stir the kind of radical national attention it did in the 1960s and 1970s. This text will argue that the 1960s were equally important to the 1970s.

The Atalissa, Iowa turkey plant story in 2014 illustrates the complicated, ongoing nature of disability identity, where men with intellectual disabilities were abused and labored without even minimum wage payment for years even in a post-ADA world where laws and cultural shifts should have prevented it.[1]

Many scholars of the DRM have attempted to identify its nascent beginnings with the ascendancy of Franklin Delano Roosevelt (FDR) to the White House, and his role was discussed in the previous chapter. From Congressional legislation to the subtle application of a complex visual disability rhetoric manipulated for public consumption, FDR and his contemporaries altered the disability landscape forever through both overt and covert means; sometimes in negative ways, but often in ways that ultimately moved a positive dialogue forward. But as made clear in the last chapter, neither Wilson nor FDR make ideal propaganda for disability rights founding figures.

[1.] Barry, Dan. "The 'Boys' in the Bunkhouse: Toil, abuse and endurance in the heartland." *New York Times*, March 9, 2014, accessed online at www.nytimes.com.

The massive influx of World War II veterans with disabilities has likewise been credited with triggering the DRM, as such vets went to school, and then to work, in giant waves that dwarfed prior immigration waves in terms of numbers and influence. In this relationship, FDR did, in fact, lay some of the groundwork for the 1950s which would manifest later in the 1960s in the identity rights movements.[2]

This text argues that it is much more salient from a broader American cultural history to date the most important period of rapid change in the DRM as occurring in the tumultuous sixties and continuing into the 1970s (perhaps better labeled 1965–1975), when a radical and leftist disability rights movement worked in tandem with and sometimes in competition with the contemporary movements in gender rights and civil rights, and in collaboration with the New Left. The Civil Rights Act of 1964, the model for the later Americans with Disabilities Act in 1990, is a central date to understanding the DRM. But there are countless other small events and even unrecorded encounters which are now swallowed by the largeness of those times, and the DRM of the 1960s remains relatively unknown, a shadow movement compared to the other identity movements.[3]

As mentioned, most histories of disability in America date the radical part of the DRM to the decade of the 1970s, and there is certainly justifiable reason to do so. However, the larger structural changes occurring in America that made the DRM possible, and even likely, are clearly anchored in the decade of the 1960s. There were two factors in particular that made that decade of lasting import: television (media) and the Vietnam War.[4]

Television had been around since the 1940s, but the visual power of the medium came of age in the 1960s. In 1936, there were around two-hundred television sets in the entire world. By 1969 when the first television video was broadcast from the lunar landing, more than 600 million people were watching.[5] The power of television to transform the way information was networked, shared, and processed, also transformed the nature of broad social movements. The 1960s were distinguished from the previous and the following decade by that media explosion. The lessons learned about media coverage in the 1960s were perfected by disability activists in the 1970s.

---

[2] Zames and Fleischer.

[3] Houck and Kiewe, p. 4; Z, Mickey. *50 American Revolutions You're not Supposed to Know*. New York, Disinformation, 2005 pp. 133–135.

[4] Interview with Dr. Michael Fischbach, June 13, 2020. Dr. Fischbach is a noted historian of the 1960s and teaches at Randolph-Macon College, Ashland, VA.

[5] "The Invention of Television." Accessed at https://www.thoughtco.com/the-invention-of-television-1992531

The second transformative factor was the Vietnam War. The lengthy conflict defined the decade in many ways, but also was a pivotal event in disability history for a number of reasons. Due to medical advancements, a higher percentage (even than WWII) of veterans survived wounding and trauma and returned home disabled. To illustrate the trend, there are a few relatively rare cases of soldiers from the Civil War and World War I living with serious Spinal Cord Injury (SCI), yet by World War II improvements in medicine meant that more than several thousand vets with serious SCI survived and reintegrated. According to most sources, more than three-hundred thousand soldiers were wounded while serving in Vietnam (not all required hospitalization); many suffered psychological wounds that are not recorded.[6]

Historian Michael Fischbach characterizes the times this way by making the link between the persistent problem of race and the more general radicalism of the 1960s:

> Certainly the civil rights movement in the '50s is the precursor to just about everything else that happened in the '60s and '70s because it was the movement that really galvanized attention on one basic question, that is are people of color equal citizens in a country where it says liberty and justice for all? And it established secondly not only a great moral question, but secondly it introduced a new kind of politics. That is not just politics in terms of voting because in the South a lot of blacks couldn't vote anyway, that wasn't an option. It put mass politics, people power in the streets, protests, it put that out there as legitimate ways of trying to bring about change outside of a traditional legislative process. It also introduced the idea of civil disobedience, if necessary actually breaking laws that are wrong. And it stressed being nonviolent.[7]

The cultural rejection that many veterans suffered upon their return was a double stigmatization for vets with disabilities. Their service and sacrifice did not cancel out their second class status as men and women with disabilities. The effect was particularly intense when considering wounded vets of color. The sheer numbers of vets, their anger, and their energetic advocacy would become critical in the 1960s for what would later bear meaningful fruit in the mainstream 1970s DRM.

Incidence of SCI remains prominent in the ongoing war on terror, where five percent of combat wounds involve some type of SCI. Although medical

---

[6.] "Casualties." Accessed at https://www.globalsecurity.org/military/ops/casualties.htm

[7.] Interview with Dr. Michael Fischbach, June 13, 2020.

technology continues to improve, many so-wounded vets experience some type of ongoing disability after such injuries.[8]

It is a challenge in one chapter to describe the width and breadth of the impact of the radical 1960s and the New Left and other social movements on the evolution of the modern DRM which culminated in a legislative 1970s and the eventual passage of the ADA. Such a survey should probably include: a brief survey of pioneers and trailblazing organizations; a brief biographical sketch of Ed Roberts, a candidate for founding figure of the DRM, and the impact of the Independent Living Movement (ILM) that he started; an analysis of the shaky alliance between some civil rights leaders and disability activists; the resistance of metropolitan transportation authorities to early accessibility challenges; the response of the federal government to disability as a civil right and the Civil Rights Act as a template for the DRM; and a brief survey of the even more eventful 1970s. All of these phenomena contributed to significant change in the context of the growing DRM, and the coming of 1990. And there was more to it than even that.[9]

Complicating matters for scholars now, current histories of the DRM understandably point out the political victories of the 1970s as high moments, but inadvertently pay less attention to the radicalism and grassroots level discontent of the 1960s that made those coming events even possible for a series of very practical reasons. Radical disability activists in the 1960s were anarchists of sorts, much more concerned with restoring a sense of belonging to the community and disentangling the hegemony of a Western governmentality of the body and mind, and less concerned with creating a historic legacy or sometimes even changing the general public's mind about a specific disability issue. They sometimes were more interested in individual causes and their own disability identity, than with others who might have radically different disability identities. Many, however, were visionaries who were ahead of their time. Much of their history comes from oral history, rather than written records.

For these and other reasons, the DRM in the 1960s was an active, but by historical standards, a shadow movement of sorts. Most histories of the period focus on civil rights, women's rights, student activism, and anti-war/anti-establishment sentiments, and often completely omit any of the characters, events, or ideas from the DRM that had their genesis, as well, in the decade. There are few significant

---

[8.] Blair James A., et al. "Spinal Column Injuries Among Americans in the Global War on Terrorism." *The Journal of Bone & Joint Surgery,* 19 September 2012, Vol. 94, Issue 18, p. 135.

[9.] Burns, Stewart. *Social Movements of the 1960s: Searching for Democracy.* New York, 1990.

movements in the 21st century which have a lower historiographical profile than the 1960s beginnings of the radical DRM. For these reasons, this chapter focuses more on the sixties and only briefly touches on the seventies which are much more extensively documented and dealt with again in the next chapter.[10]

There were a number of underground or locally produced publications about radical disability that begin to appear or circulate more widely in the 1960s. The *Toomey j Gazette* celebrated its 10th anniversary issue in 1968, and was a publication that portrayed disability in ways counter to popular culture. In a 1960 article, for example, it demonstrated how a paraplegic could be a successful businessman working mostly through the phone at home or at the institution where they received services, making the not-so-subtle point that over the phone no one can see whether you are handicapped (disabled) or not. The message, even with its cultural baggage, was that people with disabilities could be successful business people.[11]

A 1967 issue of the magazine/newsletter contained information about EXPO 67, which took place in Montreal, Canada. The list of accommodations available and efforts to make the international event accessible for people with disabilities (primarily people using wheelchairs) would seem routine by post-ADA standards, but for the time represented a significant effort and paradigm shift in thinking.[12]

Many activists in the sixties were far from shortsighted or myopic in their outlook. Ed Roberts, considered by some to be the founding figure of the DRM, was one of the first to recognize that disability came in all shapes and sizes, and that visible (physical) disabilities had many similarities and shared civil rights concerns with invisible (psychological or other) disabilities. Roberts threatened a lawsuit to gain admissions into the University of California, Berkeley (UCB) ("We don't do crips" he was essentially told) as a wheelchair user, and went on to enjoy a long career in disability activism that permanently altered the disability landscape.[13]

---

[10] Farrell, James J.. *The Spirit of the Sixties: The Making of the Postwar Radicalism*. New York, Routledge, 1997; Unger, Irwin. *The Movement: A History of the American New Left 1959–1972*. Harper & Row, 1974; Bloom, A., & Breines, W. (Eds.). *Takin it to the Streets: A Sixties Reader*. Oxford University Press, 2011; Johnson, Roberta Anna. "Mobilizing the Disabled," in *Waves of Protest: Social Movements Since the Sixties*. Lanham, MD: Rowman & Littlefield, 1983, pp. 25–45.

[11] Toomey j Gazette. "Successful businessman…" Vol. 3, No. 2, 1960, p. 18, Chagrin Falls, OH.

[12] Toomey j Gazette. "EXPO 67, Montreal, Canada." Vol. X, 1967, p. 19, Chagrin Falls, OH.

[13] Roberts, Edward. *Edward V. Roberts Papers*, BANC MSS 99/34 cz, accessed by the author online and in person June 27–28, 2014. Specific items generally came from containers 1, 3, 6, 7, 10, which had materials identified as most germane to this book. Hereafter, referred to ERP. In addition, in-depth interviews with Zona Roberts, Ed's mother, and Paul Hippolitus, Director of the U.C. Berkeley DSP which Roberts helped found in the 1960s, were completed on June 27, 2014, and will be referred to in notes as NR interview and PH interview respectively.

"I encourage everyone to go out and get arrested," he once said. "Not just for anything, but for the cause..." And in Robert's case, the cause was for *all* people with disabilities, both visible and invisible, physical and mental/psychological.[14]

Although better-known for his disability organizations and activism in the 1970s, Roberts was quite active in the 1960s as well. In 1969, for example, he was invited to Washington, D.C. to assist federal education officials in the development of new educational guidelines. Since his heavy iron lung could not go on the plane, he had to borrow an iron lung from someone else while in D.C.[15]

In the 1960s, institutionalization had finally run its most impactful course, and while arguably accomplishing some progressive goals (perhaps providing a rhetorical lever for Americans to feel as they were doing something rather ignoring the problem, or perhaps providing a convenient focal point for medical research that would bring about cures), in reality critics maintained the social costs were far outweighing the benefits in human psychological terms. Many individuals with disabilities were held against their wishes in institutions and were sorely disenfranchised by today's standards, and often abused even by the standards of the time. Students with disabilities in public schools had little access to reliable special services, and even less ability to seek education in a truly inclusive environment. Adults with disabilities attempting to live independently found transportation and other public spaces, or employment, nearly inaccessible. Wounded vets from Vietnam now disabled and returning home in a steadily increasing stream found a country in turmoil, one that sometimes rejected them both as participants in an unpopular war and as individuals who no longer fit the norm. They were now disabled both literally, and culturally. It was an environment ripe for change and unrest.

Not all of the early advocates in the sixties placed an emphasis on recording or preserving what they did or said as some would in the seventies and eighties, let alone establishing an archival scholarship of their ideas, so a historian of the DRM must sift through recollections and disparate cultural artifacts to recreate some of the excitement, anger, and uncertainty of those times. It was a radicalized time, and those on the frontlines were angry, motivated, and determined, far less concerned about Western notions of codifying and categorizing history, and more concerned about actual change. Roberts was one of the number who

---

[14] Roberts, Edward. As collected by Jon Oda in Highlights from speeches by Ed Roberts, World Institute on Disability, available online at http://www.wid.org/about-wid/highlights-from-speeches-by-ed-roberts.

[15] Toomey j Gazette, "Ed Roberts," Vol. XII, 1969, p. 21, Chagrin Falls, OH.

did record much of his activism, and fortunately his relatively extensive papers are now preserved in the Bancroft Library at UCB.

Still, there often seems to be no "Dr. Martin Luther King" of the disability rights movement. Douglas Platt, curator at the Museum of Disability, explains:

> I really don't think of any one person because there has been so much over the decades; decades and centuries now. I'm more interested in periods of time. What it's like to be *this*, *then*. ...It's not a sharp turn of the corner; it takes a long time to turn a big ship.[16]

Pioneers and Organizations

Although the 1970s would soon be filled with numerous war stories and heroes, pioneering work occurred in the 1960s. 1960, for example, saw the advent of the first Paralympic Games, held in Rome, Italy and intended to be an equal counterpart to the historic Olympic Games that had a two thousand year history. Although some forms of sport for the disabled had been in existence for quite some time—wheelchair sports, for example, trace their roots to earlier in the 20th century—it was the decade of the sixties that brought sport for the disabled into the mainstream globally.

Along with Ed Roberts, other wheelchair users like John Hessler joined together at schools like U.C. Berkeley and not only forged access to postsecondary education but also banded together to form advocacy and support groups. Roberts gained entrance to UCB in 1962; Hessler came in 1963; by 1964 the "Rolling Quads" at UCB were a significant force for change and increased access to everything from housing to recreation. Similar groups sprang up in other educational settings, in part due to the radicalism of the times; in part due to word spreading amongst the disabled.

The sixties saw a blossoming of concern and advocacy for people who today would be termed as "being on the spectrum." The Autism Society of America was founded in 1965 as a challenge to the misconception that inadequate parenting caused autism, and challenged the domination of medical expertise in controlling individual's and family's options for accommodating spectrum disabilities. This mirrored a similar movement in other countries like Great Britain, where the

---

[16.] Interview, July 12, 2019.

hegemony of doctors and other scientific specialists over people with disabilities was exposed in a series of startling exposes that undermined medical expertise and began to shift more power to individuals.[17]

In the U.S., Burton Batt and Fred Caplan published the appalling story of how individuals with developmental disabilities were treated at state institutions. *Christmas in Purgatory* would have a lasting impact that would fuel the Independent Living Movement (ILM) and inspire a wider inspection by the mainstream media of conditions in various institutions from jails to schools that housed or educated individuals with disabilities.[18]

Disability radicalism and advocacy infiltrated the arts. Federal monies helped seed the creation of the National Theatre of the Deaf in 1967, a troupe that would eventually become the longest continually touring group with original performances in the country. Dr. Edna Simon Levine and actress Anne Bancroft (The Miracle Worker) teamed with others to bring an idea dating back to the 1950s to its ultimate fruition in the sixties.

In the social sciences, "normalization" was a fresh concept that arose in the late sixties with the aim of formalizing mechanisms that could enhance mainstream integration for individuals with disabilities. Although Wolf Wolfensberger would eventually formalize his related research in the semantics of social role valorization (SRV), an early benchmark was the presentation made in 1969 by Scandinavian social scientists Niels Erk Bank-Mikkelsen and Bengt Nirje sponsored by the President's Committee on Mental Retardation. Normalization contributed significantly to the Independent Living Movement.[19]

More than anything, the 1960s were a breeding ground for public activism and an opportunity to piggyback on the successes of the Civil and Gender Rights Movements to create and foment a permanent Disability Rights Movement. College and university students were often at the forefront. The history of activism, which began at the grassroots level with single acts of rebellion like Ed Robert's refusal to accept the "we don't do crips" decision at U.C. Berkeley, to subsequent large group sit-ins and protests, began a public process that would culminate in 1977 in what some have termed, "perhaps the single most impressive act of civil disobedience in

---

[17] "Who We Are." Accessed at https://autismsociety.org/who-we-are/.

[18] Blatt, Burton, & Kaplan, Fred M.. *Christmas in Purgatory: A Photographic Essay on Mental Retardation.* Allyn and Bacon, 1966.

[19] The preceding paragraphs all are directly linked to the disability timeline "The Disability Rights and Independent Living Movement" associated with the Bancroft Library at U.C. Berkeley, accessed at http://bancroft.berkeley.edu/collections/drilm/resources/timeline.html, and are derived from Pelka, FrEd. *ABC-CLIO Companion to the Disability Rights Movement.* Santa Barbara, ABC-CLIO, 1997.

the United States over the last quarter-century," the nearly four week sit-in at HEW in San Francisco, also discussed in the next chapter, but which has earlier roots.[20]

The sixties were the birthplace for this radicalism. Although the technique of sit-in protest had been used as far back as the 1930s, it was in 1960 when the most famous civil rights sit-ins occurred in Greensboro, North Carolina, and Nashville, Tennessee. Mimicking the Civil Rights Movement, disability advocates adopted this method in the mid and late sixties, particularly on the West Coast. In 1977, the sit-in at the HEW building in San Francisco would facilitate dramatic change, and was a result of this tradition.[21]

Castles Made of Sand

Many artists and cultural critics in the 1960s touched on themes related to disability. Jimi Hendrix made powerful music that utilized innovative electric guitar rhythms and riffs; his lyrics also touched on many conscious and subconscious human desires. Disability as a form of irony (the desire for the perfect body or mind, juxtaposed with the inevitable imperfect reality) was typified by the lyrics in one Hendrix song in particular, Castles Made of Sand:

> There was a young girl, whose heart was a frown
> Because she was crippled for life, and couldn't speak a sound
> And she wished and prayed she would stop living, so she decided to die
>
> She drew her wheelchair to the edge of the shore, and to her legs she smiled
> "You won't hurt me no more."
> But then a sight she'd never seen made her jump and say
> "Look, a golden winged ship is passing my way"
> And it really didn't have to stop... it just kept on going
>
> And so castles made of sand slips into the sea
> Eventually

---

[20] Shaw, Randy. As quoted in Schweik, Susan. "Lomax's Matrix: Disability, Solidarity, and the Black Power of 504." *Disability Studies Quarterly*, accessed May 15, 2014, copyright 2009–2013.

[21] Johnson.

> Although Hendrix was far from a disability advocate in the classic sense of the term, the girl he describes in the song is confronting the reality of stigma and an inaccessible world that has little time or hope for the disabled. Hendrix's love of freedom and energetic embrace of personal truth were twin themes that many disability activists recognized and valued in the growing disability rights movement on their own terms; scholars have compared his archetypes to Jungian symbols that defied rational structures. Hendrix on an artistic level captures the irrationality of disability, and the desire to reach the end of a difficult journey.[22]
>
> [22.] Shapiro, Harry, & Glebbeck, Caesar. *Jimi Hendrix: Electric Gypsy*. St. Martin's Press, 1990; Lehtonen, Kimmo, & Juvonen, Antti. "Castles made of sand – a psychodynamic interpretation of Jimi Hendrix's life and music." *Nordic Journal of Music Therapy* 21, no. 2, June, 2012, pp. 133–152. Lyrics accessed http://www.azlyrics.com/lyrics/jimihendrix/castlesmadeofsand.html.

Ed Roberts, Founding Figure

Ed Roberts contracted polio at the age of fourteen, and came close to dying from the effects. "You should hope he dies," the doctor told Robert's mother, and Ed wrote later that he himself doubted at some points whether life was worth going on. Fortunately, "It's very hard to kill yourself in a hospital with everything set up to save your life." After deciding that he did, indeed, want to live, Roberts began a more than four decades-long career fighting every stereotype associated with disability. In 1962, he "convinced" U.C. Berkeley to admit him; he ultimately earned a bachelor's and master's degree, but never finished his Ph.D.[23]

Robert's career would eventually include an amazing array of experiences: teaching political science at U.C. Berkeley; founding the Center for Independent Living (CIL) in 1972; serving as Director of the California Department of Rehabilitation; acting as co-founder of the World Institute on Disability in 1983; and serving as ambassador for disability rights as a world traveler (including behind the Iron Curtain to promote disability advocacy in the East).[24]

[23.] ERP; ZR Interview; Roberts, Edward. "Highlights from Speeches." Collected by Oda, Jon. *World Institute on Disability*, accessed April 23, 2014 at http://www.wid.org/about-wid/highlights-from-speeches-by-ed-roberts.

[24.] ERP; ZR interview; Elliott, J. Michael. "Edward V. Roberts, 56, Champion of the DisablEd." Obituaries, *New York Times*, March 16, 1995; Roberts, Edward. In Ona.

Roberts had to threaten the university in 1962 to gain admittance with appropriate housing in a cause that eventually brought national attention to college access for wheelchair users. Although there was still practically no ground swell in administrative circles at this juncture and Roberts and others have pointed out that other students sued or challenged universities to admit them in the mid-sixties, as well, it seems that Roberts was one of the first, and because of his later well-known career, was also the most memorable. If the DRM has a founding figure, it could be Roberts, even though many other DRM leaders have pointed to the lack of a cult of personalities as a strength of the DRM, rather than a weakness. Ed Roberts, as much as any other figure, embodied the tumultuous possibilities and systemic barriers of the 1960s.

Roberts was also remarkable for his commitment to *all* human rights, not just limited to disability issues. In classic sociological terms, he saw disability as clearly intersecting with gender and race, and he worked to see that the movements helped each other, and fed off of the combined energy. Once he recovered from the initial personal and medical battles that were triggered by his polio, Roberts essentially spent his entire life from that point on not only profoundly mobility impaired, and needing an iron lung to assist with breathing. He also led an active, energetic life and was a tireless disability advocacy figure. An athlete and a daydreamer before the illness, afterwards he began to focus his energy on academics and a life of the mind. When he finally decided on physically going to school (high school at that point), he realized he had a choice: he could be intimidated by the stares, or embrace a kind of perverse celebrity that might actually work to his advantage:

> They turned and looked away. That was when I realized that maybe it wasn't my problem; maybe it was their problem. I checked myself out, and I realized two things. First, their looking at me didn't hurt, physically, and secondly I realized, hey, this is kind of like being a star... ...And I've been a star ever since.[25]

Roberts quickly took his education at Berkeley and turned it into a wider mandate to question the American and later the International disability status quo. Why were so many adults with disabilities isolated from their families and communities? Why did universities place obstacles in the way of students with disabilities attending? Why were environments still so difficult to physically access? Roberts was a unifier, rather than a divider, in spite of his disruptive

---

[25] ERP; ZR Interview.

radicalism. He wanted to get the attention of the Temporarily Abled Bodies (TABs), and he wanted to organize the disabled, but then he also wanted a unity in the larger community that included equality of opportunity. Roberts was angry, but angry for just and socially constructive reasons, and with an ultimate purpose in mind. Like Congressman John Lewis, he was interested in getting into "good trouble."

He constantly used the rhetoric of union, as in a speech given much later at the famous 1977 Section 504 demonstration in San Francisco:

> Many of you here have championed for black rights, women's rights, Chicano rights, senior citizen's rights and others. We share common enemies — discrimination, fear, ignorance and the basic reluctance on the part of the establishment to extend us our rights because it would be too expensive. Strong 504 regulations could permit us to attend any university or college, and to use every program or agency supported by federal funds. It would literally open doors for employment, education and recreation; without it we are second class citizens, living on the fringe of society, unable to participate and devalued.[26]

No single radical had a greater impact on the DRM in the 1960s than Ed Roberts, although many like Chris Palames of Boston are quick to point out that Ed Roberts was not alone. While his suit for admission at Berkeley was seminal, there were others who were part of the "rolling quads" and other similar groups. Soon there were dozens and then hundreds of students with mobility impairments across the country at universities and colleges. They were inspired by the Civil Rights Movement, the Mississippi Summer, and by the nascent Free Speech movement, as well. They were first synergized in California, but it quickly spread to other places.[27]

Other advocates also grew of age in the 1960s: Judith Heumann as a college student joined anti-war protests, but she also organized disability protests and events; Fred Fay like Roberts made the logical connection to the Civil Rights Movement as early as 1963, and his sixties activism helped point the way to the 1968 Architectural Barriers Act; or Susan Schnur, who wrote a guide to accessing New York City in a wheelchair and was active in a dozen

---

[26] Roberts, Edward. "Speech." Director, Department of Rehabilitation at the 504 Demonstration, San Francisco, Tuesday, April 5, 1977, accessed August 15, 2015 at http://www.oac.cdlib.org/ark:/13030/hb7r29n95q/.

[27] Palames, Chris. "The civil rights movement and the disability rights movement." Part 2 of 7 interview accessed on April 8, 2014 at https://www.youtube.com/watch?v=wABxTqmEWU4&list=PL2190A68DBABCB8BC.

other ways. None-the-less, Roberts' story captures almost all of the active elements of the times, and has a pathos that very much typifies the nature of the early DRM.[28]

A Shaky Alliance

In terms of intersectionality, it is not a coincidence that in 1962, James Meredith went to court to gain admission to the University of Mississippi, and in the same year, Ed Roberts threatened suit to gain access to a post-secondary university experience at Berkeley. Individuals with disabilities were heartened and inspired by those who challenged the racial status quo, or gendered stereotypes, and often made reference to them, especially when they were also known to be disability advocates. Dr. Martin Luther King, for example, understood the relationship between diverse identities, and personally advocated for black servicemen who were disabled, recognizing that they faced a double stigma.[29]

Roberts, though, had his own long history of frustration in terms of courting practical aid from the other civil rights movements, while clearly acknowledging a debt to them, particularly the race-oriented Civil Rights Movement:

> When I was at U.C. Berkeley in the '60's, I and almost every other student on campus became involved in the Civil Rights Movement. We were fighting for the basic rights of black people. But, during my involvement in that movement, I suddenly realized something that has since been extremely important to me—that I'm part of a minority that is as segregated and devalued as any in America's history. I am part of the disabled minority. I quickly found that other disabled students shared my feelings. We all felt a sense of anger, frustration, and isolation. The more we talked, the more it became apparent that we needed to organize if we were to create our own Civil Rights movement.[30]

---

[28] ERP; Griffiths. "Judith Heumann: From 'fire hazard' to top advocate for disabled people." *The Christian Science Monitor*, October 3, 2011; Schudel, Matt. "Frederick A. Fay, forceful activist for rights of the disabled, dies at 66." *The Washington Post*, Obituaries, August 31, 2011; Zames, p. 36. Note that Fred Fay's papers are also collected at U.C. Berkeley, but are "unarranged and therefore unavailable for use" as of May 15, 2014.

[29] King, Dr. Martin Luther. *Letters*. Widely published; see for example https://www.historynet.com/famous-letters-and-speeches-of-martin-luther-king-jr/.

[30] Roberts, Edward. "The Emergence of the Disabled Civil Rights Movement." Speech, May 19, 1980, 3 p. BANC MSS 99/34 cz: [Carton 1, Folder 24], http://bancroft.berkeley.edu/collections/drilm Contributing Institution:The Bancroft Library. University of California, Berkeley. Berkeley, Calif., 94720–6000

In historical terms and in moral terms, the disability rights movement also reached critical mass with the radicalization not just of individuals with disabilities, but also with ever increasing numbers of ordinary Americans who were ready to bring about change, sometimes violently, and who were ready to challenge a disability status quo that went beyond race; one that was based on a highly medicalized, individualized and increasingly out-of-date rehabilitation model. Increased numbers of disabled veterans returning from Viet Nam also fueled agitation.

The DRM in important ways began more or less simultaneously on both coasts, typified in San Francisco by Roberts and others fighting back against the "we don't do Crips" attitude to the streets of New York City where the Zames sisters and others increasingly protested the lack of accessibility to public transportation (a long-time "red button" issue for urbanites with disabilities). In fact, transportation would eventually become a grassroots, nationwide call for reform equaled only by changes demanded in the public education system.[31]

The early battles for disability rights in the 1960s were always part of a general civil rights movement, and in spite of some advocates who attempted to isolate their own cause (such as Malcolm X, who was known to suggest indirectly that the radical Civil Rights Movement didn't have time or resources to offer material aid or even spiritual collaboration with other movements), it was frequently the case that individuals who resided in more than one stigmatized identity (race, gender, disability, etc.) inevitably found themselves fighting the same battles in each area, regardless of their specific agenda for one or the other. The struggles of black servicemen, like George Monroe, to secure military disability benefits served as marked cases in point. They fought issues of race and disability stigma simultaneously. This intersectionality was not always recognized.

In another case with this same ironic twist, Dr. King argued on behalf of a black serviceman, Cosby Wallace, to keep him exempt from military service due to his disability. Disability was in this case a secondary identity that worked side by side with race to further complicate a more general civil rights dialog. The gradual normalization of disability status, sought alongside a quickly evolving attempt at racial normalization, fueled what was as a result a much larger civil rights movement.[32]

Later, to be black and to be disabled would engender a special kind of status that advocates like Leroy Moore would readily recognize: "…My ears perked up…with

---

[31] Zames and Fleischer. P. XX; Fox, Margalit. "Frieda Zames, 72, Advocate for DisablEd." *New York Times*, June 17, 2005, obituary.

[32] King, Martin Luther. "Letter to whom it may concern." January 22, 1968, accessed June 1, 2015 at http://www.thekingcenter.org/archive/document/letter-mlk-behalf-cosby-wallace.

people like Brad Lomax, Chuck Johnson, Gary Norris Gray…because they looked like me, Black and disabled." Lomax believes that Black Panther involvement was critical to the later success of the 1977 HEW Sit-in in San Francisco.[33]

Activist Fred Fay, a student at the University of Illinois at the time, remembered:

> I really understood where Martin Luther King [Jr.] was coming from. I'd read Gandhi and really believed we needed some major social change with respect to how people with disabilities were viewed and treated in our country. So many were stuck in back rooms or housed away at institutions. It just seemed a criminal waste of human life, and a horrible place for people to live, in an institution.[34]

But overall, the level of cooperation and collaboration between disability activists and civil rights activists was sometimes noteworthy for its absence, rather than its exceptions. It was very typical for disability advocates to cite civil rights leaders as inspiration (ex. Judith Heumann crediting LIU professor Ted Childs, or ADAPT founder Wade Blank crediting his training to the Civil Rights Movement); it was hardly ever the case that civil rights leaders cited disability advocates as inspiration. A perception lingers into the present, both sociologically and historiographically, that the Civil Rights Movement was the meta-narrative, and that other movements were thus subject to it, rather than fully independent, or equal partners with it.

This frustration with undervaluing humans with disabilities would remain a constant hum in the background even while Roberts personally enjoyed career success, progress within the DRM, and continued to support a greater human rights movement. He never could understand why radical blacks wouldn't fully embrace the DRM:

> I remember meeting with Leonard Pelletier before he was arrested. I met with Stokeley Carmichael, and others in the Black Power movement. When I told them that we were all fighting the same civil rights battle, they didn't believe me; they didn't understand our similarities. I did. Even now, many people don't realize it.[35]

[33.] Moore, Leroy. "Black history of 504 sit-in for disability rights: More than serving food—when will the healing begin?" *BayView National Black Newspaper*, February 11, 2014.

[34.] Fay, Frederick A.. Interviews conducted by Fred Pelka in 2001, Disability Rights and Independent Living Movement Oral History Project, Regional Oral History Office, The Bancroft Library, University of California, Berkeley, 2004, pp. 25–26.

[35.] Roberts, Edward. *Highlights from Speeches*. Collected by Jon Oda, World Institute on Disability, accessed April 23, 2014 at http://www.wid.org/about-wid/highlights-from-speeches-by-ed-roberts.

Malcolm X came to Berkeley when Roberts was in attendance there on October 11, 1963. He spoke at a Slate-sponsored forum in Dwinelle Plaza, giving a newsworthy speech outlining Black Nationalism and advocating racial separation in order to break the "vicious cycle." It is possible, perhaps even likely, that Roberts attended this talk, which ended with seventeen minutes of questions and comments in conclusion (although his mother couldn't recall him ever talking about this in her interview with the author). One cannot but help observe the great differences in personality and temperament between the two men, and yet Roberts was always drawn to Civil Rights leaders and may very well have been one of those offering up questions from the audience that night.[36]

Although the Black Panthers famously aided disability activists in the 1977 San Francisco protests, as mentioned, and there are other examples of similar collaboration, the alliance between Civil Rights leaders and disability activists remains unexplainably uneasy even into the present time. Roberts, for his part, consistently saw the greater cause of human rights and civil rights as a global cause that transcended singular identities, an attitude that remains a permanent gift to the DRM from his efforts. In tandem, Moore and others make reference to the mostly white leadership of the DRM, and a greater healing that remains to be completed.

Transportation

The right to mobility, expressed until modern times mainly through walking, has been a basic human right in unspoken common law for thousands of years. Ancient cultures recognized the long tradition of the public right of way, and Roman roads were often open to everyone even though they had been created primarily for military purposes. Roads were not built for people with disabilities, of course, but nor where they normally banned from them. Roads were universal and therefore acted as a unifying force in human history.[37]

Modernization, however, brought mechanized forms of mass transportation into being that transformed "the road" and human life, and also presented daunting barriers to many individuals with disabilities. Mass transportation

---

[36.] Malcom X. Text of the Malcolm X speech is available online at http://www.blackpast.org; "Malcolm X speaks at UCB." *ACLU News*, No. 11, p. 3, November 1963; ERP.

[37.] Von Hagen, Victor W.. *The Roads that Led to Rome*. Cleveland, The World Publishing Company, 1967, p. 71; *Final Report: Public Rights-of-Way Access Advisory Committee*. January 200, accessed http://www.accessboard.gov/prowal/commrept/index.htm.

was defined in its American form from the middle part of the 19th century onward in large cities by rail, trolley, bus, Omni-bus, subway and other types of services, most notably in New York City and Chicago. By the 1960s, access to public transportation in most major American cities had become the primary community battleground over disability rights. Because it meant access to jobs, the conflict over public transportation was in some ways *the* battle of the early DRM.[38]

Major cities such as New York and Chicago attracted large numbers of disabled citizens because they offered proximity to various kinds of services that smaller towns and rural areas simply could not. They also offered critical mass; the opportunity for a small, often stigmatized minority (such as those diagnosed with a specific disability, like Epilepsy, for example) to form bonded communities of common interests that would not be possible in other disparate environments. In theory it also improved access to medical expertise, since doctors, psychologists and social workers had enough subjects congregated to study and treat them more scientifically. The access to buses, subways, bike pathways, cabs, streets and wheelchair friendly sidewalks was often only possible in an urban environment, even when it was far from perfect in those cities. The DRM, however, began to expose the flaws in modernization, the cracks in the shine of normality and rationalism, which often restricted rather than liberated. By highlighting the flaws in what could otherwise have easily been perceived by the ablest majority as a very accessible environment, activists brought about change by showing how it wasn't.

It was also part of a larger phenomenon. The Civil Rights Movement, for example, gravitated to the cities for related and often identical reasons. The intersectionality of the Montgomery bus boycott with the later San Francisco HEW sit-in is not lost in hindsight, as one example. The task of civil rights advocates was to show those who thought "people are basically all treated okay" that in fact the truth was the complete opposite.

The records of the Metropolitan Transit Authority (MTA) in New York (1968) and its predecessors provide a case in point in terms of disability. While protestors literally parked their wheelchairs in front of New York City buses to protest the lack of access through lifts (first in the late 1960s, and then with regularity in the 1970s), city authorities issued statements of dubious validity claiming growing percentages of buses were equipped with handicap access wheelchair lifts. What authorities did not say was that many of those buses supposedly equipped were

---

[38.] Zames, pp. xv – xvi; and it continued to be a battle ground later: McCarthy, Peggy. "Disabled to Protest Transit." *New York Times*, 9/13/1987, p. 4; "After protests, bus companies reach agreement." *New York Times*, 1/3/91, Vol. 140 Issue 48469, p. B1; etc.

coincidentally "out of service" at any given time, meaning that actual access to equipped buses may have been less than one percent. Wheelchair users were often told by drivers that lifts "were out of order" even when there was no obvious physical problem with the equipment. It was not until 1995 that the MTA finally reported that one hundred percent of city buses were fully accessible, and even then some activists claimed that at any given moment, it was never one hundred percent.[39]

This was the case in spite of a massive effort in the 1960s to revamp the entire system:

> In November 1967, Governor Rockefeller asked his newly created Metropolitan Commuter Transportation Authority ('MCTA,' now the MTA) to prepare a comprehensive plan and action program of transportation improvements for the New York State portion of the metropolitan region. In its February 1968 report to the governor, 'Metropolitan Transportation, a Program for Action,' MCTA proposed a major program of rehabilitation, modernization, purchase of new equipment, and construction of new projects to extend and enhance the existing system.[40]

Sometimes inexplicable institutional resistance was often in direct contradiction to public statements, and was typical of a wider opposition amongst those in positions to easily thwart it (those who controlled public services, or even bus drivers), and whom often attempted to portray the movement as too radical, irrational, and bent on destroying common and economic sense. A spoof on the popular television show *Saturday Night Live* would later show a miles long wheel chair ramp going to the top of the Empire State Building and further proclaim the end of common sense.[41]

Later, the MTA and other urban transportation agencies would go to great lengths to try to promote a more positive image of disability accessibility, producing posters that asked people to:

- "Give up seats to elderly and disabled people"
- Remember that "Buses don't get insulted when you put them down."

---

[39] Various documents accessed through the New York Transit Museum, including MTA documents.

[40] Rosen, Allee King, & Fleming. *Manhattan East Side Transit Alternatives (MESA)/Second Avenue Subway Summary Report*. Prepared for MTA New York City Transit by Vollmer Associates, LLP, SYSTRA Consulting, Inc., October 2001, pp. 1–9.

[41] Transit Records of the New York Transit Authority [MTA]. 4 volumes, 1953–1981, New York Public Library; Zames; Johnson, Roberta Ann. "Mobilizing the DisablEd." In Freeman, Jo. *Social Movements of the Sixties and Seventies*. Longman, 1983, pp. 82–100.

- "Help: Some riders need to sit."
- Be aware "We're making it easier for people with disabilities to ride the bus."
- Or note that "It is so much harder for them to stand."[42]

Such posters were well-intentioned, of course, but on another level revealed the second class status that people with disabilities had long occupied, and the critical role that transportation played in the battle to mitigate or perpetuate that status, depending on the level of accommodation.

Even sidewalks were a vital part of the access effort dating to the sixties. In 1961, the first national standards for accessibility were published, following on the 1959 work done by the President's Committee on Employment for the Physically Handicapped and partners. The standards were based on "anthropometric, ergonomic, and human performance data." This led directly to accessibility regulations and guidelines for sidewalks, trails, and pathways. The major feature over time would be curb cuts, and any time major improvements were made to any byway, the standards for accessibility were from then on in force.[43]

From an intersectional and sociological perspective, the Kennedy presidency was highly significant. Simultaneously with disability policy and advocacy, the administration was promoting evolving civil rights enhancements, promoting gender equity, and addressing systemic social problems such as poverty. A disability history can only be told completely by recognizing that these collective efforts were not being worked on in isolation from each other.

Dennis Cannon and Transportation Advocacy

The Urban Mass Transportation Act of 1964 recognized that for many Americans public transportation was the sole means of accessing a wide range of basic services, from access to food supplies to medical care. Even today, the history of transportation advocacy remains centered in the dramatic protests of the 1970s.

[42.] Archive Records, New York Transit Museum, dates ranging from undated pre-ADA to late 1980s and 1990s, Object IDs: IA-3394, IA-9, XX.2010.606.6, 2012.13.3.29, IA-12325, XX.2010.606.104, and 2011.5.15. Accessed online September 15, 2015.

[43.] U.S. Department of Transportation. *Designing Sidewalks and Trails for Access*. Chapter 1, accessed September 1, 2015 at http://www.fhwa.dot.gov/environment/bicycle_pedestrian/publications/sidewalks/chap1.cfm.

Many advocates like Dennis Cannon, however, were involved in the nascent period of protest in the 1960s, and provided an invaluable impetus for change. Cannon joined the San Fernando Valley chapter of the California Association of the Physically Handicapped [CAPH] in the early sixties:

> We talked about was bills that we were sponsoring in the state legislature and other kinds of things. I got involved in the transportation issues just because I found them interesting and I became the chair of the transportation committee for the state. I was also the president for the San Fernando Valley chapter for a while. One of the biggest significant things we did is we lobbied heavily the Southern California Rapid Transit District [SCRTD] to buy accessible buses. That was ultimately successful.[44]

Cannon and other wheelchair users "crashed" other meetings organized around what were perceived to be dissimilar causes, like anti-war protests, or civil rights, and instead brought up disability issues. They weren't always popular for doing so.

> That was sort of our original interest in this new stuff called disability rights. And the biggest thing was, here was an organization that was actually doing something in terms of getting laws passed, that was politically active, and that was kind of interesting because I had been involved early on with the grape strike with Cesar Chavez's United Farmworkers Union and a few other things on campus.[45]

Although activists like Cannon were pioneers who remain largely unheralded, their groundbreaking efforts paid off later when transportation rights made the national agenda in the media, and in politics of the media-covered 1970s.[46]

---

[44] Cannon, Dennis. *Disability Rights and Independent Living Movement Oral History Project, Shaping National Disability Policy: Transportation Access and Social Security Reforms.* Cannon, interview; Cannon, Dennis. "Advocate for Accessible Public Transportation in California and Washington, D.C." Regional Oral History Office, The Bancroft Library University of California, Berkeley, 2004 by The Regents of the University of California, Accessed online August 15, 2015 at http://content.cdlib.org/view?docId=hb2j49n5h3&query=&brand=calisphere.
[45] Ibid.
[46] Ibid.

Transportation became a similar battleground for activism in Canada, simultaneous with growing activism in the United States. In 1966 when the Montreal subway system opened, a long battle over access ensued that exposed structural barriers and confirmed that popular (but misplaced) ideas from the earlier eugenics era were far from dispelled. Repeated calls for improvement in the system documented a nascent disability rights movement within Quebec that mirrored much larger North American and even Western forces.[47]

In the field of architecture, Universal Design (UD) principles had already quietly proven that the environment could be much more accessible with minimal financial cost, and only modestly more intellectual expense. In 1961, the American National Standards Institute accessibility guidelines already mentioned were a UD breakthrough, and targeted transportation resources, but also a broader way of thinking about the environment.

Urban decay and resistant city bureaucracies kept transportation improvements in flux and individuals with disabilities frustrated with authorities. DRM advocates confronted economic and discriminatory arguments with the only weapon they had: their lived experience and postmodern adaptations of Foucault's governmentalities of the mind and body which rejected normality. They protested, often loudly. This in turn helped make the issues more public, and exposed the network of stereotypes and discrimination enforced by powers that remained firmly entrenched in government, education, and in the media. The world would not end if Ed Roberts were admitted to UCB, and bus service in New York City could be just as convenient and inexpensive even with wheelchair lifts installed.[48]

It required a radicalization congruent to the other identity rights movements, and a philosophical wedding of leftist politics ranging from anarchists to Marxists. Disability advocates such as Ed Roberts, the Zames sisters, Fred Faye, and Judy Heumann, and others knew that many elements of the radical left, perhaps ironically, needed just as much education about the lived experience of disability as everyone else. But the left also had political resources, social capital, and organizational experience that the DRM desperately needed. The radical left also had the attention of authorities, who feared that the disabled, in spite of their diversity in backgrounds and widely varied experiences of disability, would essentially "unionize" to combat discrimination and ignorance, and become part of the active fight against the establishment.

[47.] Reaume, Geoffrey. "Disability history in Canada: Present work in the field and future prospects." *The Canadian Journal of Disability Studies*, Vol. 1(1), 2012, p. 46.

[48.] Davis, Lennard. "Introduction: Normality, Power, and Culture." In Davis, L. (Ed.) *The Disability Studies Reader*. Routledge, 2013, pp. 1–14.

Hence the DRM fought battles in the streets of America like other radicalized minorities did, blocking access to non-accessible services, showing up in mass at public events to garner attention with signs and chants, and intentionally make an already nervous public more uncomfortable; radicalizing college and university campuses where they demanded access to education and to possibilities; and generally making their voices heard.

In fact, the term learning disability—now obsequious—was introduced for the first time in 1960s. Samuel Kirk introduced the term in 1962 in the first edition of his text Educating Exceptional Children. Thanks to Ed Roberts and other students with disabilities, colleges and universities everywhere began to see increasing numbers of applicants with physical and psychological-oriented disabilities; in K-12 the structures that would become a formal special education system with parent organizations, formal definitions of learning disorders, school system initiatives, etc..

Transportation remained an arena in the center of the public eye; the protest movements of the 1960s were often photographed at rallies in city streets, frequently with city buses, trains, or cabs in the background; the media covered radicalism in the streets, and not inside public schools or inside institutions for the mentally ill. Later, advocates would speak of the transportation battle nostalgically, often stating that "the public right of way is an ancient concept," or that "all users have the right to equal access to public rights-of-way." But in the 1960s, it was a street-level battle over the tyranny of the norm and the outright discrimination by those in power, whom individuals with disabilities dared to ask for what couldn't be had, even it were as simple a matter as requesting a seat in a taxi cab to go out to dinner.[49]

Transportation issues sprang up everywhere, even beyond the major cities, although the two cites that most typified the phenomenon of protest and provided stages for nationally-centered disability radicalism were San Francisco and New York City. Appropriately, both cities remain places today where one can encounter the best in disability accommodation and universal design, and also find innumerable instances where significant barriers and discrimination still remain. Transportation may, according to some, be a battle that was won in the 1970s, but it began in the sixties, and the brush wars continue today.[50]

---

[49] Public Rights-of-Way Access Advisory Committee. *Final Report*. January 2001, accessed at: http://www.access-board.gov/PROWAL/commrept/index.htm on October 15th, 2012.

[50] Zames, pp. xv – xvi.

President Kennedy, Disability, and Civil Rights

Although this text has very intentionally avoided strict timelines whenever possible, as they imply a linear element to history that can be very misleading, the era of the 1960s comprises several factors which make an arguable exception to that rule. First, the 1960s saw an unprecedented degree of individual and collective activism that is nearly impossible to completely document except in general media accounts and some broad historical secondary sources; secondly, events sped up in the sixties to the point that it was felt both at the time and still today, that more happened in a ten year period than had occurred of equal significance during many previous decades (or perhaps even centuries); and lastly, progress was defined more in this period by benchmarks and firsts, as well as by small victories that DRM activists used as launching pads for the next assault on the status quo. For these reasons, a list of major events in the 1960s is a useful list to become familiar with.

In November of 1960, John F. Kennedy was elected President. No president since FDR had taken as active a role in supporting disability rights. The Civil Rights Act he crafted set the standard for other legislation and led to the creation of the EEOC, the Equal Employment Opportunity Commission, which become responsible for enforcing non-discrimination in hiring practices, and also provided a model for de-stigmatizing other institutions like education.

President Kennedy was symbolic of the growth of the so-called New Left, a liberal cross-section of middle class citizens who experienced a growing social conscience and concern for the welfare of historically stigmatized minorities, including individuals with disabilities. Postsecondary students were particularly active, forming the well-known group Students for a Democratic Society (SDS).

Sociologist C. Wright Mills codified the term "New Left" in an open letter that would set the tone for many in the movement. Many amongst the New Left rejected the rigid labor and management structures associated with Marxism or Sovietism, for example, but accepted the dialectical need for significant change and a larger degree of radicalism (including skepticism about aspects of capitalism). Individuals in the New Left could endorse the Civil Rights Movement, for example, even if they were removed from racial discrimination by their own privileged status, and in fact could use the social capital of their status to actively lobby for social change.

Mills stated:

> These criticisms, demands, theories, programs are guided morally by the humanist and secular ideals of Western civilization — above all, reason and freedom and

> justice. To be "Left" means to connect up cultural with political criticism, and both with demands and programs. And it means all this inside every country of the world.[51]

It was in essence a call to activism, which many students and intellectuals answered. (For example, the author's parents were college students in the 1960s who marched and protested.)

Kennedy used his executive influence through the President's Committee on Employment of the Physically Handicapped to encourage the media to promote increased rates of gainful employment of individuals with disabilities through a large-scale public service media campaign. Although the program initially began under President Eisenhower, it was under Kennedy and the influence of the emerging New Left that results began to be felt. In a 1962 press release, this was quantified in startling dollar amounts, as the committee prepared to recognize what broadcasters and networks had accomplished thus far:

> ...The "Hire the Handicapped: campaign has been a top NAB [National Association of Broadcasters] special project. And NAB's support has been enthusiastic...

> ...During the past decade alone, broadcasters have donated MORE THAN FIVE BILLION DOLLARS WORTH OF PUBLIC SERVICE TIME to the cause. At present, the dollar value of donated time is running about $5 million a year...

> ...Broadcasters are playing leading parts in citizens' movements to further jobs for the handicapped... ...The ideas have grown; the ideas have been converted into action. And the handicapped have been finding jobs, in greater numbers.[52]

The emerging DRM was quite comfortable within the American framework of the New Left, and the other identity rights movements. It was far from purely socialist, revolutionary, or labor-based, but it was reactionary, boundary challenging, leftist, and utterly rejected the status quo. It relied heavily on the influence of liberal middle class whites, who were sympathetic to the Civil Rights and Women's Rights movements, and soon also on returning veterans from Viet Nam who represented a new class of disabled soldiers that would shape politics in Washington.

---

[51] Mills, C. Wright. "Letter to the New Left." *New Left Review*, No. 5, September-October 1960.

[52] Committee on Employment of the Physically HandicappEd. *Report*. 1962, John F. Kennedy Presidential Library and Museum, Digital Identifier: JFKPOF-093-005.

The Civil Rights model for advocacy was adopted early on by disability activists, and has been maximized in the past several decades, culminating most recently in the passage of the Amendments Act (2008), a reauthorization of the Americans with Disabilities Act (1990) necessary due to lingering stigmas and the erosion of disability rights in myriad court cases.

The Civil Rights model moved beyond the individual, where the intersectionality of defect and disorder had been firmly situated for centuries and was centered in medical practice, and instead focused on a larger cultural context. The aim was generally to grant equal access, or in colloquial terms, to "level the playing field." Activist Fred Fay provided one of the siren calls in the sixties for rejecting the medical model; others joined him, mirroring a similar rejection of medical power and expertise simultaneously occurring in Great Britain.

Kennedy's role in the passage of the Civil Rights Act is well documented. Although the Civil Rights Act of 1964 made no specific reference to disability, it was and is considered still to be the model for such legislation, and disability activists have been tireless in adapting the semantics of disability accommodation as a basic civil right as a result. Consistent with the philosophy Ed Roberts and others adopted, and the foundation of the Independent Living Movement, the focus remains on access to basic life activities: housing, education, voting, public transportation, and the right to live outside of oppressive institutions (both physical institutions and socially constructed institutions).[53]

Like other types of civil rights, disability rights landed in court where litigation became an important tool in forwarding the cause, educating the public, and defining the specifics of what disability rights actually consisted of. A number of cases in the 1960s influenced the radical period, including two that are mentioned in the U.S. Commission on Civil Rights' own history of the movement.[54]

The first involved a school teacher in NYC, who sued the school system for denying him a position due to his blindness. The court found on the side of the school system, stating:

> Whether a blind teacher may satisfactorily perform classroom duties in a particular school may not be left for the determination of the school principal

---

[53] Foreman, Michael L., et. al.. *Sharing the Dream: Is the ADA Accommodating All?* U.S. Commission on Civil Rights, 1998).

[54] Ibid.

> or other supervisory official, as the minority opinion suggests. The statute requires the Board of Examiners to determine whether an applicant has the ability to perform satisfactorily the duties of a teacher. The Board of Education is concerned with the effective performance of duties by a teacher both inside and outside the classroom. Although my sympathies are with this petitioner because of his unfortunate affliction, it is my opinion that the refusal to certify petitioner as eligible for a teaching license was within the power of the Board of Examiners.[55]

The radical DRM rejected sympathy (or charity), while courts such as this one codified it. The use of the term "affliction" with all that it implies is representative of the governmentality of oppression that was at stake.

The second case involved exclusion of mentally retarded children from school in Utah. In this case, Wolf v. State Legislature, Civ. No. 182646 Utah, the court sided with the parents, indicating that students with disabilities were under Utah law and therefore entitled to free and appropriate public education (FAPE). These cases were typical of the tensions and contradictions of the times, and overall progress.[56]

Perhaps most visibly, Kennedy championed the cause of children, especially those with intellectual disabilities:

> Mental retardation ranks with mental health as a major health, social, and economic problem in this country. It strikes our most precious asset, our children.[57]

Kennedy's own sister, Rosemary, was born with intellectual disabilities, and Kennedy made this particular cause a priority throughout his administration. As a progressive, President Kennedy up until his untimely death was a president who quite visibly and psychologically supported the major social movements, including the DRM.

President Johnson continued Kennedy's work. A story from Life magazine illustrates this in a personal fashion:

---

[55] "Decision." Accessed April 30, 2015 from http://www.leagle.com/decision/19658023AD2d57_170

[56] U.S. Commission on Civil Rights. *Sharing the Dream: Is the ADA Accommodating All?* Chapter 1, The Road to the ADA, 1998; Russo, Charles J., & Osborne, Allan G. Jr.. *Essential Concepts and School-Based Cases in Special Education Law.* Corwin Press, 2008, pp. 8–9.

[57] "JFK and People with Intellectual Disabilities." Accessed April 30, 2015 http://www.jfklibrary.org/JFK/JFK-in-History/JFK-and-People-with-Intellectual-Disabilities.aspx.

> Not long ago Johnson noted a newspaper story about a small girl who had passed all the government physical fitness tests except chin-ups; these she could not do because she had lost part of her arm in an accident. She could not get her certificate. The President picked up the phone and ordered the Physical Fitness Council to change the rules for handicapped people, and then he wrote a tender letter to a determined little heart.[58]

The Civil and Women's Rights Movements have dominated the cultural and political landscape for more than fifty years since their dramatic growth in the 1960s, but the Disability Rights Movement co-existed side by side with them, sometimes striving for collaboration, but sometimes in competition for attention and resources. The three movements in sum radically changed identity politics, along with the social and cultural landscape, and it was in part due to the leadership of the executive office.

The Storm Breaks

In the 21st century, the DRM has manifested in ways that would have amazed the activists of the 1960s. Information now spreads through networks at the speed of the Internet, and demonstrations are organized online. But the fundamental desire to see social justice and to combat stereotypes remains strong, and similar to the spirit that broke out in the sixties. Although the actions of the 1970s would be dramatically captured and displayed by the national media, and eventually become enshrined in the emerging disability history that explained the ADA, the activism of the sixties was the true training grounds and incubator for those events.

---

[58] Hugh Sidey, "The Presidency," Life (magazine), September 1, 1967, p. 26B.

CHAPTER 7

The 1970s and 1980s and a New Civil Rights Act

The radicalism of the 1960s made the leap forward in disability rights in the 1970s and 1980s possible. Although disability issues had been simmering as a result of a more general civil rights movement, in the mid-1970s disability as a mainstream identity suddenly crystalized and formed more completely on the national stage. Although this historical narrative has also argued for the seminality of the 1960s, many chroniclers of the DRM have traditionally seen the 1970s as the "leap in consciousness of people with disabilities."[1]

This movement was not limited to America, and a fascinating aspect of the DRM was to see similar activities taking place in Great Britain, Canada, other Western nations, and even in more remote places such as Antigua and Barbuda in 1957 with a Mental Treatment Ordinance, or South Africa's 1968 Blind Persons Act, as just two of many examples.[2]

The 1970s was an intense period of advocacy, change, and legislation key to the wider progress of the DRM. Judith Heumann, for example, was radicalized in the 1960s, but formed the organization Disabled in Action (DIA) from 1970–1972 in New York where her efforts would translate into practical and measurable action:

> I think DIA was a very important organization at the time because it was cross disability, it did deal with multiple issues, it was a political activist organization, made no bones about it, wasn't shy about it. [I] really felt that we had to take what we considered the anger and oppression that we were experiencing as disabled people and not sit around and complain about it.[3]

---

[1] Zames, p. xiii.

[2] A fascinating list at the time of this writing is maintained at: https://dredf.org/legal-advocacy/international-disability-rights/international-laws/ by the Disability Rights Education & Defense Fund.

[3] Heumann, Judith. "Interview." Accessed at http://www.disabledinaction.org/heumann.html. Note that some people date the founding of DIA to 1970, although in this interview Heumann states that she thinks it was 1972. DIA actually appears to be a formalization of what had been going on less formally for quite some time.

Heumann and others recognized that laws were important, but that attitudes could only be changed through education, agitation, and organization. Oppression was a call to action. It was a call for legislation, as well. But as it would turn out, laws could and would be passed, but without enforcement or regulations to guide their use, they could potentially be little more than suggestive ideas, glorified statements of principle, rather than impactful paradigm shifts.

The idealism of the New Left, although not in the exact same guise as earlier in the 1960s, was still running on the reform fumes left over from the Kennedy administration and anti-war protests that continued into the new decade, and fueled action for broader education as well as movement within the federal government and its programs for greater accessibility. The year 1972, for example, saw the passage of changes to the Social Security Act which expanded disability benefits, supplemental social security income (which impacted people with disabilities disproportionately), and attempts to pass what would eventually become the Rehabilitation Act of 1973 (it was initially vetoed by Richard Nixon).[4]

In educational circles, north and south of the border, change was occurring. In Canada, a commission on emotional and learning disorders in children began the process of what would ultimately be called "inclusion" in public education. In the U.S., experts as well as parents began to challenge the paternalistic and long-held belief that segregated classes or schools were simply better for students with disabilities. The philosophy and social theory of normalization continued to gain a following during this period, pioneered by social scientists like Wolf Wolfensberger, which ultimately would be expressed in the 1975 Individuals with Disabilities Education Act, which essentially created special education.[5]

In the mind of the disabled public, and in the mind of many activists, the sixties had only set the stage for victories that were not yet fully obtained by any means. Although the Americans with Disabilities Act was the ultimate prize still down the road, there were many other victories that characterized the leading battles of seventies and eighties, and they were only possible as a result of the work done in the radical sixties.

---

[4] Zames, p. xxiii; *Presidential Vetoes: 1789–1988*, Washington DC: U.S. Government Printing Office, 1992, pp. 483–494.

[5] Winzer, Margaret A. *The History of Special Education: From Isolation to Integration.* Washington DC: Gallaudet University Press, 1993, pp. 366, 380–381; Wolfensberger, W.. *The Principle of Normalization in Human Services.* Toronto, Canada, National Institute on Mental Retardation, 1972.

Devil in the Details: Section 504 Regulations

Disability activists realized fairly quickly that the Rehabilitation Act of 1973, which included Section 504, was only a partial victory. Aside from the fact that it only covered entities that were connected to federal funding, and hence exempted most private businesses, it also failed to be implemented at the federal level through any meaningful regulatory process. The complaints about lack of specific regulations grew from a murmur over the coming years to a loud rallying cry in the mid to late seventies. What good was a law, people asked, that had no enforcement mechanisms, or even guidelines for enforcement?

The Section 504 protests reached a dramatic climax in 1977 in San Francisco. It was different from other cities where the planned protests that were to be in conjunction with each other were mostly unsuccessful; very few people actually showed up, and there was little if any media coverage of the events. In those cases, the routines in offices like the Health, Education and Welfare department where attempted sit-ins fizzled, mostly continued normally as if the protests hadn't even taken place.

But something very special did ultimately happen in San Francisco, and what transpired there forced a different interpretation of all of the other efforts:

> Most of the protests ended that day as planned. The San Francisco protest did not. After marching past the security guards at the local HEW office without resistance, over 100 protesters unpacked their knapsacks and began what became known as the 504 Sit-In. The landmark takeover remains the longest non-violent occupation of a U.S. federal building in history. Though there is some disagreement about the exact length of the protest, it is often cited as 26 days. (Some protesters stayed in the building a few days after the larger group dispersed.)[6]

Ultimately, it appeared that a single straw had finally broken the camel's back. Many people made the obvious connection between the earlier success of the Independent Living Movement (ILM) pioneered by advocates like Ed Roberts on the West Coast, and the sudden success of the protests for 504 regulations in 1977.

---

[6] Shoot, Britta. "The 1977 Disability Rights Protest That Broke Records and Changed Laws." Atlas Obscura, November 9, 2017, accessed at https://www.atlasobscura.com/articles/504-sit-in-san-francisco-1977-disability-rights-advocacy.

Herb Levine, a disabilities rights activist whose career spanned five decades, and who worked at the Independent Living Resource Center in San Francisco, remembers getting involved in the protests:

> Somebody said to me, 'You know, Judy Heumann and a bunch of people are down there at the Federal Building at HEW; we hear something's going on down there.' This was the Civil Rights act. It wasn't 1964, it was 1977![7]

Levine, like thousands of other Americans with disabilities could not believe that four years had passed since the ground-breaking disability rights legislation, and yet there were still no practical means of implementing its statutes (regulations). Levine later connected it directly to the ADA:

> You know, the ADA [1990] really said, 'Don't discriminate.' So it was important! Starting to fill in some gaps. But, yeah, not as important as 504. And you know, isn't it amazing that a bunch of crips in the federal building for almost a month, and they, they won over the federal government! And I... I remember being there just so happy to be there. You know? When I've told this story, people say, 'what... is there one message in that story?' I say, 'yeah.' The message was: 'you don't need to be some extraordinary person.'

Kitty Cone, another participant, remembers that the protestors felt some of the enormity of what was happening; in spite of *just wanting to be treated like ordinary people*, some knew that what was happening was extraordinary:

> At every moment, we felt ourselves the descendants of the civil rights movement of the '60s. We learned about sit ins from the civil rights movement, we sang freedom songs to keep up morale, and consciously show the connection between the two movements. We always drew the parallels. About public transportation we said we can't even get on the back of the bus. A high point was Julian Bond's visit to the building.[8]

An important aspect of Section 504 was that it was civil rights legislation that looked both backwards and forwards. First, it recognized the historical

---

[7] Levine, Herb. "Interview." Personal Interview with Jessie Lorenz, accessed June 10, 2015 at http://disabilityvisibilityproject.com/tag/section-504/; Senior and Disability Action. "Bio of Board member Herb Levine." Accessed June 10, 2015 at http://sdaction.org/about/board-members/.

[8] Cone, Kitty. "Short History of the 504 Sit In." Accessed June 10, 2015 http://dredf.org/504site/histover.html.

discrimination that people with disabilities (of all types) had been subject to for hundreds of years in the American experience (and perhaps even further back in the Western experience). But secondly, it aimed forward; it reified a vision of a more accessible world. The failure to implement meaningful regulations essentially denied the spirit of the law; it was worse than a Presidential veto.

Joseph Shapiro has famously documented the events of this period in his ground-breaking book, *No Pity*. Shapiro points out that the disability civil rights component of 504 was not part of the initial planning in the legislation, and advocates had not originally asked for it. It was in essence a later editorial addition with a very unclear legislative genealogy. But that language led to dramatic events and demonstrations, even at the personal residence of HEW Secretary Joseph Califano, who had the unhappy task of taking the Ford administration's unfinished regulations and trying to make something manageable out of them. Califano became a Bogeyman of sorts to the disability community.[9]

In memory and at the time, the legislation was commonly referred to as "Section 504," or simply "504," rather than the broader Rehabilitation Act, and this was not simply for convenience' sake, and Section 504 was not the only section of the larger law. It was because that part of the law represented the change sought so long. In fact, the rehabilitation model for managing disability was exposed in the radical sixties for what it had come to symbolize: institutionalization; marginalization; and medicalization. So passing a "rehabilitation" law could be seen as a semantic regression.

Section 504 altered that. Although perhaps rehabilitation could arguably be seen as a positive step forward on the grand stage of Western history, by the time of the HEW protests in the 1970s the semantics and the reality of rehabilitation were seen as problematic by the disability community. They implied that something within the individual needed fixed, or cured, and that the solution must come through charity, or government paternalism. Section 504, on the other hand, represented a new mantra for independence, respect, and equal access—it codified a disability identity as legitimate.

Judith Heumann said shortly afterwards, as recounted by Doris and Frieda Zames:

> The 504 demonstrations last year in California were successful for a number of reasons: because the disabled community was united; because the disabled

---

[9.] Shapiro, Joseph P., *No Pity: People with Disabilities Forging a New Civil Rights Movement*. New York: Times Books, 1993, specifically pp. 64–70.

community unequivocally believed that 504 was our civil rights provision; because we knew if we did not fight for this civil rights provision, we were in fact going to slide backward instead of making further progress.[10]

The protests were also successful because they brought together unlikely partners as part of the coalition, ranging from the Black Panthers and a local grocery store chain, to former students (now adults) left over from the civil rights battles of the sixties and the New Left, and all of whom communicated through diverse vantage points and technologies, ranging from American Sign Language (ASL) to electronic speech technology. It was a rainbow coalition that represented a distinctly unique human rights movement.[11]

Justin Dart and the Road to Freedom

The disability advocacy of the mid to late 1970s and throughout the 1980s took on an increasingly more sophisticated and highly organized nature. Although the 504 protests in 1977 had succeeded largely because of an outlier group in San Francisco, they had also displayed an increasingly integrated approach and intentional degree of collaboration that was usually not present in the more spontaneous activism of the 1960s.

It is true that most of the disability activist leaders in the 1970s and into the 1980s had actually learned their craft of activism in the 1960s, many of them as university students swept up in the New Left and student protest movements for civil rights and following anti-war agendas. Justin Dart, who became a central figure in the eventual passage of the ADA, and helped define the 1980s, has been called the "father of the ADA." Dart attended college in the 1950s, where the University of Houston refused him his teaching certificate due to disability. He brought historic scope of vision to disability advocacy.[12]

---

[10] Zames, p. 54.

[11] "Patient No More: An Interactive, Multimedia Exhibit." Accessed on June 25, 2015 at http://longmoreinstitute.sfsu.edu/patientnomore.

[12] Lehrer-Stein, Janice. "Honoring the Legacies of Olmstead and Justin Dart." Representing the National Council on Disability, accessed online June 25, 2015 at http://www.ncd.gov/newsroom/2013/06212013; Dart, Justin. "Prepared Statement." From the National Council on Disability, accessed online June 25, 2015 at http://www.ncd.gov/newsroom/2012/06222012.

For Dart, the personal turning-point moment did in fact come during the 1960s, on a 1966 visit to war-torn Vietnam to compare rehabilitation services to those that were available back in the U.S. for individuals like Dart who contracted polio. While there, examining the extraordinarily crude and harsh conditions in which Vietnamese children and adults with polio were forced to live every day, he realized that the world for those with disabilities would never be ideal without a vigorous activism to challenge the highly medicalized and stigmatized status quo.[13]

> That scene is burned forever in my soul. For the first time in my life I understood the reality of evil, and that I was part of that reality.[14]

Dart would never be the same, and what began as a personal revelation became a public revolution:

> I call for solidarity among all who love justice, all who love life, to create a revolution that will empower every single human being to govern his or her life, to govern the society and to be fully productive of life quality for self and for all.[15]

Like Ed Roberts, Dart believed that the cause of human rights included primarily disability rights, and he also supported sister movements for women, people of color, and LGBTQ. Dart was a believer in the mantra that Martin Luther King espoused: "Injustice anywhere is a threat to justice everywhere."

For Dart, and many other activists, the question of the early 1980s was a practical one: had enough been accomplished with the 504 victories, or was something even bigger on the horizon? Many, like Dart, intuitively understood that the battle was far from over. Sweeping civil rights legislation for disabilities was still not fully accomplished. 504 had many gaps and shortcomings, and lack of access and discrimination remained commonplace.

Dart played a pivotal role in the steps that led to the passage of the ADA, and later reminded people that its passage was never a given and that it did face significant critics. Even while working in Texas in the early 1980s on long-range

---

[13] Disability Social History Project. "Justin Dart – Activist." Including an obituary written by Fred Fay and Fred Pelka, accessed June 1, 2015 at http://www.disabilityhistory.org/people_dart.html.

[14] Ibid.

[15] Ibid.

planning for disability policy, he recognized the dangers of passing federal laws that were weak or through their lack of effect actually unintentionally codified segregation. When he was appointed by President Reagan to the National Council on Disability (NCD) in 1982, many people (including the president) still didn't fully realize the extent to which disability experience transcended political party and ideology. Mentored by Judith Heumann (a former council member), Dart became a key advocate on the council for a federal disability civil rights law that was free of exemptions, and not weakened by a lack of concrete statutes (like 504).[16]

An NCD report issued in 1986 became the basis of a first version of the ADA which was Congressionally introduced in 1988, and which failed in part, according to Dart, because many in the disability activist community still despaired about enforcing laws that already existed (like Section 504), or perceived that the disability rights movement had peaked in the late 1970s and was now losing steam. New legislation was perhaps an overreach. Dart countered by working with the Task Force on the Rights and Empowerment of Americans with Disabilities, and broke new ground by including advocates for learning disabilities, and appointing members with AIDs.[17]

In other words, he refused to give up. When the ADA finally passed in 1990 and was signed into law, much of the credit belonged to people like Dart, who had moved beyond initial efforts and roadblocks, and persisted in a broader vision. Dart near the end of his life recalled:

> We are so proud to have passed the ADA built on the 504. And that attitudes of all Americans have changed about people with disabilities. We are real human beings in the human race. That's different than it used to be. However, now we have to get out and get our rights enforced. While no minority has all their rights enforced, we have to do it, because nobody ever gave rights away. We have to get out of life as usual and become fully 24 hour a day, 365 days a year passionate single-minded advocates for disability rights.[18]

---

[16] Zames, pp. 88–89.

[17] Zames, pp. 91–92; various National Council on Disability documents accessed June 25, 2015 at http://www.ncd.gov/newsroom.

[18] *"On A Roll: Reflections from America's Wheelchair Dude with the Winning Attitude featuring his last media interview."* Accessed at http://www.thestrengthcoach.com/remembering-justin-dart-birthday/.

ADAPT

Adapt was founded in 1974 by Wade Blank, a minister (without any known disabilities at the time) who began an advocacy for disability rights group called the Atlantis Group in Denver, Colorado. The group initially targeted transportation as their impact issue, although over several decades the organization would expand with many chapters and take on much wider issues. The acronym originally stood for Americans Disabled for Accessible Public Transportation (ADAPT). Over time, leadership become primarily by disability activists and people with disabilities themselves.

On July 5th and 6th, 1978, the so-called "Gang of Nineteen" protested over accessible public transportation in Denver, laying down in the street in some cases, and blocking transit service, demanding change. But the defining moment for ADAPT, and perhaps for the DRM, came closer to the eve of the ADA, when ADAPT members left their wheelchairs and crawled their way up the steps of the capitol building in protest. It was a DRM defining moment.

Robert Shapiro describes it best:

> The sight of paraplegics dragging themselves across each step was both fascinating and repelling. At the end of the day, some activists, including editor Mary Johnson, worried that the grueling "crawl-up" had conveyed precisely the image disabled people wanted to avoid... ...Yet the network that night stressed exactly the message ADAPT wanted to get across: that disabled people were demanding civil rights.[19]

[19.] Shapiro, p. 133.

More Transportation Confrontations

The unrest in 1960s which centered on the so-called "transportation disabled" only grew in the 1970s and into 1980s. This was in part because of the growing urban decay which would eventually result in the "rust belt," and a crisis in human services in many large cities, which served to expose the sorry state of mass transportation and the challenges it faced. But it also grew out of the Independent Living Movement (ILM) and was a result of cultural forces that inherently demanded more access to better transportation, especially for people with disabilities.

Dating back the Middle Ages in Europe, the Western tradition included a unique role for the city in accommodating individuals with disabilities. Cities grew as a result of "critical mass" benefits in economic, educational, entertainment, and practical terms. The best shoes, for example, could be purchased in cities, generally, where tradesmen gathered, markets encouraged innovation, and guilds set standards, and true competition could flourish. Likewise, innovation with prosthetic devices often occurred in guild workshops in cities. Cities, in the Western tradition, have served a major driving force in support of classic liberalism and free market capitalism, presumably benefiting everyone.

However, markets in themselves do not make decisions about who should have and who should have not. The radicalism of the sixties in the U.S. that brought disability issues into the national dialogue focused first and foremost on transportation, for without that primary resource, the beneficial resources and community opportunities of the city were essentially reserved for the able-bodied and wealthy, or those who had private transportation. What good would educational reform do, for example, if individuals with disabilities simply could not get to where the schools were?

Coming out of the federally funded studies of transportation in the sixties and seventies, metropolitan transportation authorities across the country began to come under the public microscope with increasing scrutiny. The Urban Mass Transit Act of 1964 had been intended to address wider concerns, with "assistance for the development of comprehensive and coordinated mass transportation systems, both public and private, in metropolitan and other urban areas…" Although some read the improved "techniques" of delivery of services as also meaning more equitable services, the sixties were a period where mass transit bureaucracies were often resistant to fundamental change.[20]

It is also interesting to note that many planning commissions not only identified access as a key area of reform, but also as a necessity for public safety. This was a case of fear (ex. urban violence) actually being treated as a functional barrier to access to public services, and was addressed openly in many transportation plans. Essentially, fear of personal safety was treated

---

[20] Public Law 88-365. From the National Archives online collection.

in some cases like another type of disability, or from the administrative point of view, fear of mob violence.[21]

By the 1970s, urban transportation reform normally included bus systems, light rail, and subway systems, but also increasingly attempted to address private services like taxis and private buses. Recent international studies of taxi service show that even as late as 2007 access to taxi service in Western countries lagged far behind other forms of public transportation. "Access to taxis remains a particular challenge, largely due to the structure of the trade and its operations, as well as the design of the taxi vehicle itself," according to European officials. In America, disability advocates often made taxis the punchline in a sarcastic accessibility joke. The numbers of accessible taxis and/or vans in the 1970s was negligible.[22]

With even government agencies calling for overall transportation reform, an angry disability lobby finally took to the streets over the issue of transportation access.

One ADAPT member recounts how the militant protests in Denver finally made a difference:

> They blocked off the intersection of Colfax and Broadway, the busiest intersection in downtown Denver, blocking buses with their bodies, and getting out of their wheelchairs and lying in the street. That action eventually led to RTD making all of its buses wheelchair accessible. That was the "shot heard 'round the world"; once people with disabilities in other cities heard about that action, they wanted to learn how to do direct action to bring about change.[23]

Hale Zukas, honored by BART (Bay Area Rapid Transit) for his disability and transportation activism in 1970s (he co-founded the ILC at Berkeley) in 2012, recalled even after the 1977 demonstrations how many battles were still left:

> General Motors had just come out with its new transit bus, and General Motors was very opposed to TransBus [a proposed accessible bus design]. One day in 1978, they brought one of their buses to Capitol Hill to demonstrate. That morning a group of us met with the chairman of GM and they gave a group of

---

[21] New York Department of City Planning. *Transportation for the Elderly and Handicapped of Harlem*. 1979.

[22] European Conference of Ministers of Transportation (ECMT). *Improving Access to Taxis*. Paris: OECD Publishing, 2007; other ECMT documents.

[23] "Angry Black Womyn." Accessed at http://www.angryblackwomyn.com/.

congressmen a tour. I raced down the street--their bus had the lift in the back door. So I went to a mid-block bus stop where buses could not pull in, and the designer of the lift had to get me off the curb.[24]

Zukas, and many others as well, continued to demonstrate for transportation access throughout the 1980s and into the post ADA era. In cities like New York, which had converted to buses in 1947, it would be up to fifty years later that ramps and accessible buses routinely became available. Although some consider the battle for transportation access to be a major victory for the DRM, the truth is that it was a gradual, grinding, hard-fought and often incomplete victory that still is being fought in the present.[25]

Transportation access varied wildly from city to city; Seattle had a reputation for innovation and ease of access; St. Louis, the opposite. Some cities, due to population and sympathetic media coverage, were more battlegrounds than others. In New York, Mobility Through Access continued sit-ins against the MTA into the 1980s. In 2000, activists protested against the inaccessibility of Greyhound buses (and did so with the sympathetic help of drivers and employees). As of 2011, only half of the Yellow Cabs in New York City were accessible, so the victories in disability transportation protest still must be considered partially incomplete.[26]

Special Education

Nowhere was the Disability Rights Movement more sorely needed than in the public schools, where the accommodation of exceptionality varied widely from state to state, and system to system. In some progressive, wealthier systems advanced reading programs and other sophisticated interventions could be found; in others, often rural, there were no special programs and alarming drop-out rates. The Education for All Handicapped Children Act (later known as the Individuals with Disabilities Education Act, or IDEA), or Public Law 98–142 as it was known popularly at the time, was a landmark attempt to set a national agenda for

---

[24] Cowan, Kathy, & Bonney, Sharon (interviewers). *Builders and Sustainers of the Independent Living Movement in Berkeley: Volume III, Eric Dibner, Advocate and Specialist in Architectural Accessibility, Hale Zukas, National Disability Activist: Architectural and Transit Accessibility, Personal Assistance Services* (Disability Rights and Independent Living Movement Oral History Series). 1997–1998, Copyright © 2000 by The Regents of the University of California; "BART honors disability rights activist Hale J. Zukas.", April 18, 2012, accessed at www.bart.gov.

[25] Zames.

[26] Zames, pp. 58–59.

disability accessibility for young people—it in essence formally created special education as a national, federalized initiative even though special education had long existed in specific schools and systems, as well as being represented by professional organizations like the Council for Exceptional Children founded in 1922 by Elizabeth Farrell which by this time had been advocating for decades.[27]

IDEA was passed in large result as a consequence of the wider disability civil rights movement that gained significant strength across the board in the seventies and was supported by many of the most visible disability activists. People with disabilities had historically been neglected in education, but children with disabilities were always a special case of the special case; sometimes for the better, sometimes for the worse. Even in the 1970s examples could be found where infants of normal intelligence and ability who were abandoned by their parents were unilaterally institutionalized and neglected to the point where that neglect actually contributed to them becoming disabled. On the other hand, there were some established schools for disability that enjoyed success. In a state and culture where universal access to education for the non-disabled was increasingly the norm, this kind of inconsistency was no longer unacceptable.[28]

Although psychological and education testing has been and still can be abused and misused, the use of such tools in the 1970s proved it also could be used to liberate and connect young people to new resources and forms of help they otherwise would not have received. The revolution behind IDEA was in part that the science of psychology and social science of education could be combined to improve access and student learning outcomes, and should be made available to those who qualified. The other element following on Brown vs. Board of Education was a growing moral imperative to rectify a long-standing unfairness in educational access.

In the 1970s it was still common for parents of children with special needs to have schools refuse to accept their child for enrollment. Children with developmental disabilities, for example, might find some success in early grades when the pedagogy was more developmental by design, but often were ignored and discriminated against actively in middle grades (if they got that far). IDEA provided tools for the first time to address the situation across state lines and without regard to socio-economic status (although all current special educators know that the system is still fraught with inequities).

---

[27] Winzer, Margaret A. *The History of Special Education: From Isolation to Integration.* Washington DC: Gallaudet University Press, 1993, p. 335.

[28] See for much of this section: "Archived: A 25 year history of the IDEA," available from the U.S. Department of Education, and accessed June 13, 2015 at http://www2.Ed.gov.

Special education was an attempt at the marriage of modern social science and modern sociological theory—the theory of learning disabilities, for example, could now work hand in hand with the theory of role valorization, and normalization.

The IDEA (originally EHA) would become known for several key philosophical and practical requirements. One of them was the idea that a child should be educated in the least restrictive environment (LRE). This notion led to mainstreaming and inclusion, frameworks that let students with disabilities be "normal" students wherever possible, and be educated with their peers whether they had disabilities or not. Although there are always cases where a student can't meet learning objectives in a "regular" classroom (arguably they are few and far in-between), critics have been surprised to see just how well students with disabilities actually do in many inclusive situations. Such successes, hard-won, and often in the face of adversity, clearly expose the cultural bias about disability that continues to persist into the present time, but that the IDEA was clearly intended to address.

The law also required that schools provide at least one meal per day to students with disabilities, ensuring that wellness would be seen as a physical and educational requirement for success. For some students with profound disabilities, even when they couldn't be educated in the same academic classroom (for math, for example), they could still eat, exercise and socialize with their peers in other areas.

IDEA was also the first serious attempt to smooth out socio-economic inequities in public education. Students with disabilities came from all types of family backgrounds, like other students, but their parents generally incurred more medical and other related expenses, and the cultural bias built into many educational and psychological tests and measurements continues to mean that many students in marginalized categories are found eligible for special education at higher rates than others. IDEA embraced the notion of free and appropriate public education (FAPE), which clearly indicated that the parent's ability to pay for something should not determine what types of educational accommodation their child could receive at school. Although FAPE has not been a panacea, by any means, it was a sea-shift that was just as important as the evolution of new testing tools to diagnose and address diverse learning needs.[29]

[29.] Jones, Thomas N., & Semler, Darel P. (Eds.). "School Law Update." *Preventive School Law*, pp. 179–188. For complete document, see EA 016 748.

To the federal government's credit, there had been movement in the 1960s and even earlier to embrace elements of these crucial philosophical ideas. Key legislation and programs that the Department of Education identifies in their own history of special education include: the Training of Professional Personnel Act of 1959 (PL 86-158) which attempted to help set standards for professionalizing teachers of children with disabilities (and 85-926 did something similar for teachers of students with mental retardation); or the Teachers of the Deaf Act of 1961 (PL 87-276) which helped with the improvement of training for teachers of the deaf. Before IDEA, the key overarching legislation was the 1965 Elementary and Secondary Education Act (PL 89-10) which directly aided states in educating students with disabilities.[30]

Beyond children and education, PL 98-142 was hardly the only legislation impacting the handicapped/disabled in the 94h Congress. Between 1975 and 1976, there were some 140 bills or resolutions introduced that impacted disability directly, ranging from determinations about historical building waivers (which DRM activists opposed in many cases) to reduced airfares for the disabled (which many DRM activists supported). As with nearly every Congress, the vast majority of these did not leave committee and never became laws, but the impact of PL 98-142 was out of proportion with everything else. It was quickly understood to be a landmark for education, the way 504 was for transportation.[31]

Many parents of children with disabilities at the time were overjoyed with the passage of the IDEA. In the 1980s, the law was expanded to include parent training, as well as more services for early childhood. Most recently, IDEA legislation has worked in tandem with other sweeping reforms such as No Child Left Behind, to individualize and accommodate students in a wide variety of educational situations who are struggling to learn.

Not everyone was as enthusiastic about the 98-142 legislation as some parents and educators were. President Ford, for example, apparently signed it reluctantly:

> I have approved S. 6, the Education for All Handicapped Children Act of 1975. Unfortunately, this bill promises more than the Federal Government can deliver, and its good intentions could be thwarted by the many unwise provisions it contains.[32]

---

[30] Zames.

[31] Congressional Records, 94th Congress. Various summaries.

[32] "President Gerald R. Ford's Statement on Signing the Education for All Handicapped Children Act of 1975." December 2, 1975 [NOTE: As enacted, S. 6, approved November 29, 1975, is Public Law 94-142 (89 Stat. 773)] accessed July 2, 2015 at http://www.fordlibrarymuseum.gov/library/speeches/750707.htm.

In spite of that, Barbara Keough, an educator at the University of California, Los Angeles, recalled that the law was clearly seen by special educators and others as a broad and important civil rights victory:

> PL 94-142 and subsequent legislation are best understood against the backdrop of political unrest and the civil rights movement. The United States Supreme Court had ruled earlier that "separate but equal" education for different racial groups was not constitutional, and in the 1960s and 1970s education became part of the controversy over civil rights...[33]

As a result of the IDEA, and subsequent legislation and advocacy, public education in the United States is more seamless and inclusive than it has ever been before (which isn't to say there still aren't inequities—but there has been progress). In the present time, expanded legislation allows educators to design interventions based on individual student need, including students without disabilities who might have been ignored even a decade or two previously—such as the thousands of children who speak English as a second language, or ESL learners. The legacy of the IDEA, like the overarching DRM, is a civil rights victory, fostering inclusion, growing acceptance, and a wide public agreement on the goal of equal access.

The Uprising at Gallaudet in 1988: "Deaf President Now!"

No recent disability protest captures as many elements of the modern Disability Rights Movement as the student uprising at Gallaudet University in 1988. Although almost exclusively a school for deaf students, the president of the institution had traditionally been a hearing person. When the search committee met to begin the process for selecting a new president, a group of young alums decided to take matters into their own hands; they demanded a deaf president now.

---

[33] Keogh, Barbara K. "Celebrating PL 94-142: The Education of All Handicapped Children Act of 1975." *Issues in Teacher Education*, Volume 16, Number 2, Fall 2007, pp. 65–69.

The alumni and student uprising would eventually encompass a number of DRM firsts and notables, including:

- First widely reported disability protest that was clearly linked to a wider civil rights perspective
- First major injection of deaf culture and issues of disability identity conspicuously seen in the national media
- Educated the nation collectively about deaf culture

Prominent leaders, like Senator Tom Harkin, an architect of the ADA, wrote letters of support:

AN OPEN LETTER TO STUDENTS, FACULTY, STAFF, ADMINISTRATORS, ALUMNI AND BOARD OF TRUSTEES OF GALLAUDET UNIVERSITY

Dear Folks:

Congratulations. You have succeeded in educating the world about deafness, the concerns of deaf people, and the simple truth that we all need and are entitled to dignity and respect. You communicated your message with clarity and forcefulness. Your actions will have a positive impact on future generations of hearing and deaf persons both here and abroad. By your actions, you have brought the deaf community together. You are my heroes. I look forward to meeting the next President of Gallaudet University -- who I expect will be deaf.

Sincerely,
Tom Harkin
Chairman

Although the students used traditional techniques like sit-ins, blocking traffic on the street, and writing letters (with demands), and eventually accomplished their goal, it was the impact on the wider American culture that left an indelible mark that is part of the fabric now of the DRM.[34]

[34.] Baynton, Douglas. "Disability and the Justification of Inequality in American History." Baynton, Douglas, & Umansky, Lauri (Eds.). *The New Disability History: American Perspectives*. New York University Press, 2001; Zames, pp. 28–29; "Issues." Accessed at http://www.gallaudet.edu/dpn_home/issues/history_behind_dpn.html; documents at the Gallaudet history of DPN site; http://www.washingtonpost.com/local/education/gallaudet-marks-deaf-president-now/2013/02/07/17666740-6fdc-11e2-8b8d-e0b59a1b8e2a_story.html.

Psychological Disability

The term handicap, and later disability, and all the preceding terms had primarily meant physical difference for thousands of years. Humans (at least in the Western Tradition) had difficult separating physical disability from psychological or invisible disabilities. To go mad was to defy labels, logic and medicine, and although there were cases in almost all periods when certain types of madness were associated with prophecy, gifted insight, or certain artistic abilities, the rule by and large was a stigmatization that was more pervasive and less charitable than that which usually accompanied clearly physical disabilities.

The failures of two waves of institutionalization—first, in the antebellum period from 1820 to 1860; the second from 1875 to 1925—to neatly resolve the tension between medical advances with the utter lack of integration into mainstream society, ultimately led to the de-institutionalization movement, specifically for mental-health oriented patients. Building on the wider Independent Living Movement, which had often focused on physical disabilities, this movement spawned a branch of the DRM that specifically targeted individuals with invisible, psychological-orient disabilities for activism, independence, and freedom from the oppressive stigma and institutional structures they had endured for centuries even dating back to the Old World.

Author and researcher Seth Farber recounts the significance of the shift, and one of the social scientists responsible for it:

> In early 1970s the mental patients liberation movement was spontaneously launched in America. The movement was organized by people who had read and embraced the theories of Thomas Szasz. Mental patients' liberation organizations started in Portland, in New York and Boston in 1970 and 1971 and spread up and down the coasts and even to parts of the heartland. Reading Szasz's books made it possible for the "mentally ill" to redefine themselves in ways many of them could not have imagined before Szasz - as survivors of psychiatric oppression, as heroes in the anti-psychiatric Resistance.[35]

What is now referred to sometimes as the mental health "consumer/survivor movement" made steady progress, building on the Independent Living Movement

---

[35] Farber, Seth. *The Spiritual Gift of Madness: The Failure of Psychiatry and the Rise of the Mad Pride Movement.* Inner Traditions, 2012; "Szasz and Beyond." Accessed at http://www.madinamerica.com/2012/11/szasz-and-beyondthe-spiritual-promise-of-the-mad-pride-movement/.

and advances in medicine and pharmacology that helped normalize many types of mental illnesses. More importantly, the movement allowed individuals more freedom to come together and share their stories, and then to organize.

The advocacy of the seventies continues today as a result of the movement. More recently in 2006, for example, grant monies funded the creation of the National Coalition for Mental Health Recovery (NCMHR), a wide-ranging initiative to bring diverse mental health oriented groups under one umbrella to education and lobby for change. There are presently thirty six member organizations, and the NCMHR is a partner with the National Disability Leadership Alliance (NDLA), which also includes groups like ADAPT, the American Association of People with Disabilities (AAPD), and Not Dead Yet, to name just a few. The creation and growth of the NCMHR was a result of the mental health revolution that began in the 1970s.[36]

Addiction recovery, or simply "recovery," evolved into a highly specialized medical, counseling, and human services field in its own right. Addiction, as much as any disability or medical condition, highlights the ongoing semantic complications between the terms disease and disability. Addiction is frequently referred to as a disease, but its effects are more disabling than some traditional "disabilities." Addiction has been litigated in disability courtrooms, with sometimes less than clarifying results, although alcoholism is more accepted as a genuine disability than it was when the ADA was initially passed. The truth test for recovery is quantified by the explosion of resources devoted to it, ranging from a proliferation of non-profits to federalized and state-funded resources to train counselors and modify behavior, as well as new support for families going through recovery.[37]

The growing awareness of the problematic dichotomy between physical and psychological disabilities, or in many cases visible verses invisible disabilities, allowed later architects of the disability rights movement to build on the efforts of those like Ed Roberts who had argued in the radical sixties that disabilities of all types shared more in common than they were held separate by their "minor" differences. It was a radical argument to make in the sixties when groups of individuals with specific conditions had been congregated in single purpose institutions for the sake of streamlining services; it was a neo-modern argument in the 1980s that would ultimately become a mini movement within the larger

---

[36] NDLA. "History of the National Coalition for Mental Health Recovery;" "National Disability Leadership Alliance." Documents accessed on June 25, 2015 at http://ncmhr.org.

[37] The Virginia Department of Behavioral Health & Developmental Services. *Peer Recovery Specialist Training Manual*, 2nd edition. Office of Recovery Services, 2019.

DRM that focused specifically on normalizing, and de-stigmatizing mental health-related disabilities.

The implications and effects of the Mad Pride or wider psychological disability rights movement are still currently being felt in great force. Colleges and universities, for example, who geared programs in the 1970s for students with learning disabilities, started programs in the 1980s and 1990s for attention deficit disorders, are now designing programs and interventions for students with psychological disabilities like Bi-Polar Disorder, and students on the Asperger's/Autism Spectrum (ASD) who are appearing in record numbers in new freshmen classes. These are largely students who would not have accessed higher education before the DRM, or Mad Pride.

There is also a growing school of thought in the present that recognizes the complexity of the human condition, suggesting that ability and disability are present in every individual in varying degrees and that in some more exceptional cases, the two elements cannot be neatly separated. The theory of Twice Exceptionality (2E) is a theory that promotes the benefits of the dyslexic brain, for example, or highlights how many famous leaders and innovators throughout history have used their psychological challenges to further their success. In the theory of 2E, giving up the disability might also mean giving up the giftedness, or the essence of who the special person is. This idea had its roots in the seventies, when psychiatric patients were being mainstreaming and coping with a world that did not always see their abilities.

This is consistent with the concept of intersectionality, which increasingly sees our multiple identities in constant byplay with each other, as well as with external forces. A relatively new field entitled DisCrit (a combination of Critical Race Theory and Disability Studies) places such byplay at the forefront of its knowledge-gathering efforts. Such scholarly efforts are now increasingly reflected in the mainstream media, where conversations about race and disability in tandem appear more frequently and in greater depth of analysis.[38]

Michel Foucault, author of *Madness and Civilization*, and many other postmodernists, would be astonished if they were alive today to witness the degree to which concepts of identity relating to psychological conditions have shifted. Nowhere is that accomplishment highlighted more profoundly than in the area of psychological disabilities, where a disorder like Attention Deficit Disorder (ADD) which was poorly understood and heavily stigmatized in the seventies, has now become a "designer" disability where some college students or their

---

[38] Gupta, Shalene. "You have to scream out" part of "Inheritance." *The Atlantic*, Sept. 21, 2021.

parents "fake it" in order to receive academic, testing, and even social benefits from it; ADD/ADHD is the ongoing target of million dollar pharmaceutical ad campaigns.

This change can only be understood in the context of the radical sixties, the ILM, deinstitutionalization, and an evolving social construction of disability in the 1970s.

Addition and Recovery

The rapid expansion of disability definitions and protections in the 1980s quickly brought addiction and related conditions into the mainstream public discourse. Alcoholism, illegal drug use, drug abuse, addition and related problems had long been seen as poor choices rather than medical afflictions that were deserving of medical treatment, and just as importantly, worthy of the de-stigmatization that was taking place with physical disabilities and a little more slowly with psychological disabilities, as well.

Opponents of disability legislation often cited substance abuse, alcoholism, and even AIDs as fundamental exceptions to disability protection, in spite of the growing medical information that suggested many situations were not a result of so-called lifestyle choices, or just illegal behavior, but rather were firmly rooted in neuropsychology, a deep cultural bias, sometimes genetics and family history, and were sometimes even more highly stigmatized than overt physical disabilities. The recovery movement has converted many celebrities and notable politicians in recent history to the cause of addressing these public (mis)perceptions, even as an underground therapeutic movement has continued to move above ground regardless of political trends.

Landmarks in the history of recovery and addition include:

- Mid 1700s Native American "recovery circles"
- 1784 Benjamin rush authors "An inquiry into the effects of ardent spirits"
- Late 1800s growth of inebriate asylums
- 1908 professionals begin regularly using the term "alcoholism" (coined in 1849)
- 1935 founding of Alcoholics Anonymous (AA)

- 1950–1953 founding of Narcotics Anonymous (each coast)
- 1978 First Lady Betty Ford announces her struggle with addiction

In the late 20th and early 21st centuries, the recovery movement has continued to gain strength and numbers and currently represents a sizable lobby group, promoting legislation and wider education about recovery and addition.[39]

[39.] White, William. *Slaying the Dragon: The History of Addiction Treatment and Recovery in America*, 2nd Ed. Bloomington, IL: Chestnut Health Systems, 2014, pp. xvii, xviii, 507–508, 520, etc.

The Battle in Congress for the ADA

Section 504 had been a success in many ways; it had also been a failure in other significant respects that exposed the need for an over-arching legislative law or constitutional amendment. Although it was in its own right ground-breaking civil rights legislation, it also left many access areas unaddressed, including the behavior of private businesses and corporations, as well as organizations which did not directly receive federal funding. The need for a broader civil rights statement was made crystal clear by the challenges that the Section 504 victory uncovered, including the painful quest to see regulations actually implemented (or accommodations actually made, if you will).

In 1988, a Congressional hearing considered the current need for additional disability legislation. Arlene Mayerson recounted:

> A room which seated over 700 people overflowed with persons with disabilities, parents and advocates. After the hearing, a commitment was made by Senator Kennedy, Chair of the Labor and Human Resources Committee, Senator Harkin, Chair of the Subcommittee on Disability Policy, and Representative Owens of the House Subcommittee on Select Education, that a comprehensive disability civil rights bill would be a top priority for the next Congress. At the same time, both presidential candidates, Vice President Bush and Governor Dukakis, endorsed broad civil rights protections for people

with disabilities. The disability community was determined to assure that President Bush would make good on his campaign promise, and re-invoked it repeatedly during the legislative process.[40]

Some of the battle to bring forward broader initiatives has already been discussed in this and previous chapters, and was essentially street-level, sometimes scattered public activism. The real battle for the ADA ultimately took place on the floor and in committee within Congress, where a mostly unanimous final vote on the ADA (377 to 28 in the House; 91 to 7 in the Senate) belied the initial uncertainty and extent of potential opposition that really existed.[41]

After initially passing in the Senate, the proposed bill passed through an unusual number of committees in the House, making some proponents nervous about possible attempts to stonewall the process. Amendments were proposed and failed, and in the meantime corporations and business owners, fearful of unfunded mandates that would force them to close doors, lobbied hard to see the bill stay in committee and put tremendous public pressure on legislators. Disability activists, for their part, tried to fill the galleys and hallways outside for every hearing or public event, and maintain a strong voice in support.

Ultimately, legislators were able to cross the aisle and go against the pressure of lobbyists for business interests, and send the bill out of committee to be considered on the floor.

Representative Steny Hoyer proudly reported:

> Madam Speaker, yesterday the Education and Labor Committee, by a vote of 35 to 0 passed out the Americans with Disabilities Act. I want to observe that that event occurred because of the bipartisan work of a number of us, the support of the President of the United States, and the overwhelming vote given to the document by the U.S. Senate. The Americans With Disabilities Act will fairly and reasonably extend civil rights protection to 43 million disabled Americans and insure that the words, 'and justice for all,' will ring true for all Americans. Madam Speaker, yesterday's markup and the support of the gentleman from Texas and the minority whip of the House reemphasize the bipartisan support for this

---

[40] Mayerson, Arlene. *The History of the Americans with Disabilities Act: A Movement Perspective, Disability Rights Education & Defense Fund.* DREDF, 1992, accessed July 2, 2015 at http://dredf.org/news/publications/the-history-of-the-ada/.

[41] Congressional Records. "Senate Bill 933." Accessed at https://www.congress.gov/bill/101st-congress/senate-bill/933/all-info.

landmark legislation. I expect and hope that the three remaining committees of jurisdiction will soon complete their work. I look forward to House passage and enactment of the bill sponsored by our former majority whip, Tony Coelho, the Americans with Disabilities Act, early next year.[42]

Ultimately, the year 1990 represents a significant watershed event in American history. A large proportion of Americans are alive today who have never known an America without significant civil rights protections for individuals with disabilities. Children attend schools not knowing there was a time when there was no special education. The 2008 reauthorization of the ADA in the face of court losses only served to underscore what a dramatic event the 1990 law had actually been (and how difficult it was and is for any civil rights law by itself to deconstruct underlying stigmas and structural barriers).[43]

Conclusion

The 1970s and 1980s saw significant changes in the amount of media coverage, exposure in popular semantics and discourse, and a heightened degree of legislative debate surrounding disability. Attention deficit disorders, for example, became household words, and the interventions for psychological disabilities including pharmacological treatments grew into a multi-billion dollar industry (which some compared to the pill craze of the 1950s). Schools were suddenly accommodating students under the Section 504 legislation, or IDEA, in record numbers; resources were stretched; mistakes were made. Disability began to be a more common feature element in film and art, and medical terminology shifted as a result from handicapped people to individuals with disabilities (IWD or PWD).

These cultural shifts, even with some opposition, were pervasive, and explain in part why the debate in Congress over the ADA ultimately became a lop-sided affirmative vote. They were changes that fueled further radicalism. They were changes only made possible by the work of pioneering activists with disabilities and their supporters in the earlier, stormy sixties.

---

[42] Representative Steny Hoyer. "Bipartisan Support Noted for American With Disabilities Act." House of Representatives, November 15, 1989, Page: H8637, Congressional Records.

[43] Pear, Robert. "Congress Passes Bill with Protections for DisablEd." *New York Times*, September 17, 2008.

CHAPTER 8

Conclusion 21st Century Strands of the DRM

The social history of disability in America is a story which contains many connected threads. In practically every phase, for example, veterans have played a prominent role in it. Disabled veterans have sometimes had the social capital to make demands for accommodation that were not easily denied by a grateful nation. They have sometimes returned home in sheer numbers that turned their rehabilitation or reintegration into a national expediency. Because they were often the target of federalized resources, they often were the first to benefit from new technologies, treatments, and accommodations that were facilitated by the massive capabilities of the federal government. Although trickledown economics may have its own set of historical complications, it appears that trickledown accommodations for individuals with disabilities who were *not* in military service has arguably been a success and made a major impact on the overall disability landscape. Veterans, wittingly and sometimes unwittingly, have been on the frontlines of the American disability experience since the American Revolution and eventually became an active part of the American DRM in 1960s and 1970s.[1]

The social history of disability in America involves people, but it also involves ideas. One of those ideas, which has an ironic twist to it, is American rugged individualism. For hundreds of years American and Colonial North American culture emphasized the individual conquering the daunting physical environment and overcoming personal challenges to ultimately persevere. While such mythmaking resulted in dramatic rags to riches stories, frontier survival tales, and small-town heroes who rose to the presidency or to generalship, it also fostered and sustained a negative stereotype where individuals with disabilities were routinely blamed for their own plight, and perceived as needing to

---

[1.] Gerber, David A. (Ed.). *Disabled Veterans in History*, Enlarged and Revised Edition. Ann Arbor, MI: The University of Michigan Press, 2012.

"do their part" to address their own situation. When individuals with disabilities did triumph over long odds, or "pull their own weight," it tended to reinforce the cultural norm (rugged individualism), rather than challenge the flawed status quo (inaccessibility and lack of accommodation).

This can be considered a peculiarly American form of the "normate." The term normate is singular, ironically, and highlights the lack of communal responsibility sometimes typical of the American experience as it relates to people with disabilities. The radicalism of the sixties ultimately demonstrated the necessity of shared responsibility between the disabled and non-disabled, and began to deconstruct the notion of individualism, yet even so the idea remains strong in American culture even into the new century. The charity model for understanding disability also worked in tandem with individualism to imply that somehow people with disabilities just couldn't do it for themselves—unless "we" helped them do it—ignoring the vast untapped possibilities in human capital, and impeding agency for people with disabilities.

Another theme that evolves from studying American disability history is the competitive spirit of the American people. The race to develop prosthetic limbs after the Civil War, the booming business of special education in the public schools in the 1980s, or the Veteran's Administration-driven traumatic injury revolution of early 21st century all demonstrate how Americans often "send a man to the moon" metaphorically speaking when major problems are identified and collectively addressed. This, again, has had both positive and negative impacts. On the one hand, no one wants to see their child born with a disease or disability that can easily be prevented; on the other, it perpetuates the cure model mentality which suggests that curing a disability is the only solution, rather than accepting and accommodating and hence fully valuing the human being as they are, disability or not.

Competition is also part of capitalism, and combined with the Protestant work ethic, Americans have sometimes been suspicious or even discriminatory towards those who don't work, compete, and contribute to the "system." In this book, Civil War veterans returning home with disabilities after the war experienced great angst about their (in)ability to work productively. This angst has been an ever-present anxiety for people with disabilities throughout the American experience for several hundreds of years. As you are reading this text, people with disabilities are *still* up to four times more likely to be unemployed despite comparable education levels and skillsets. If competition in the American system means getting the best job and making the most money people with disabilities are automatically moved further behind the starting line for the race.

Advances in healthcare and medical accommodations for disability also have been an evolving American theme, whether Colonial doctors adopting new Native American techniques hundreds of years ago, or 21st century geneticists who are identifying neurological triggers for psychiatric disorders. Although radical disability activists have often correctly questioned strictly medical understandings of disability, there is also no empirical reason to deny that medical advances based on modern scientific techniques have eliminated, mitigated, and spread understanding of a significant number of chronic human disabilities and diseases. No one need die of a papercut anymore since the advent of antibiotics.

On the other hand, expansion of healthcare resources and technical medical advances create another inequality loop, especially in America. The very nature of American federalism means that some states have better disability resources than others. Some treatments and medical assistive devices are more readily available to the affluent. There is also little room to deny the lack of full and fair access to beneficial medical science that individuals with disabilities still confront in spite of new healthcare laws and continued civil rights efforts to the contrary.[2]

There is also the ever-present danger of technology and medicine becoming an end unto themselves and scratching the long festering itch of eugenics. There are ample historical examples—including in this text—that an improved human race is not always a *better* human race, or a more equitable and loving human race. America remains at risk of falling into medical solutions and new technologies that are ripe for this seduction.

What does this mean about this time, and about this new century?

More than fifty years after the Disability Rights Movement began in earnest in the 1960s, America is now journeying into neomodernism (see Appendix A), a place where disability remains about physical difference, and physiognomy (judging a book by its cover) cannot apparently be fully engineered out of humans, but also a place where social justice, education, the study of identity in sociology, and universal design principles provide important counter narratives. In spite of the many shortcomings in a long disability history, America stands on the other side of a 1990 ADA divide, where the conversations now turn to much more sophisticated, complicated, and important moral aspects of disability issues, and less often deny that the conversations should actually be taking place or attempt to repudiate the complicated history.

---

[2] Peacock, Georgina: Lezzoni, Lisa I.; & Harkin, Thomas R.. "Health Care for Americans with Disabilities: 25 Years after the ADA." *The New England Journal of Medicine*, 373, No. 10, 2015, pp. 892–93.

The intervening years since ADA were not always filled with successes, so the future should not be foreseen necessarily as smooth. Immediately after the 1990 passage of the Americans with Disabilities Act, complainants (often private businesses or their employees with accommodation complaints) took their cause to court, and to the media. In 1992, for example, disability activists protested the barriers to accessibility at the iconic Empire State Building in New York City. Later, they took the management of the structure to court. In fact, between 1990 and the reauthorization in 2008, hundreds of court decisions were necessary as a result of similar complaints, more than ninety percent of which were judged by the court against the person or group with disabilities bringing the complaint (and therefore almost always supporting employers or bureaucracies, who quicky learned that the odds were on their side), which gutted the initial strength and meaning of the original legislation. The reauthorization in 2008 negated that court history and re-established, again, for the second time, the priority for disability access as a basic human civil right.[3]

The amendments also attempted to deconstruct the label, or the tattoo, as the original Greeks linguistically described it. For most individuals in America seeking accommodations in the last fifty years, having a label or a specific diagnosis was the key to unlocking services or gaining official approval for accommodations. The 1990 legislation codified this, but the unintended outcome was the creation of a system where labels could actually be used to keep people locked out of services like special education, or denied accommodations in the workplace.

If you are thinking "without the label you can't get accommodations" but "with the label you will be discriminated against," then you are contemplating a small piece of the frustrating contradiction that drove the DRM. Labels are the ultimate expression of modernism, Westernism, empiricism, and standard medical history. Traditionally, symptoms and supporting data are gathered in order to culminate in a label (or diagnosis). Then a course of treatment can be developed. The postmodern, and then the neomodern DRM, were from their roots intensely interested in rejecting labels at the cultural level (still often recognizing their importance at the practical or medical level). Neomodernism is in many ways a rejection of labels, and the subsequent hierarchies associated with them, and is consistent with the language of the 2008 reauthorization. It is consistent with the philosophies of disability studies and intersectionality in sociology and how they confront power and hierarchies.

---

[3] Andrews, E. L.. "Disabled people protect lack of accessibility at Empire State Building." *New York Times*, 01/28/1992, Vol. 141, Issue 48859, p. B1.

In the future, for better or worse, there will still be labels and hierarchies. An indicator of how hierarchies work in Foucauldian terms is exposed when examining the treatment of deaf prisoners, to show just one small structure within a much larger paradigm. Incarceration rates for individuals with disabilities are much higher than the general population would predict, yet even within that prison population there are hierarchies. Some sources suggest that there are significantly higher rates of disability lawsuit prison complaints amongst the deaf, for example. Yet at a recent large correctional science convention, no sessions were offered addressing the situation of the deaf in prison. ADHD, on the other hand, is routinely studied in prison populations, and the availability of treatments and accommodations fairly wide spread, and growing rapidly.[4]

The 21st century in America presents a number of new critical issues that the founding figures would never have anticipated, but which the ongoing neomodern DRM must address: genetic engineering and potentially designer babies; growth of replacement organs and possibly even replacement limbs; designer drugs designed for the specific person's brain; cloning; a universal design (UD) revolution sweeping into remote corners of popular culture (ex. designer prosthetics, and even intentional disablement); and a possibility that soon more humans will be alive at one time than had previously existed altogether in written history, and a record number of them will be disabled. Although Social Darwinism and Malthusian notions of population control presumably died stillborn after two World Wars and the Holocaust, the specters created by that science still haunt the halls of laboratories, universities, and pharmaceutical manufacturers in spite of the hard lessons learned.

Disability, as it has for thousands of years, will likely remain a human constant. In this sense, disability is not an accident—it is an ordinary/extraordinary expression of human individuality and difference. This new century will be a century of disability.

Lennard Davis believes that America has entered into or perhaps now has even passed through a period of Dismodernism, a time when the experience and identity of disability is so powerful and openly recognized as a universal human experience that it creates a new meta-narrative; one that will perhaps end once and for all any notion that empirical explanations alone of disorder and disability can fully explain the lived experience of disablement. Moreover, the increasingly public familiarity with disability, along with perhaps a gradual softening of the hard wiring of the brain, suggests that we are living in a different kind of era.

[4.] Deaf Digest. "American Correctional Association ignoring the deaf needs?" 2014/01/14, accessed http://deafdigest.net.

Identity, as sociologists often claim, may be inherently unstable. Humans continue to evolve, as studies show that children who have grown up keyboarding instead of writing by hand have a new neural understanding of language unique in human history; the plasticity of the brain has become the 21st century metaphor for shifting constructions of identity and perhaps, increasingly, disability.[5]

Science, for its part, now provides amazing accommodations and adaptations that few would want to argue should not be available humans. Science and medicine continue to dazzle. Sometimes, people with disabilities reject forms of help that might seem logical or obviously beneficial to the non-disabled. Although many doctors and social scientists continue to shelter in the purely empirical and rational explanations of disability, which allow many very intelligent people to sleep soundly at night, there is still an irrationality about the disability experience that flirts with and sometimes enters into the monstrous sublime. Sometimes, disability (like humans in general) must be irrational.[6]

There is also the persistent problem in America, as elsewhere, of social and economic inequality. If advances in science, medicine and technology are a beacon of light on the one hand, they are also the harbingers of inequality if access remains limited to those with economic means or good healthcare, which would seem to be the case at this point in time. The capitalist system in general has yet to resolve the problem of fairness in terms of economic benefits and the persistence of political and cultural Otherness that limits who gets it.

In the 21st century is has become apparent that some forms of Otherness still matter more than others, and whether they are defined legally or culturally as a disability is a matter for debate. ADD/ADHD has been identified by some anthropologists as a survival advantage in pre-agricultural societies, while it has been labeled as a medical disorder in the late 20th and early 21st century. Some disabilities, however, are an advantage in some cultural contexts. Some argue now that disability can be economic, or cultural, or even other forms of stigmatized identities. DisCrit argues that race and disability are practically synonymous in many ways. It can also be argued that people can be economically disabled.

In America, disability has never been defined *completely* by legal dictate, or by medical expertise, but has also been defined by the functionality of individuals, their quality of life, and increasingly over time by the spirit of equity typified in the better parts of our constitutional tradition. Disability is arguably, still, mostly

---

[5] Davis, Lennard. *Bending over Backwards: Disability, Dismodernism & other Difficult Positions.* New York University Press, 2002.

[6] Kearney, Richard. *Strangers, Gods and Monsters: Interpreting Otherness.* Routledge, 2003.

socially constructed. If we all had one leg instead of two, our escalators would be ten inches wide, and having two legs would be a disability.

Increasingly in the 21st century, disability will be defined by personal choice and personal identity, and by the mass media, as much as it is defined by scientific or medical labels. Although perhaps too optimistic, the arc of disability equity and awareness has moved over time as I hope this text shows. Neomodernism may in essence (hopefully) be science with a socially constructed moral conscience.

Disability in the Media

One of the most unique variables in the disability 21st century story is social media and a highly evolved mass media. Never has there been a time comparable to the one in the new century in terms of overall disability media coverage; control, manipulation and portrayal of personal disability identity; volume of disability content in the streaming, cinematic, and visual mediums; and the overall level of public discourse about disability. In that sense, the DRM is now in uncharted territory. Whereas one hundred fifty years ago the profoundly disabled were often hidden way, now they are often presented in overtly public ways that are largely an erstwhile attempt to normalize attitudes. Today, audiences are increasingly presented with noticeable and perhaps dramatically unexpected changes, ranging from the new Gerber baby to characters with disabilities in Disney movies. Disability activists rightly see the new media coverage and Hollywood portrayal of disability as a double-edged sword, both opening new opportunities and creating unforeseen objectifications and new stereotypes.

Studies of media coverage and disability clearly reveal an exponential increase in the number of stories about disability, the number of shows that feature characters with or themes about disability, and the amount of disability narrative in the general public discourse. Media analysis studies confirm this continuing trend. Disability has debuted on Broadway. The sociology of disability in the new century should focus largely on this media barrage.[7]

A shift has occurred in this media expansion that is likely to continue in the coming years moving away from an emphasis on medical definitions of disability, toward social acceptance, and in some cases, even a semi-privileged status. The example of Attention Deficit Disorder/Attention Deficit Hyperactivity Disorder

---

[7] Haller, Beth. *Representing Disability in an Ableist World: Essays on Mass Media*. Louisville, The Avocado Press, 2010.

(ADD/ADHD) is the ideal example to point out. At the turn of the 20th century, when ADD/ADHD was first studied by British researcher Sir George F. Still, the disorder was classified as an "abnormal defect of moral control," or even as a damaged brain. At the turn of the 21st century, ADD/ADHD is often being treated as a "designer disability," which one can easily obtain a prescription for, has become much more socially acceptable, and has even had documented incidents of "cheating" where people faked the disability to gain an accommodation or advantage on an entrance exam or similar requirement. Ironically, this same problem troubled legislators designing benefits for disabled sailors in the 18th century and has been a quiet but consistent criticism of the ADA.[8]

The explosion of disability characters in the media has resulted in a new pride movement that sometimes is specific to the disability—such as ADD/ADHD. Viewers often identify with someone "like them" and feel more comfortable in their own identity. Characters and actors with disabilities appear much more frequently than in the past, ranging from blind New York homicide detectives to a variety of characters routinely using prosthetics; twice as many appeared in 2013 as in the year previous, and the trend is expected to continue. McDonalds' recent Super Bowl television ad featured Down syndrome. The disability identity of the 21st century will include more mainstream media coverage and targeted advertising.[9]

The media, including now social media, has created a virtual reality proposition out of proportion with individual lived experiences in the past. In social media, people can literally choose to be something else other than who they physically are. Disability advocates who once eagerly courted media coverage and saw social media as a leveler now are beginning to understand the other side of that phenomenon. The media defines disability in ways that are beyond the control of any single group, or law, and objectifies simply by its own mandate to "tell the news," entertain, or literally create new identities. A great deal of normalization has taken place; on the other hand, a great deal of control of the meta-narrative about disability has been lost to structural forces beyond the reach, it sometimes appears, of any one advocacy group.

---

[8]. Lange, Klaus, et. al.. "The history of attention deficit hyperactivity disorder." *Attention Deficit Hyperactivity Disorder*, 2010 Dec, 2(4), pp. 241–255, published online 2010 Nov 30; Trammell, Jack. "The Anthropology of Twice Exceptionality: Is Today's Disability Yesterday's (or Tomorrow's) Evolutionary Advantage? A Case Study with ADD/ADHD." In Ambrose, Don, et. al. (Eds.). *A Critique of Creativity and Complexity: Deconstructing Clichés*. Rotterdam, Sense Publishers, 2014, pp. 227–237.

[9]. Disability Scoop. "TV Disabilities Rise." Accessed at http://www.disabilityscoop.com/2013/10/14/tv-disabilities-rise/18802/.

There is now enough sheer bulk to create a growing canon of orthodox disability media that is accepted by scholars and activists as critical to the overall history of the DRM. The existence of such a canon serves to reify the DRM and the field of disability studies itself. Two films that commonly appear in disability readers, for example, are Tod Browning's *Freaks* (1932) and Andrew Niccol's *Gattaca* (1997). Although neither received the types of critical acclaim sought in the film industry, within the world of disability they are considered "classics" that demonstrate the myriad and timeless complexities and ethical conundrums associated with disability, and especially the stigma that remains associated with it.

Browning's 1932 film essentially ended a successful career that had included such hits as *Dracula* and *Iron Man*, and silent films earlier than that. The film was banned in some locales, including Great Britain, and appalled both audiences and the studio higher ups. Its shock effect was amplified by a number of unique qualities: the circus freaks, many of them also "disabled," were essentially the heroes, while the non-disabled characters were portrayed as villainous and vindictive; the freaks were diverse in color, gender, and abilities, while the "normals" were white and privileged; the "normals" were often portrayed by professional actors, while the freaks were real circus freaks Browning intentionally cast as themselves; the freaks represented a radical counter-culture, while the "normals" represented the corruption and hegemony of an entrenched elite. All of this was shown in dramatic, exaggerated fashion, and audiences who typically could not bring themselves to admit or talk about the fact that the United States had a "handicapped" president (FDR) were unable to process it. Browning turned the comfortable world of normality inside and out and dared people to face it.

Gattaca, which portrays a dystopian new world where your resumé is literally your genes, was one of the first serious Hollywood efforts to fully capture the myriad implications of genetic determinism. It is filled with subtle references to the negative American experiences with race, eugenics, physiognomy, medicalization, class stratification, modernity, and of course disability. It overtly mocks the statistical error rates that social science routinely embraces as official.

As the new century unfolds, it would be natural for the disability media canon to expand and diversify, to the benefit of all, from dating apps to serialized shows. The canon will likely keep expanding. To borrow a current phrase, we will be "binge watching" disability in the 21st century.

New Identity Politics

Sociologist Erving Goffman, who studied identity, famously said that one should "choose your self-representations carefully, for what starts out as a mask may become your face." The DRM helped spark an identity revolution in the U.S. that has emphasized heightened individuality (not rugged individualism) and acceptance of self "as is" in ways manifesting from tattoo crazes to gender transformations. Rather than masks, identity might be better said in the present to be complete body suits or even a new virtual self.[10]

The implications for disability are myriad, as prosthetics become better than actual limbs, and students without disabilities use their roommate's medication so they can study more effectively. There will be legal challenges in the coming decades, as culture stretches to incorporate the neomodern disability experience. In fact, it is even possible to envision the 2008 amendments and its attempt to shed labels as a first step in eliminating disability altogether as a legal category (I am aware that may sound radical). If you don't need a label to receive special treatment, then anyone can be disabled or choose to identify that way; if universal design is implemented to its capacity everyone is accommodated. In theory it removes oppression from the system and instead heightens agency.

Goffman was perhaps looking into the future when he wrote in 1963 that:

> Stigma management is a general feature of society, a process occurring wherever there are identity norms. ...One can therefore suspect that the role of normal and the role of stigmatized are part of the same complex... ..persons wonderfully diverse who share nothing but a need to control [identity] information.[11]

The expansion of medical and scientific technology, along with the evolution of a virtual world stemming from the Internet and social media, combine to result in a new environment where people can increasingly choose to identify as disabled or not in major parts of their lives. This was simply not possible in the past without going to great lengths to "wear a different mask." This is evidenced in daily news items reporting individuals who claim identities that they previously might not have been culturally or legally entitled to, and span all of the major

---

[10] Erving Goffman (1959) as quoted in Smith, Eliot R., et. al.. *Social Psychology*: Fourth Edition. Psychology Press, 2014, p. 123.

[11] Goffman, Erving. *Stigma: Notes on the Management of Spoiled Identity*. Englewood Cliffs, NJ: Prentice-Hall, Inc., 1963, p. 130.

identity categories including race and gender. Disclosure, which remains a legal act, is quickly becoming a social choice in many arenas.

In ways that the DRM founders may not have ever envisioned, their movement has helped establish and promote a much larger identity-based civil rights movement that places the old identity politics in a precarious position and leaves a new one (I am calling neomodernism) in an uncertain space.

Twice Exceptionality and Neurodiversity

Part of the new (neomodern) identity landscape is an acceptance of neurodiversity that mirrors the growing acceptance of physical difference/diversity that the DRM has traditionally supported. Some anthropologists and psychologists suggest that the ADD/ADHD arrangement of the pre-frontal cortex, for example, may have been an evolutionary advantage many centuries ago, when humans had a greater need to respond rapidly to stimuli in the environment and consider creative or non-linear approaches to solving immediate issues of survival. In the 21st century, that same brain arrangement is often treated as a disability, according to the *Diagnostic and Statistical Manual*, 5th Edition (APA), and the potential giftedness or simple advantages associated with it sometimes overlooked. Can a brain arrangement be a disability in one culture and timeframe, and an evolutionary advantage in another?[12]

Some doctors, for example, examine the historical etiology of ADD/ADHD and based on current neuroanatomical perspectives suggest that the degree to which the brain arrangement is medically disabling is problematic. In tandem with this, there is abundant cultural evidence which advocates that the popular concept of ADD/ADHD as a disability is rapidly being transformed into an experience that is something other than purely a negative disability-based experience.

All of this suggests that ability and disability may be two sides of the same coin, and therefore inseparable in a truly empirical sense (remember the problems with IQ tests). Many theories of the late 20th and early 21st century examine the whole person as not just a sum of the various parts, but as something more in total.

The technical definition of twice exceptionality itself (the co-morbid diagnosis of ADD/ADHD and giftedness, for example, and referred to in the vernacular as 2E), may actually be an obfuscation of a rapidly evolving human brain where

---

[12.] Trammell, pp. 227–37; Hartmann, Thom. *The Edison Gene: ADHD and the Gift of the Hunter Child*. Rochester, VT: Park Street Press, 2003.

today's disability may easily represent yesterday's, or tomorrow's, special ability. The idea that disability and ability may be two sides of the same coin potentially obliterates modernity's obsession with the label and returns to an ancient and formerly well-respected view of humans as complicated, capable of both good and bad, flawed and wonderful, sometimes irrational, and ultimately responsible for their own choices and pathways. The theory of 2E (twice exceptionality) has a slowly growing neuro-scientific backing although the power of the tattoo (label) remains strong.

Neurodiversity also increasingly appears to be a logical outcome of a successful DRM. Different brains are quite analogous to different bodies—with varieties of shapes and sizes, eye and hair colors, and even features of personality. The idea that someone who was visually impaired shared a common cause with someone with diabetes struck many in the 1970s as illogical. Yet the case was made in the DRM that something bigger was going on. People vary widely, and the dominant culture should be able to accommodate that variability without defaulting to the tyranny of the norm. 2E is arguably a logical outcome of that thinking.

Oliver Sacks, in interpreting Gerald Edelman's *Neural Darwinism*, summarizes how we *must* be different from each other neurologically:

> Individuality is deeply imbued in us from the very start, at the neuronal level. Even at the motor level, researchers have shown, an infant does not follow a set pattern of learning to walk or how to reach for something. …We are destined, whether we like it or not, to a life of particularity and self-development…[13]

The DRM argues in part that we "should like it" to answer Sacks' question. Whether it be individuals on the Autism spectrum, or individuals with psychiatric disorders, the 21st century has opened access and greater cultural acceptance to neurodiversity. Some anthropologists and educators are now arguing that neurodiversity may become the most important diversity of all in the coming times.

Universal Design

As consideration is given to what disability will look like in the 21st century, a return to the concept of Universal Design (UD) is crucial to the conversation. UD began in the world of architecture after World War II, where a postmodern

---

[13] Sacks, Oliver. *On the Move: A Life*. Alfred A. Knopf, 2015, pp. 368–369.

design exercise was to rethink form and function in terms of more imaginative and practical spatial access. Architects in essence began to move away from defaulting to "l'homme moyen" or the average man, and moved toward thinking in broader human terms.[14]

In the American construction business, for example, the standard sized door had been fitted for generations to a consistent model, designed for a man of average height and build (five foot seven inches and one-hundred forty pounds in the 19th century), and with no consideration to the anti-normate, such as a wheelchair user, to cite just one example, or even a taller or larger man with no obvious disability.

Architects realized and accepted the premise that just because a door (or any other object or design element) had always been designed and built one way, did not mean that it had to always be drawn or imagined that way. UD was an attempt to move beyond the "normate," and account for the diversity of human bodies, human experiences, human needs, and their impact on each other in physical environments. Aging Americans often choose to live in homes without stairs, or where they can access kitchen, bathroom, and bedroom without climbing, for example.[15] The fruit of UD in architecture was immediate and profound. Spaces and environmental elements could be designed and imagined in such ways that anyone (or at least many more than before) could inhabit or readily use them. The concept of UD by now has spread to other areas and major life activities beyond architecture, and is even recognized as a key element in more ephemeral areas, from curriculums that schools teach to airplane seats, or in the way that media is designed, or even the ways that teachers teach, or postsecondary environments are designed.[16]

The concept that an environment, service, or product can be re-imagined in ways that make it more broadly accessible is egalitarian, equitable, positive, and democratic in almost every sense. It also can foster creativity. It is consistent with the overall American experience. It is true that UD may cost more money to "retrofit" in some cases, and this has been a widely used argument against UD

[14.] Davis, Lennard. "Introduction: Normality, Power, and Culture." In Davis, Lennard (Ed.). *The Disability Studies Reader*. Routledge, 2013, p. 5., pp. 1–14; an interesting side note is that the standard American door stems from several hundred years ago when the average male was 5' 7"!

[15.] Thomson, Rosemarie Garland. "Seeing the Disabled: Visual Rhetorics of Disability in Popular Photography." In Longmore, Paul K., & Umansky, Lauri (Eds.). *The New Disability History: American Perspectives*. New York University Press, 2001, pp. 335–74.

[16.] Bowe, Frank. *Universal Design in Education: Teaching Nontraditional Students*. Westport, Conn: Bergin & Garvey, 2000; "Postsecondary Education and UDL." Accessed September 29, 2015 at http://www.udlcenter.org/implementation/postsecondary

as a wider initiative. However, many see now that UD as a mindset is now the next frontier, and capitalist processes are beginning to see the possible profits and embrace it.

UD as a philosophy is also the beneficiary of emerging new technology, which makes everything from designing and producing a door, to teaching in the public schools, much easier on the strategy and production level, and often far less expensive in the long run. As technology improves, costs go down, and the world of UD has continued to evolve in spite of concerns about financing it. In fact, more recent experience even suggests that UD often *saves* money, since retrofitting and reactionary solutions often cost more in the long run than brand new innovative construction.

Although deinstitutionalization and the Independent Living Movement resulted in a drastic reduction in the number of traditional institutions for individuals with disabilities, specialized institutions remain a very important part of the landscape in the 21st century. Universal design has implications for every aspect of daily life in such facilities, too, and will impact the next phase of institutional development. The first waves of institutionalization came out of the Enlightenment and for our purposes can be simplified as comprising the periods of 1800 to 1850 in the U.S; and then from 1875 to 1935 the second wave came post-Civil War and ran its course through the Progressive era. The latter half of the Progressive era was the heyday of the Eugenics Movement.

Both periods were underpinned by very concrete assumptions about the design of the physical space (often prison-like, which wasn't originally seen as a bad thing), the use of the space (often driven by the needs of the experts running the institution), and the levels of basic accessibility, as they related to the function of the institution rather than the needs of an individual patient (ex. private bathrooms were not to reward patients but to avoid riots and unwanted fraternization).

From 1935 until the major outbreak of the Independent Living Movement (ILM) in the late 1960s, institutions remained in operation, but infrastructure deteriorated, and the public generally had declining awareness of abuse or mismanagement. A great deal of the research-oriented resources were channeled by the Cold War agenda into military and industrial infrastructure, rather than human services, which also further marginalized the importance of institutions as front-line centers for change. By 1970, Ed Roberts and others found the system outdated, run-down, ignored, and filled with problems. It was ripe for a change.

Universal Design principles now suggest that people who live in institutions should have not only basic medical, psychological supports, and access to experts, but should also be able to have the environmental freedom to make decisions for themselves about basic daily living, including productive employment and more independent housing options, even within the institution itself. They should be given ways in which to give their consent to choices that are available to them. The spaces should be designed for the patients and humans in general, rather than for the doctors and psychologists who help run them. Institutions will remain with us, but they no doubt will look different in positive ways due to the influence of UD design and philosophy.

Universal design principles even apply to the "normal" methodologies historians have long used, which in the past largely ignored many stigmatized identities including individuals with disabilities. Increasingly, historians and social historians design their methodologies to be more inclusive of those voices which have remained primarily unheard. American disability history does exist, persist, and demand a voice in explanations of the American experience, and American Exceptionalism.

2008 ADAAA

Most Americans are familiar with the idea that there is a law that protects people from disability-based discrimination; some even know that it is called the Americans with Disabilities Act (ADA); very few know that it is a law that has actually been passed twice (1990 and 2008), and that it may be passed again a third time soon if the accessibility to the physical environment and persistently negative attitudes people harbor about disability don't significantly improve.

The original ADA was modeled on the 1964 Civil Rights Act, and its proponents crossed political party, gender, age, and racial lines. Although the Civil Rights Act had been used to generally defend disability rights, its lack of specificity left disability activists clamoring for their own legislation. Section 504 provided disability legislation in 1973 as part of the Rehabilitation Act, but it was limited in who it covered. When the grass roots movement behind the ADA gained steam publicly in the 1980s, aided by supporters like Justin Dart, Congress began to slowly pay attention. Senator Tom Harkin (D-Iowa) and Representative Steny Hoyer (D-Maryland) were the primary guides for the legislation; President George H. W. Bush signed it into law.

The ADA was not, however, a panacea, and it came with caveats. For example, it excluded people who were "current drug addicts." It came with no funding, or obvious mechanism for enforcement beyond the courts. Some feared that it would ruin businesses who were forced to adapt their environments and practices to accommodate individuals with disabilities for the first time.

None-the-less, students of the Disability Rights Movement (DRM) now can state with hindsight that 1990 marked a great turning point in American history. In terms of disability history, especially, there is a "before" ADA and an "after" ADA way of seeing the world. College-age students in the present time have never known an America where disability was not protected in theory, and often in practice.

Unfortunately, the original ADA was gutted over time in an endless series of court cases. Individuals with disabilities generally lost suits more than ninety percent of the time, and a sequence of seemingly punitive findings emboldened employers and organizations to make accommodations increasingly difficult, if not impossible in some cases, to obtain. For example, in Sutton et al. v. United Airlines, and in similar cases, the U.S. Supreme Court ruled that if a condition was not permanent, or was easily correctible, then it did not qualify as a disability.

In 2008, the Amendments Act was passed in order to reinvigorate the original intention of the ADA, and vacate harmful court cases. The ADAAA broadened the definition of disability, and made it easier to document such a disability. It made it much easier for temporary disabilities to be accommodated. It took twenty years of erosion to bring about a reset, but it then allowed the reinforcement of the original foundational pieces of the law and its intent.

"The either/or categorization [disabled or not disabled] is a… fiction," Doris Zames and her sister wrote recently. The ADAAA acknowledges that disability is something we all must contend with, and it is a law that allows us to demonstrate daily why humans are unique, and exist in communities that seek equal opportunity under the law. The 2008 amendments expanded the definitions of disability, and liberalized documentation processes.[17]

---

[17] Zames.

The International Community and Disability

The late 20th and early 21st century disability experience in America has in part been defined by the growing international nature of the DRM. Although, ironically, the U.S. to this point has failed to sign the United Nations convention on disabilities for political reasons, many of the principles in it will seem familiar and comfortable to those who know the history of the DRM in the U.S.

Article 3 is typical:

> The principles of the present Convention shall be: Respect for inherent dignity, individual autonomy including the freedom to make one's own choices, and independence of persons; Non-discrimination; Full and effective participation and inclusion in society; Respect for difference and acceptance of persons with disabilities as part of human diversity and humanity; Equality of opportunity; Accessibility; Equality between men and women; Respect for the evolving capacities of children with disabilities and respect for the right of children with disabilities to preserve their identities.[18]

The full document is an intriguing artifact that Ed Roberts and general civil rights leaders from earlier generations would have found remarkable, and yet it is still what many consider just a beginning. This growth in international disability rights is all the more notable when one remembers the checkered history of the past two-hundred years *outside* of North America, where individuals with disabilities were victims of the Holocaust in Nazi Germany, were infantilized or openly neglected in many less developed areas of the third world, and positioned as victims in continuing cultural wars related to ethnicity (ex. In Eastern Europe, where Roma children are educated in schools for disabilities in spite of the fact that they often *don't* have disabilities, other than cultural disadvantage).

More recently, many other countries have added disability legislation modeled on the ADA in the U.S. (and the analogous laws in Britain, Canada, etc.) which really stemmed from the Civil Rights Act in 1964. The European Union now is promoting disability access in Eastern Europe post-Cold War, and as a trans-European human right. Although the U.S. still remains exceptional in some ways, it is likely that in the new century the American disability experience will become much more synonymous and seamless within the global disability experience.

---

[18] The full text of the U.N. Convention on the Rights of Persons with Disabilities can be seen at http://www.un.org/disabilities/convention/conventionfull.shtml

Social Media and Disability News

As the 21st century continues to unfold, the way we process "normal" continues to change dramatically. Nowhere is this better illustrated than in the stories that frequently appear in the publication/social media outlet entitled *Disability Scoop*, "The Premier Source for Developmental Disability News," which is also a chronicle of the disability-oriented changes that occur daily on a wider cultural basis.

An article from 2015 will serve to illustrate the point: "Boy Scouts accused of kicking out teen with Asperger's." A young man with seven years of experience in the Scouts was mysteriously revoked as a member, for no apparent reason. The parents of the young man were suing. Within this story are several relatively newly evolving paradigms: the changing (some would say eroding) definitions of disability and Autism Spectrum Disorder (ASD); the increasingly isolated corners where discrimination still lurks (traditional, long-established organizations are often the last to change); and the increasing public shaming for overtly discriminatory behavior (the online comments were almost uniformly scathing towards the organization).

Another story from 2015 came out of a Ted Talk given by a young woman who introduced a wider world to the shock term "inspiration porn," implying that the old worn-out stereotypes and medical definitions still predominant in many forms of disability media actually serve as a prop to make an ablest world feel better. "Objectifying people with disabilities creates the wrong kind of hero." Essentially, helping people with disabilities makes "normal" people feel good; but does nothing to make attitudes change or the environment more accessible.

Like the Boy Scouts story, this Ted Talk reveals that discrimination is still "in the water" that we all drink, our language still laden with it, our forums for research and science still mired in its negative ontology (world view), and some people still somewhat isolated from the lived reality of it. The positive aspect of both stories is that a vibrant disability media shared them widely with a diverse audience who can then continue to react to them.[19]

[19.] Brisco, Tony. "Boy Scouts accused of kicking out teen with Asperger's." *Chicago Tribune*/TNS, June 2, 2015, as reported in Disability Scoop, http://www.disabilityscoop.com; Perry, David M.. "Inspiration porn further disables the disabled," *Aljazeera America*, June 2, 2015, accessed online at http://america.aljazeera.com.

A 21st Century DRM

Most advocates for disability rights in the new century would argue that a great deal of work remains to be done. An argument can be made that social science has advanced understanding and acceptance of disability; that science and medical technology have done much to offset the effects of disability; that the humanities have brought empathy to disability; and it is hard to imagine those trends will not continue, especially in academia.

Science remains at the center, for better or worse. Recently, researchers have begun to develop saliva tests, or other physical exams, which can reveal the presence of disorders or conditions that heretofore had only been diagnosable through extensive psycho-educational testing, or elaborate interviews and symptom reporting processes. There is particularly impactful research being done in the area of Autism and other spectrum disorders like Asperger's Syndrome in terms of causal factors.[20]

For countless centuries human behavior was judged primarily using outward physical appearance as the means of rhetorical leverage, so that now the idea of medicine and science literally seeing inside such conditions as depression, or ADHD, promises a fundamental alteration in the way that the narrative of those disabilities are perceived and treated culturally; perhaps even a shift in understanding of what it means to be human. The significance to the Disability Rights Movement, and to democracy based on classic liberalism in the U. S., cannot be overstated.

The distinction already discussed between disease and disability remains a 21st century dilemma. With the onset of the COVID-19 pandemic, and then the subsequent discovery of "Long COVID," the lines continue to blur between what might have once been considered a stable identity of disease OR a disability, and instead created a moving target, a day to day variation in degree of disablement that may or may not meet certain definitional thresholds. This hearkens back to experiences mentioned in this text with diseases like TB.

Disability in 21st century is likely to look very different from disability in the past in the world of entertainment. Gone are freak shows and menageries, and replacing them are more serious characters in film and literature and entertainers with disabilities. Perhaps another president with a disability like FDR *can* be elected in the 21st century.

---

[20] Rizzo, Alan. "Saliva test shows promise for diagnosing Autism." *Watertown Daily Times*, February 17, 2015.

Research breakthroughs will continue to mitigate conditions and disabilities that have heretofore been stable identities for centuries. For example, it was only in 2003 that the draft of the entire human genome was mapped out; an event that now seems in the distant past when compared to new genetic research advances. Every congenital disorder or condition from a millennia or more of human experience is now potentially targeted for new interventions and accommodations, and breakthroughs have also opened the door to equally ambitious sequels, such as the Human Microbiome Project, which examines humans and bacteria, or so-called stem cell programming, which can recreate any type of human cell. Early failures at eye transplants may led to innovations that initiate a decline in blindness.[21]

Disability in America will increasingly rely on the online or virtual environment not only for entertainment, but to mitigate the effects of disability stigma. The advent of telecommuting, especially during COVID-19, and acceptance of virtual personalities, has resulted in a new type of social community for work and play where disability is less visible, less impactful, and almost totally accommodated through technology. Physical and often psychological disabilities simply don't exist in cyberspace in the same way they do in physical office spaces, schools, or in public venues. New masks are available, to paraphrase Goffman. For some activities, like work, or education, the online environment has become one of the great leveling influences in the new American/global experience.[22]

Some types of disorders will be reframed as "normal" or even seen as "giftedness" in the coming decades. There is already evidence of this with Attention Deficit Disorder/Attention Deficit Hyperactivity Disorder (ADD/ADHD). Not only has the medical definition of the so-called disorder remained contentious, the popularity of the general brain-type has grown exponentially—college students fake it for test advantages, parents take their children's medications, and quippy pop culture references to it have inundated the media. Some anthropologists and doctors question whether or not the ADD/ADHD brain type might actually serve important purposes that remain evolutionarily relevant in the post-modern world. Others question the long-term stability of the medical diagnosis.[23]

Disability in America will be transformed in the new century… How can it not be so, given our complex and colorful history?

---

[21] "Lifeswork Medical Advances." Accessed at http://www.cnn.com/2013/06/05/health/lifeswork-medical-advances/.

[22] Foreman, Abbe E., et. al.. "Beautiful to me: Identity, disability, and gender in virtual environments." *International Journal of E-Politics* 2, no. 2, 2011, 17 pages.

[23] Trammell.

Conclusion and Predictions

There are a number of general lessons from American disability history that we can draw on in conclusion, and perhaps a few of them should be mentioned again, because they are likely to continue to be evolving themes. Access to public transportation has been a constant theme. The ancient attraction to the "right of way" seems embedded in the DRM. American cities have been critical access points for mass transportation and centers for innovation, but because distances are greater than in Europe and parts of Asia between cities, access has typically been more limited outside of major cities. We are likely to see a continuing change as highspeed transportation systems are upgraded and technology transcends demographics. Rural disability will perhaps be redefined by technology.

Students and Scholars of disability in the 21st century will need to account for a number of complex cultural variables, even as technology and biomedical breakthroughs transform human life and notions of "normal." For starters, the brain and its evolution will be at the forefront. One aspect of the human brain is the rapid hardwiring for visual stimulus that is partially a long-placed cognitive pre-set, but also quickly occurs in babies and toddlers as they explore the world visually. For example, an area of the pre-frontal cortex wires for facial recognition, explaining in part why babies cry when their mother hands them to someone else. A prejudice for the visual over the other four senses is built into many eons of our language and culture and is the cause of much misunderstanding and faulty judgement even in the present time. The Greeks "invented" the science of physiognomy, or judging people by their physical appearance, and we still use this sometimes-automatic reaction quite commonly as a first response to someone new. Can we overcome visual bias in the coming decades?

As a primitive survival tool, vision is arguably indispensable in some scenarios. It allows one to recognize immediately family and tribe, or enemies and threats. It coordinates the actions of the hands with the physical environment. It permits a sense of time and space that would be otherwise difficult. It allows for immediate recognition of many physical human differences. Yet millions of humans in the 21st century live with limited vision or blindness and are usually not limited in any of life's major activities. There is car technology, for example, that aids the visually impaired in driving, or literally drives itself. Perhaps the ongoing issue of why we privilege sight so much will be questioned anew, and we can argue more vociferously that you can be fully human without it.

Our brains still are wired for vision, so our world reifies that sensory dominance, language reinforces it (if you "see what I mean"), and our immediate future will not likely change that hegemony. It is for this reason that people like Rosemarie Garland-Thomson and Richard Kearney (and many others) challenge the visual hegemony. They challenge us to first acknowledge our visual bias, but then default to the pre-frontal cortex and make a conscious decision to move beyond the bias. In addition to wiring for the visual, we also have an advanced pre-frontal cortex where we can decide not to make important decisions based purely on the visual or on immediate stereotypes. Babies learn not to cry when their mothers hand them to someone else. We can fight our instincts to judge. This means that the 21st century DRM is in part a battle over the brain, and what we are wired for, and what we have to fight for; even what we might intentionally rewire ourselves for.

One controversial aspect of the American experience already discussed is the evolution of so-called "rugged individualism," or the notion that pioneers can survive without cities and industrial comforts, and either invent what they need or simply go without. Although seriously flawed as a 21st century paradigm, and now truly outdated, vestiges of this cultural bias remain present in the 21st century. It is related to the rice culture (communal) verses wheat culture (individual) conversation that some sociology students may be familiar with.

We still sometimes expect people with disabilities to "just deal with it." Europeans, on the other hand, have for centuries generally lived closer together in tighter communities, and whether fighting or collaborating, generally accepted humans as needing to interact with each other regularly, and more often than not sharing communal responsibility. This is also true in many Asian cultures. This may explain in part why healthcare is universal in most European countries, but still curiously not so in the United States (although Canada does have a European-style system).

For people with disabilities, rugged individualism (or the vestigial impacts of it) places tremendous pressure on the individual to adapt to the world, rather than to advocate for the world to change. The two major divisions amongst the blind community, represented by the American Federation for the Blind (AFB) and the National Council for the Blind (NCB), demonstrate how these forces are in tension with each other in terms of a specific disability, with one group more traditionally focused on helping people navigate in an unfriendly sight-privileged world, and the other advocating more for accommodation and transformation of the world. In the new century, students of disability history might hope to see a change in perceptions about individualism.

The notion of consent is not the same as rugged individualism and has evolved in extremely important ways in the early 21st century. Whether a formal informed consent to participate in a research study, or simply the informal consent to talk about a personal disability situation with someone, a revolution has occurred recently in which social scientists, educators, and others are re-thinking who can give consent, under what circumstances they can give it, and how much self-determination they should have in any given situation. The DRM maximizes the emphasis on personal agency (choice). The concept emerging from that revolution is a greater respect for individual autonomy (fewer "other" people making decisions for an individual with a disability); a deeper appreciation of the myriad ways and communication networks people can use to give consent (someone who is non-verbal has other ways to communicate consent); and the importance of access to things that TABs (temporarily abled bodied people) take for granted, like deciding which flavor of ice cream to eat, or what podcast to watch. It fosters greater community by allowing individuals to choose themselves to participate.

We are likely to see changes in public and higher education as they relate to disabilities, both students who need accommodation, the working faculty and staff, and the place of disability in the curriculum. The general trend has been toward increased access, and toward increased interest in disability policy and social history. There are now courses and programs for disability studies. Sociology has a disability branch. College can be an option for everyone, and our history indicates that is the direction we are going.

We are also likely to see special education in the K12 environment continue to change. Enabling youth should be a core mission of any K12 system, and the shortcomings of special education as it currently functions sometimes interfere with that mission. In addition, the 21st century DRM needs more youth leading youth, and people with disabilities in policy-making positions.

Self-determination might best be thought of as a basic human right in the new century, along with the ADA tenants including access to gainful employment, education, and other major life activities. Although the United Nations accords, as well as the ADA itself, encourage this line of reasoning, the functional reality of the American landscape falls short of the expectation. The ILM, for example, is not over yet; nor are the arguments about how much control individuals with disabilities should have over their own bodies, minds, and lives. A priority from an advocacy standpoint remains training and education about personal information management—who to tell, how much to tell, when to tell—in order to maintain true individual autonomy in a culture that though although increasingly accessible remains biased towards ableism.

The 21st century is likely to see a growing appreciation of the rich political and cultural history of the DRM. The universality of the disability experience means that its history and social narrative are germane to everyone. Disability is becoming, slowly, the place where common ground can be found, including the semantics of how to negotiate identity. The explosion of independent streaming entertainment has opened viewership up to the world of disability.

Corporate America will increasingly normalize the disability landscape, ultimately because it is in their interests. Companies like Ford and Dominion Energy have already realized that it helps them be more profitable to hire people with disabilities (PWD), and it helps them look more like the America they market to. Leadership training at the corporate level now increasingly includes disability components. Corporations and businesses also need to utilize the power of social media to promote the efforts already being made to accommodate and assimilate. Even the largest corporations, like Capitol One, are starting to prioritize the benefits and historical imperative of normalizing disability.

As we learn more about and become more accepting of disability, there is a nuanced challenge that arises increasingly. This is the sometimes-inflated claims of counter-productive or competing accommodations. For a simplified example, a teacher with severe dog allergies is required to allow a student who is blind and uses a service animal (usually a dog) to be in his or her classroom. Whose accommodation wins in the accommodation battle? Although a separate argument could be made about whether the severity of the allergies rises to the standard of ADA case law and guidelines might be interesting, this is actually a false dichotomy, even though the dilemma for each individual with a perceived or documented disability (and even the other classroom community members) is real and impacts the entire environment. Instead, the principles of respect that came out vividly in the 1960s, and the de-stigmatization (ongoing of course) of disability instead means that a new dialogue must occur. This kind of "complication" can only arise in an advanced culture where disability is better understood and more openly accepted.

Other challenges remain, of course, ranging from improved access to the benefits of technology to improved access to "old" services like taxis. The biggest challenge of all, however, remains the stigma associated with disability—no one (or very few people) wants to be disabled in the old sense, even in the better world that is evolving—and money and resources don't take away the tattoo, or the mark, as the early Greeks called it. Bridge programs and media campaigns have certainly made their impact felt, but the problem remains—of all the major identities, disability is arguable the most universal but also the one that inhabits the most persistently negative universe of ideas and semantics. This is not just an American problem, but a human problem. This is in part why Critical Race Theory examines race as a disability.

Still, the American experience with disability has been a remarkable one to date, and it remains for us to make the most of it in the yet unwritten future. In the meantime, there are triumphs to be celebrated and serious warnings of what could go wrong with which we should continually take heed. Disability is in America, it has a compelling story, and it has not yet fully unfolded. Disability is here and it's here to stay.

APPENDIX: NEOMODERNISM FOR UNDERGRADUATE STUDENTS

Neomodernism for Undergraduate Disability Studies Students

Jack Trammell

The concept of *modernity* is a sweeping ontological paradigm (basic framework for interpreting reality) that has hundreds of different meanings and interpretations. Within the liberal arts, for example, art historians have a particular timeframe, set of human actors, artistic styles, and trends that are particular to their expertise and comprise for them what modernism or modernity is; their ideas and assumptions about modernity are sometimes divergent from a content area like sociology, where modernity has a different set of assumptions and actors for social scientists to tinker with and argue about. The potentially confusing aspect to this is that ALL forms and interpretations of modernism or modernity share some core characteristics, and it can be argued that when mashed together they are the totality of modernity. Are you confused yet? It is confusing, but for our conversational purposes, we can bookend several points of relative certainty and combine them with a working definition that will be particularly useful for a sociological or a broader social science perspective, including an area of inquiry like disability studies.

Before modernism, there was primitivism. In this period there were tribes, small collectives, and crude forms of anarchism, but generally no organized political entities. Mankind emerged from primitivism in a historical sense in the age of literacy and with the formation of cities and empires. Following the collapse of the largest and most successful of these, the Roman Empire, Europe entered a period of fragmentation and diffusion. (Note that this story has a strong bias toward Westernism, but that is unavoidably part of how modernity came to be created and defined.) For many hundreds of years, human existence was largely demarcated at the village level, with highly prescribed social hierarchies, and with only a few bigger cites and centers of learning attracting most of the serious intellectual activity. Europe eventually began to emerge from this long sometimes chaotic period and became increasingly more structured during and following the Renaissance, which was a peculiar celebratory rebirth of the old (classical) world combined with the something new, and soon led to a period known as the Enlightenment. Almost all core concepts of modernity can be traced to the Enlightenment, and the following discussion about timelines should be firmly rooted in that primordial period.

The new world would eventually supplant the old one almost entirely, and this process was the beginnings of modernity. Hans Kung, a scholar of the history of the Catholic Church, describes emerging modernity this way:

> Everything was dominated by geometry, which became virtually a characteristic of the era; the state as a rationally constructed machine, from the building of cities and fortifications and the architecture of gardens to exercises, music, and dance. All this was connected with the first of those revolutionary impulses which brought in a turn of the ages, the epoch-making shift to modernity. Europe would no longer orient itself, as in the Renaissance, on antiquity as its model, but rather on autonomous reason, on technical progress, and on the nation.[1]

Historian and author Stephen Greenblatt is perhaps more elegant and sweeping in a similar assessment. According Greenblatt, modernity was propelled forward dramatically in all human areas:

> ...Shaped the dress and etiquette of courtiers; the language of the liturgy; the design and decoration of everyday objects. It suffused Leonardo da Vinci's scientific and technological explorations. Galileo's vivid dialogues on astronomy. Francis Bacon's ambitious research projects, and Richard Hooker's theology. It was virtually a reflex, so that works that were seemingly far away from any aesthetic ambition at all—Machiavelli's analysis of political strategy, Walter Raleigh's description of Guinea, or Robert Burton's encyclopedic account of mental illness—were crafted in such a way as to produce the most intense pleasure [an Epicurean rather than erotic pleasure]. ...Painting, sculpture, music, architecture, and literature—were the supreme manifestations of that [pursuit of] beauty.[2]

---

[1] Kung, Hans (2003). The Catholic Church: A Short History, New York: Modern Press, p. 143.

[2] Greenblatt, Stephen (2011) . The Swerve: How the World Became Modern, NY: W.W. Norton and Co., p. 8.

Although modernity evolved in fits and starts over hundreds of years, it's most powerful impact on the world has arguably been in the past several hundred years. For those who like time-frames, let's begin by calling modernity a phase of human experience that generally ranges from about 1850 to about 1950. Why those dates? Even though there are many dates that would work, I chose these for a few reasons. 1850 places America and Europe squarely in the industrial revolution, but before the American Civil War (argued by some to be the first "modern" war) and at the embryonic stages of the modern sciences (sociology was "invented" in the 1880s according to some). It was a time of dramatic advances. Darwin published his *On the Origin of Species* in 1859, for example. In 1850, many of the concepts that would later become core characteristics of modernity were beginning to become absolutely central to human existence. An example of this would be the importance of naming and ordering things of the world. The Swedish scientist Carl Linnaeus had already invented a system for classifying plants and animals (a taxonomy) but by 1850 this new form of nominalism (emphasizing the name, or the classification) was occurring in all areas of intellectual and recreational pursuit, from poetry to politics.

In 1850, Great Britain, Europe, and America collectively dominated global culture so that the growth of modernism is, as mentioned previously, again closely associated with Westernism, imperialism, colonialism, and capitalism (not always a happy set of relationships to be sure). These associations are vitally important to framing modernity. Speaking of capitalism, Karl Marx co-authored *The Communist Manifesto* in 1848, close (enough) to our beginning date under discussion.

So to wrap up the time conversation about beginnings, it becomes clear upon reflection that a lot was happening around 1850 that was new to the human experience, and even people living at the time often expressed the opinion that the world was changing, distances shrinking, inventions promising to solve problems, or that something really big and different was occurring (at least in the West). There was generally optimism about the whole development of mankind, and people viewed it as true evidence of human progress—the antithesis of primitivism. In a metaphorical sense, man was evolving into a new species in a brand new world.

Why stop or close this ambitious period around 1950? By 1950, the epic failures of modernity were finally becoming evident to all. Two monstrously destructive world wars, capped by the horrors of the Holocaust, left the world in shock, and when the dust finally settled it became clear that some elements of modernity were just not that progressive or more advanced at all. Primitive humans didn't drop atomic bombs on each other and hold the day-to-day capacity to end the world. The now problematic science of eugenics, for example, had demonstrated that perfectly rational processes could be based on terribly immoral assumptions and result in unthinkable crimes and tragedies. The nuclear destruction of Nagasaki and Hiroshima had shown that perfectly rational science could result in unthinkable human horror.

In the midst of the Cold War between the West and the Soviet Union, some intellectuals continued to reframe, criticize more thoroughly, and reinterpret modernism. You may have heard of postmodernism, which was a knee-jerk response across disciplines to the failings of modernity even before the Second World War. By 1950, the specter of nuclear destruction was a daily cloud of anxiety over the entire globe. If I'm not careful, things will begin to sound pretty gloomy, and they weren't exactly that—your great grandparents may remember the economic prosperity, television, and good times of the 1950s with nostalgia. They may not remember so much the creation of nuclear fallout shelters and required civil defense training…

The point for us is that in the intellectual history of humans, something fundamentally changed by 1950 after the Holocaust and after the bombs. Many of the fundamental elements of modernity that we can originally identify in the 1850s—even Westernism itself—were now subject to extensive reinterpretation or even outright rejection (as in the case of eugenics, for example).

If we can agree roughly on the importance of this one-hundred year window, then it makes it easier to list (yes, like a good modernist we'll make a list and order it) the key elements associated with modernity, as they will be most useful for sociologists and other social scientists in their work. There is a twist. Because sociologists are both scientists and champions of social justice, they must wear two hats and both use the tools of modernity and critique them at the same time (a little bit of a circus balancing act that we'll return to later). Elements of modernity include but are not limited to:

- Industrialization
- Urbanization
- Rationalization
- Medicalization
- Growth of technology including forms of A.I.
- High speed communication
- Globalization
- Capitalization

- Automation
- Rise of the nation state
- Growth of wealth
- Specialization (creation of experts)
- Systems thinking
- Empiricism/Positivism
- Emphasis on cause and effect
- Emphasis on ordering, labels, hierarchies, measurement, and norms

Perhaps this is a list of things that could be seen as somewhat agnostic. In other words, many of them are not good or bad in and of themselves some would argue, it is only the unintended consequences that come along with them that have created or perpetuated human problems. High speed communication allows grandparents to be "face to face" with their grandchildren on the other side of the globe any time they want to be; on the other hand, email is now ninety percent of most people's jobs. The consequences of modernity go well beyond the obvious wealth, convenience, gadgetry, and privilege we take for granted, and they STILL have not been fully explored. (Thank goodness we have sociologists!)

For those of you convinced of at least some of the problems of modernity, you may be wondering why postmodernism didn't just go ahead and solve all of the shortcomings of modernism. First of all, postmodernity remains more of an intellectual pursuit than a true human revolution, while modernity was (and some would say remains) a true revolution, a fundamental change in how humans live and understand reality. Secondly, postmodernism fails to address the tremendous benefits that we all have reaped from modernity (would you like to go back to pre-antibiotic days and die from a simple paper cut?) Postmodernism also doesn't offer an alternative life or world view—it simply condemns the one we live in. Ultimately, postmodernism remains an interesting critique of capitalism and modernity, but it leaves us unsatisfied in trying to understand the good that has come with the bad, and how we can embrace individuality AND the collective good.

You've probably heard that you can't put the genie back in the bottle. That is why we need a new way of thinking about this. I propose the term neomodernism, or the "new" modernism, to help us understand and explore it. Even scientists recognize that modernity itself has shortcomings and even outright flaws that are potentially quite consequential. Michio Kaku, a popular physicist who studies string theory, believes that many physicists (and other scientists) "…Suffer from the mechanistic process of thinking… …which tries to understand the workings of an object [or person, my emphasis] by examining the mechanical motions of its individual parts... ...It blinds one from seeing the overall picture [or the true picture of something or someone, my emphasis]."[3]

What is neomodernism? Neomodernism is the "new" modernity, or a recognizable "beyond" the 1850—1950 modernism. It means using antibiotics on paper cuts, but rejecting the best-looking family eugenics contest at the county fair (yes, they used to routinely have those). It means striving to reach Mars, but addressing famine and poverty on our own planet. If it sounds a little bit like a political agenda, I should point out that it is actually a moral agenda. Neomodernism recognizes that we have the power to do almost limitless "things." But just because we *can* do something (like bomb the planet out of existence) doesn't mean that we *should* do something.

Neomodernism is not to be confused with other "isms," such as neoliberalism (which essentially is focused on free markets, deregulation, and has drastic social consequences associated with it), or postmodernism (which rejects much of modernity outright). Neomodernism perhaps means recognizing that Nietzsche was wrong; God isn't dead. In more practical terms, it means that humans aren't reducible in the sense that our best current science still can't fully explain everything about us down to sub-atomic levels. In spite of the genius of scientists like Brian Greene, who wrote the wonderful book Until the End of Time, neomodernism argues that we are more than the sum total of our individual parts. There is something in each of us that defies completely rational explanations. (Greene works very hard in his book to refute this; I recommend reading it).

There are many competing ideas to replace, criticize or reimagine modernity. For example, Anthony Giddens' concept of the reflexivity of modernity essentially grants it the equivalence of social immortality (it keeps responding to itself, and changing, but never really goes away); postmodernism as a critique is unlikely to go away; dismodernism, a concept developed by disability studies scholar Lennard Davis, argues that disability has permanently thrown a wooden shoe into the gears of modernity; identity politics projects itself as winning a war for individualism that has negated aspects of modernity. The list goes on.

But none of them adequately reimagine the current epoch we live in as comprising both important rejections of modernity fully existing side by side with normal and live-enhancing acceptances of modernity. None of them fully speak to the place of antibiotics curing a paper cut, but not fundamentally altering our "humanness" as a result. Even Marxism, the most violent and damning critique

---

[3.] Kaku, Michio, and Thompson, Jennifer (1995). *Beyond Einstein: The Cosmic Quest for the Theory of the Universe*, New York: Anchor Books, p. 106.

of all of modernity (and obviously capitalism), doesn't leave enough space for the tedious balance of the good and bad; the rational co-existing, albeit sometimes uneasily, with the completely irrational.

The physicist Michio says that the challenge in part is that we can't keep up mentally with technology and that this is unlikely to change: "…Technological progress proceeds geometrically. However, our brains and our imaginations cannot comprehend geometric growth." In other words, modernity might be uncontrollable and difficult to understand or study under the best of circumstances. That makes it extremely difficult to imagine something new—like neomodernism.

So… Why is it important for students of disability to consider something like the concept of neomodernism? It is important because you are studying social science (which still often relies on many positivist and "scientific" tools) at the same time that you are studying the fundamentally irrational behavior of humans. Such behavior can't routinely be approached without looking at socially constructed norms and an ethical code of some sorts that most of us can agree upon. You are at that awkward place where you might argue that preventing birth defects is good, but accepting babies with disabilities and freeing them to pursue a meaningful life is also good. Both of those things can be true in a neomodern framework. In modernity, they often can't be. Neomodernism also provides a safe space to explore globalization and a firm move away from Westernism.

If we don't escape the full clutches of modernity, there may be another world war, or God-forbid, yet another genocide in the name of improving mankind. But if we abandon modernity, it might be just as disastrous. We need vaccines to combat epidemics; we need sophisticated technology to keep people connected and safe. Neomodernism is the new "think space" that is being created in-between the extremes. It is actually a good way to make more sense of the other competing theories already mentioned, which each in their own way have been seeking a similar kind of place somewhere in-between revolutionary change and complete surrender to modernity.

Finally, neomodernism also has the advantage of semantics. The term modernity, in some circles (certainly not all), has a little bit of a pejorative sound to it. Not necessarily anything like the term "eugenics," which can't be used in any positive way anymore, but not fully politically correct either. As I've already mentioned, modernity will likely never shed some of the human catastrophes that were facilitated by its shortcomings. But neomodernism has a slightly different ring to it. It sounds almost progressive, as if perhaps maybe we can avoid another wave of eugenics, world war, or Holocaust.

Neomodernism reframes disability as neither something to be sought intentionally, nor to be disowned when present. The negative world disability previously has inhabited for thousands of years can be different in a neomodern world. We can come up with gadgets and cures, but we can also value every human life equally. We can accommodate, but we also can do things which make unintentional disability less likely. If these combinations sounds difficult, it is because they are, but that is the space neomodernism is creating where they can co-exist.

I'm sure if this little pamphlet spreads wider than just my undergraduate students, it will likely be picked apart, battered, and bruised—for often that is what we social scientists do with theories. In fact, a good sociological theory class experience can leave you loving and hating someone like Marx at the same time. Such is the territory. But I like neomodernism because it is hopeful and more optimistic, rejects reductionism, liberates disability from a negative ontology, but still allows us a lot of room to keep growing and exploring with the scientific methods and medical tools we have. I think it's a better way of understanding where we are, and if someone doesn't like that, while phooey on them.

INDEX

A
Accommodation(s): 12, 88, 108, 127, 155, 158, 161, 178, 192, 196, 211, 212, 212
ADAAA: 32, 203-204
Adams, Abigail: 33, 42-44
ADAPT: 151, 173, 175, 183
ADHD/ADD: 38, 44, 108, 185, 193, 194, 196, 199, 207-298
AIDS: 130, 172, 185
Allen, Hannah: 1, 23, 27
American Exceptionalism: 16, 28, 50, 107, 110, 203
American Sign Language (ASL): 63-64, 170
Americans with Disabilities Act/ADA: 32, 81, 105, 107, 136, 168, 170, 186-188, 196, 203-204, 211
Architectural Barriers Act: 148
Asthma: 45, 47-48
Autism Society of America: 143

B
Baynton, Douglas: 30, 108
Bierce, Ambrose: 80
Beverly, Robert: 11
Bi-Polar Disorder (BPD): 184
Black Panthers: 152, 170
Blindness: 8, 17, 19-20, 55, 58, 66, 89, 161
Browning, Tod (Freaks): 197
Bruegel, Peter the Elder: 58
Bush, President George H.: 136, 186-187, 203

C
Camps for the Disabled, Civil War: 83, 91-92, 106
Canada: 25, 58, 67, 70, 74, 110, 117, 123, 141, 157, 165-166, 205, 210
Cannon, Dennis: 155-156
Capitalism: 123
Charity/Charity Model: 105, 129, 190
Civil Rights Act of 1964: 32, 138, 140, 159, 161, 203, 205
Civil Rights Movement (CRM): 78, 105, 139, 145, 148-153, 168, 173, 180, 199
Clerc, Laurent: 62-63
Cone, Kitty: 168
Consent, and Disability: 52, 103, 203, 211
Constitution of the Iroquois Nation: 6-7
Constitution, U.S.: 30, 32, 53
COVID-19: 13, 207-208
Critical Race Theory (CRT): 109, 184, 213

D
Dart, Justin: 76, 170-172, 203
Davis, Lennard: 105, 193, 220
Deafness: 7, 17, 21, 55-62
Deinstitutionalization: 58, 76, 185, 202
Democracy, American: 28, 30, 82, 207
Demonstrations/Protests: 78, 111, 139, 144, 148, 155-156, 163, 167-169, 175
Developmental Disabilities: 55, 122, 144, 177
Disability Rights Movement (DRM): 28, 81, 104, 108, 115, 125, 130, 136-148, 152-153, 165, 172, 184, 198-201, 205
Disability Studies (DS): 36, 108, 133, 184, 192, 197, 211, 215
Disability verses Disease: 24, 107-108, 121, 130-132, 183, 207
Disabled in Action (DIA): 165
DisCrit: 190, 184, 194
Dismodernism: 193, 220
Doctors/Physicians, early: 8, 10-12, 23, 35
DuBois, W.E.B.: 73
Dyslexia: 38, 112-113

E
Elderly/Ageism: 5, 135, 154
Enlightenment: 1-3, 6, 8, 12, 14, 18 ,28, 30 ,38, 52, 55, 57 ,69, 202, 216
Eugenics: 20, 55, 76, 107, 112, 119, 121-123, 133-134, 191, 202, 218
Evangelical healing: 8, 17

F
Faye, Fred: 157
Fischbach, Michael: 139
Foucault. Michel: 60, 67, 73, 86, 133, 184
Franklin, Benjamin: 3, 33-42
Frederick, MD: 9
Free and Appropriate Public Education (FAPE): 162, 178
Freemasons: 80

G
Gallaudet, Thomas: 62-63
Gallaudet University/Uprising: 77-78, 180-181
Garland-Thomson, Rosemarie: 31, 68, 96, 210
Gattaca (Movie): 197
G.I. Bill: 82, 98, 105
Globalization, of Disability: 107, 111, 121, 218, 221
Goddard, Henry: 122
Goffman, Erving: 133, 198, 208
Governmentality: 37, 52 ,60, 73, 140, 162
Graham Bell, Alexander: 21, 111
Grand Army of the Republic (GAR): 103-104
Great Awakening: 56, 59
Great Britain: 13, 19, 33, 62, 98, 119, 143, 161, 165, 217
Greece, ancient: 3, 61

H
Harkin, Senator Tom: 181, 186, 203

Hendrix, Jimi: 145-146
Henry, Patrick: 3, 10, 16-17
Henry, Sarah: 10, 16-17
Heumann, Judith: 148, 151, 157, 165-169, 172
Holocaust: 78, 110-111, 133-135, 193, 205, 217-218, 221
Hood, Confederate General John B.: 90, 102
House of Burgesses/General Assembly (VA): 2, 4, 10-11, 64, 67, 77
Hoyer, Congressman Steny: 187, 203

I
I.D.E.A. (Individuals with Disabilities Education Act): 176-180, 188
Independent Living Movement (ILM): 58, 140, 144, 167, 174, 185, 202, 211
Indian (Native-American) Sign Language: 64
Insane Asylums: 22, 52, 59-60, 67-78, 108, 185
Institutions/Institutionalization: 14, 20, 25, 56, 58, 61, 63, 66-82, 121, 142, 169, 182, 202
Intersectionality: 8, 16, 36-37, 43, 73, 109, 149-150, 153, 161, 184, 192
Inventions and Improvements: 40, 109

J
Jacksonian Era: 56, 66-67
Jefferson, Thomas: 24, 34-37, 43
Johnson, President Lyndon B.: 32, 162-163

K
Kennedy, President John F.: 32, 136, 155, 159-162, 166
King, Martin Luther: 26, 119, 143, 149-151, 171
Kirkbride Plan: 70-71

L
Ladd, Anna Coleman: 116
Learning Disability(ies): 38, 113, 158, 172, 178, 184
Least Restrictive Environment (LRE): 178
Left-handed Penmanship: 97, 102
Levine, Herb: 168
Lincoln, Abraham: 73, 86-87, 89

M
Madison, James: 3-4
Mad Pride: 184
Malcolm X: 150, 152
Manual Signing: 62
Marshall, Polly: 37
Martha's Vineyard, MA: 21-22, 55
Media, Disability in: 195-197
Medical Model: 41, 105, 161
Mexico: 10, 28, 64, 67
Mills, C. Wright: 73, 159
Mississippi State Lunatic Asylum: 70-73, 82
Mobility Impairments: 49, 85, 92, 119, 126, 147-148
Modernity/Modernism: 78, 120, 130, 133, Appendix
Morris, Gouverneur: 33, 48-51, 67

N
National Council on Disability (NCD): 172
Native Americans: 4-12, 35, 64, 185, 191
Neomodernism: 191-195, Appendix
Neurodiversity: 199-200
New France/Canada: 67, 70, 74, 110, 117
New Left: 138, 140, 159-160, 166, 170
New Spain: 10, 28, 64, 67
No Child Left Behind: 179
Normalization: 44, 56, 144, 150, 166, 178, 190, 200-201
Norm/Normate: 12, 31, 96

O
Old Testament: 58
Oralism: 62-63
Other(ness): 16, 23, 26, 28, 61, 67-70, 194

P
Pengilly, Mary Huestis: 74-75
Perkins School for the Blind: 65
Physiognomy: 56, 108, 117, 191, 197, 208
Post-Hoc Disability Analysis: 34, 44-45
Postmodernism: 129, Appendix
Post Traumatic Stress Disorder (PTSD): 89, 94, 106, 117
President's Committee on National Employ the Physically Handicapped Week: 136
Progressivism: 25, 115, 119, 130
Prosthetics: 51, 96, 116, 174, 190
Psychological Disabilities: 1, 15, 60, 70 ,77, 89, 141, 158 ,182-188, 208
Public Hospital for the Persons of Insane and Disordered Minds (Williamsburg, VA): 10, 71

R
Recovery (Addiction): 183-186
Rehabilitation: 13, 60, 81, 92, 95, 111, 120-121, 150, 171
Rehabilitation Act of 1973: 81, 166-169, 203
Roberts, Ed: 58, 76, 113, 140-143, 146-152, 157, 161, 183, 202, 205
Rolling Quads: 143, 148
Roosevelt, Franklin Delano (FDR): 108, 114, 125-129
Rugged Individualism (American): 39, 96, 189-190, 198, 210-211

S
Sacks, Oliver: 200
Salem Witch Trials: 15-16, 23
Section 504 (1973 Rehabilitation Act): 81, 148, 167-172, 186, 203
Semantics: 2-3, 33, 77, 121, 126, 144, 161, 212
Service Animals: 124
Shapiro, Robert: 57, 169, 173
Shay, Jonathan: 106
Slavery/Slave Trade: 13, 25-26, 36, 45-46, 56, 68, 79
Smith-Hughes Vocational Education Act: 120
Smith-Sears Veterans Rehabilitation Act: 111, 120, 125
Social Capital: 157, 159, 189
Social Darwinism: 78, 107, 111, 121, 193

Index

Social Media, and Disability: 129, 137, 195-198, 206, 212
Social Model/Social Construction of Disability: 41
Social Security: 129, 166
Special Education: 158, 166, 176-179, 190, 211
Spinal Cord Injury (SCI): 139
Stephenson, Michael: 75
Sterilization: 110-111, 121, 123, 134
Students for a Democrat Society (SDS): 159

T
Temporarily Able Bodied [person] (TAB): 27
Texas School for the Blind and Visually Impaired: 66
Toomey Gazette: 141
Transportation Access: 140, 142, 150, 152-158, 161, 168, 173, 176, 209
Treatments, early Asylums: 10, 12, 23, 35, 48, 69
Twice Exceptionality (2E): 35, 37, 44-45, 57, 86, 184, 199-201

U
Universal Design (UD): 113, 157, 193, 200-203
Urban Mass Transportation Act: 155, 174

V
Veterans: 13, 79-97, 100-105, 110, 115-120, 125, 135-136, 160, 189-190
Veterans Administration: 105, 190
Vietnam War: 99, 105-106, 138-139, 142, 171
Virginia School for the Deaf and Blind: 65, 76

W
Washington, George: 3-4, 31, 34, 46, 48-50, 81
Wheatley, Phyllis: 45-48
Wheelchairs: 108, 111, 123-127, 141, 145, 148, 154, 156, 201
Wilson, Woodrow: 108-109, 111-115, 127
Wolf v. State Legislature: 162
Women's Rights/Gender Rights Movement: 138, 140, 144, 148, 160 ,163
World War I: 13, 82, 104, 111, 115-121, 124
World War II: 82, 98, 104-105, 133-135

Z
Zames, Doris and Frieda: 28, 31, 150, 157, 169, 204

www.ingramcontent.com/pod-product-compliance
Lightning Source LLC
Chambersburg PA
CBHW030825230426
43667CB00008B/1381